D0821619

Mexico City

World Cities series

Edited by
Professor R.J. Johnston and Professor P. Knox

Forthcoming titles in the series:

Mexico City

*The production and reproduction
of an urban environment*

Peter M. Ward
*Department of Geography, University
of Cambridge and Fellow of Fitzwilliam College*

G.K. HALL & CO.
70 LINCOLN STREET, BOSTON, MASS.

Published in the United States by
G.K. Hall & Co.,
70 Lincoln Street, Boston, Massachusetts.

Published simultaneously in Great Britain by
Belhaven Press
(a division of Pinter Publishers)
London and New York

ISBN 0-8161-7259-5

Library of Congress Cataloging-in-Publications Data

forthcoming

For Victoria, whose collusion in not taking no for an answer
made it all happen.

Contents

List of plates

List of figures

List of tables

List of abbreviations

AURIS	Acción Urbana y de Integración Social
BANOBRAS	Banco Nacional de Obras
BNH	Banco Nacional de Habitação (Brazil)
BNHUOPSA	Banco Nacional Hipotecaria Urbano de Obras Públicas
CANACINTRA	Cámara Nacional de la Industria de Transformación
CAPFCE	Comité Administradoa del Programa Federal de Construcción de Escuelas
CAVM	Comisión del Agua del Valle de México
CEAS	Comisión Estatal de Aguas y Saneamiento
CFE	Comisión de Fuerza y Electricidad
CNC	Confederación Nacional de Campesinos
CNOP	Confederación Nacional de Organizaciones Populares
CODEUR	Comisión de Desarrollo Urbano
CONAMUP	Coordinadora Nacional del Movimiento Urbano Popular
CONAPO	Comisión Nacional de Población
CONASUPO	Companía Nacional de Subsistencias Populares
CONCAMIN	Confederación de Cámaras Industriales de los Estados Unidos Mexicanos
CONCANACO	Confederación de Cámaras Nacionales de Comercio
COPARMEX	Confederación Patronal de la República Mexicana
COPEVI	Centro Operacional de Poblamiento y de Vivienda
COPLADE	Comisión para la Planeación del Estado
COPLAMAR	Coordinación General del Plan Nacional de Zonas Deprimidas y Grupos Marginados
CoRett	Comisión para la Regularización de la tenencia de la tierra
COTREM	Coordinación del Transporte en el Estado de México
COVITUR	Comisión Técnica de la Vialidad y Transporte
CTM	Confederación de Trabajadores Mexicanos
CUD	Coordinación Unica de Damnificados
DDF	Departamento del Distrito Federal

List of abbreviations

DF	Distrito Federal
DGAyS	Dirección General de Aguas y Saneamiento (DDF)
DGCP	Dirección General de Centros de Población (SAHOP)
DGCOH	Dirección General de Construcción y Operación Hidráulica (DDF)
DGHP	Dirección General de Habitación Popular (DDF)
ECLA	Economic Commission for Latin America (United Nations)
FIDEURBE	Fideicomiso de Interés Social para el Desarrollo Urbano de la Ciudad de México
FINEZA	Fideicomiso de Netzahualcóyotl
FOGA	Fondo de Garantía de Vivienda
FONHAPO	Fondo Nacional de Habitación Popular
FOVISSSTE	Fondo de la Vivienda ISSSTE
HCP	Secretaría de Hacienda y Crédito Público
IBRD	International Bank for Reconstruction and Development
IMF	International Monetary Fund
IMSS	Instituto Mexicano de Seguro Social
INDECO	Instituto Nacional de Desarrollo de la Comunidad
INFONAVIT	Instituto Nacional del Fondo de Vivienda para los Trabajadores
INPI	Instituto Nacional de la Protección a la Infancia
INVI	Instituto Nacional de Vivienda
ISSSTE	Instituto de Seguridad y Servicios Sociales de los Trabajadores al Servicio del Estado
MRC	Movimiento Restaurador de Colonos
OPEC	Organisation of Petroleum-Exporting Countries
PAN	Partido de Acción Nacional
PARM	Partido Auténtico de la Revolución Mexicana
PCM	Partido Comunista Mexicana
PCP	Procuraduría de Colonias Populares
PDM	Partido Democrático Mexicano
PEMEX	Petróleos Mexicanos
PFCRN	Partido del Frente Cardenista de Reconstrucción
PFV	Programa Financiero de Vivienda
PIDER	Programa de Impulso de Desarrollo Rural
PIHLU	Public Intervention, Housing and Land Use in Latin American Cities
PMS	Partido Mexicano Socialista
PMT	Partido Mexicano de Trabajadores
PNR	Partido Nacional Revolucionario
PPS	Partido Popular Socialista
PRI	Partido Revolucionario Institucional
PRM	Partido de la Revolución Mexicana
PRONAL	Progama Nacional de Alimentación

PRUPE	Programa de Reorganización Urbana y Protección Ecológica
PST	Partido Socialista de Trabajadores
RHP	Renovación Habitacional Popular
SAM	Sistema Alimentario Mexicano
SAHOP	Secretaría de Asentamientos Humanos y Obras Públicas
SARH	Secretaría de Agricultura y Recursos Hidráulicos
SEDUE	Secretaría de Desarrollo Urbano y Ecología
SEPAFIN	Secretaría de Patrimonio y Fomento Industrial
SPP	Secretaría de Programación y Presupuesto
SRA	Secretaría de Reforma Agraria
SRH	Secretaría de Recursos Hidráulicos
SSA	Secretaría de Salubridad y Asistencia
SUDENE	Superintendency for Development in North-East Brazil
UAM	Universidad Autónoma Metropolitana
UNAM	Universidad Nacional Autónoma de México
WHO	World Health Organisation

Preface

When you travel to Mexico City go POSH (Port Out, Starboard Home). Ask for a window seat on the left hand side when you fly into the city's international airport; and sit on the right hand side of the plane when you leave. That way you will get a marvellous view across the city as the aircraft takes a flightpath down the west side, before turning and banking across the south of the city to land in the east. At nighttime, or if the pollution is not heavy, you will see everything. Flying out of Mexico City towards the north east there is less to see. But with a starboard window seat you will certainly see the swathe of irregular settlement that is Netzahualcóyotl, where over one-and-a-half million of the city's poorest people live. Craning your neck and looking south, you may also get a view of the snow-capped volcanos of Iztaccíuhuatl and Popocátepetl. And, if you've stayed long enough, you may even be able to pronounce their names correctly.

But many people come to Mexico City with some trepidation. This is not surprising in the light of the adverse publicity that the city receives. In the early 1970s I wrote a paper in which I described the pollution levels in downtown Mexico City as the equivalent of smoking two packets of cigarettes a day – as it was put to me by one expert. Rather like a Chinese Whisper this 'fact' has reappeared many times in the international press, often in exaggerated form. Would that reporters followed my other work so assiduously. Nevertheless, I still feel a little guilty about identifying the 'fact', and I hope that the more serious analysis in this book may go some way to setting the record straight.

One of today's 'buzz' words is 'megacity' (over 10 millions), and Mexico City with 19 millions in 1989 is certainly mega-big. Undeniably it has enormous problems: of population size and growth, poverty and under-employment, inadequate housing and servicing, pollution and traffic congestion. For the tourist this does not make it a terribly pleasant or comfortable city to visit. My advice would be to spend three days in the city and do the obvious sites. But if one is sensible and reasonably sensitive, then it is not a particularly dangerous city. Nor is it an easy city in which to live permanently. People often challenge me and ask, 'Would you want to live permanently in Mexico City?'. 'Hell, no!', I reply, but then nor do I want to live in London, New York or any other large metropolitan area where many of the same hassles and problems apply.

But for some reason – perhaps because it will shortly be the largest city in the world – Mexico City attracts attention and publicity. *Time* magazine (2 January 1989), describes the city as 'the anteroom to an ecological Hiroshima' and as an 'urban gas chamber'. This is grossly irresponsible reporting. Owing to temperature inversions in the Central Valley, pollution is likely to be especially severe at the beginning of the year, prompting the authorities to initiate such drastic measures as to stagger school hours, ban cars with particular license plates from being used one day a week, etc. These may be *ad hoc* measures, but often, also, they are considered **responses** that city authorities and citizens undertake while seeking to remedy the problem in the longer term. Call it muddling through if you wish, but it is these state-initiated responses that are an important element of evaluation in this book.

My aims in this text are to offer a serious analytical account of the nature of the urban structure of Mexico City, and to provide an accurate diagnosis of why it exists in the first place. I examine Mexico's recent economic development strategy in Chapter 1 as this, more than any other factor, determines the dynamic of Mexico City's emergence; and of its poverty. Rapid population growth, and often uncontrolled spatial expansion, are analysed in Chapter 2, as is the spatial segregation between rich and poor. Chapter 3 analyses Mexico's political structure and, in particular, evaluates the rationale for existing political and managerial structures and their capacity to respond to the city's needs. Transportation policy and planning experience in general are examined in the following two chapters. Both exemplify well the way in which decisions are taken in Mexico: behind closed doors and with low levels of public debate and involvement. But the rationality, nature and outcomes of city policy in the fields of access to land for self-build, and access to urban services and health care (Chapter 6), suggest that, while the city's administration has become more technocratic and sophisticated in matching policy to needs, it has done so in ways that are politically convenient to the maintenance of the *status quo*. Social control is the order of the day, not a political commitment to improve conditions as rapidly, and as efficiently, as possible. Finally, in Chapter 7 I show how the city's architectural structure both reflects the city's evolution and its philosophies, and, in so doing, helps to reproduce inequality and ideology.

This idea of reproducing and sustaining inequality is a central theme throughout the book. I show how the spatial structure, as well as the architecture and architectonic processes recreate and, in some cases, intensify, poverty. The same applies through the systems of delivery whereby urban resources are distributed and people's needs are met. These systems act to accentuate stratification patterns and to resist other forms of organisation, solidarity and collective action. Indeed, I will show that the very management structure of Mexico City has evolved and is designed to head-off social unrest and to retain political control for the government and its Party (the PRI). But the election results in 1988 and the breaking of the PRI's stranglehold over the electoral process, particularly in the Metropolitan Area, raises important questions over whether the city's political structure can survive by making minor concessions, or whether it must be completely reconstructed. In short, I argue that genuine empowerment of the city's population together with a party-based political agenda for the city's future development is required, if the city is to thrive. The alternative is survival through policies that will comprise more-of-the-same (i.e. muddling through). I do not write the city's epitaph in Chapter 8. There is some cause for optimism, and much to applaud in recent policies.

My own personal involvement with the city began in 1973 when I embarked upon research for a PhD. Soon after arriving in the city I moved into one of the many peripheral squatter settlements in order to analyse at first hand the process of self-build. Since that first year I have returned to the country many times to conduct further research, to attend conferences, to adopt a child, to advise successive governments, to lie on beaches etc. Although the city is too large to know like the back of one's hand, I know it better than any other in which I have lived. Whether as researcher, adviser, tourist or supplicant, the country and the city have been enormously kind to me. I hope that this book is one way of giving something back.

Living in Mexico, and particularly in its capital, can be an exasperating and, sometimes, a frightening experience. I often visualise the country as a mischievous *Genie* who plays with you until you think you can stand no more. Then, just as you feel you are about to die or break down, or get on the first plane home; the *Genie* puts you down – gently. It is as though it is a way of teaching you respect for Nature and for a country that is volatile, and sometimes violent. Not everyone is so lucky. Periodically disasters such as the gas explosion in Azcapotzalco in 1983, and the earthquake in 1985 result in a huge loss of life. Personally, too, I have lost too many close friends to take the *Genie* for granted.

It is a country to which I feel very committed. Yet I had always been slightly disappointed (and surprised) that, although much has been written about Mexico City in journal articles or chapters to books, there was no serious or comprehensive academic text on its contemporary development – with the exception of the recently published *Atlas de la Ciudad de México* (DDF/Colégio de México, 1987). Even this superbly informative study fails to provide an integrated analytical view, written as it is by over 80 different authors. Thus, when invited to contribute an early volume to the 'World Cities Series' I jumped at the opportunity. I was especially eager to write a good book: one that was both analytically strong and perceptive. I wanted it to reflect the **essence** of the city: its guts; its frustrations, its violence and its beauty. I wanted to show that, while not an easy city to live in, the consequences are less dire than some would contrive to have us believe. And although heavily engaged in the city and committed to it, I wanted this book to be as objective as I could make it. As a scholar I was determined to describe the city as I saw it, even if the result was to offend those with whom I have worked, and whom I admire. I hope they will respect this intention and forgive any errors of fact or of interpretation that may have arisen. Responsibility for the errors are, of course, mine alone.

Above all, I wanted this book to be enjoyable to read, so that it reflects some of the fun and pleasure that I had in the making of it. Although it carries a lot of data and statistical material, I have tried to avoid jargon or concepts that would make it impenetrable for the lay reader. Although designed for the specialist student, I would like to think that Mexican politicians and officials, newspaper reporters, analysts of all kinds, and perhaps even the occasional tourist might read it and be stimulated by some of the discussion.

PMW, 6 November 1989
Cambridge, England

Acknowledgements

As I indicated in the Preface, this book is the outcome of 15 years' involvement with Mexico City as researcher and sometime resident. It is impossible, therefore, even to begin to acknowledge all those who have contributed information, ideas and criticisms throughout such a long period. Inevitably, those thanked here are likely to be those most recently embroiled in the making of the book.

Several funding bodies should be acknowledged for having financed research at some stage. Specifically, the UK Overseas Development Administration financed the research project entitled 'Public intervention, housing and land use in Latin American cities' (PIHLU) which I co-directed with Alan Gilbert between 1978 and 1982. The British Academy supported two separate periods of fieldwork in Mexico City in 1982 and 1984. The Nuffield Foundation also supported a visit in 1986. And the bulk of the actual writing was done during sabbatical leave early in 1989 while I was a stipendiary Visiting Research Fellow at the Centre for US–Mexican Studies, at the University of California, San Diego. I am extremely grateful to all institutions and to anonymous referees who, throughout, have been prepared to back my proposals financially and intellectually. Responsibility for the views expressed in this book is mine alone and these views do not reflect those of any funding body.

In Mexico, many institutions have assisted in one form or another. The *Instituto de Geografía*, at the National Autonomous University in Mexico City provided an office and a physical base for fieldwork in 1978–9. My period as an adviser in the Human Settlements Ministry (SAHOP) provided a unique insight into the inner workings of government and planning in Mexico and I should like to acknowledge the support I received then, and subsequently, from Arq. Roberto Eibenshutz, ex-director of the Population Centres Directorate (SAHOP), and of FONHAPO. I also thank Noemí Stolarski, a colleague and friend from that time. I benefited, too, from the invitation to advise the reconstruction agency (RHP) in 1986, when it was engaged in the most dynamic period of its earthquake rebuilding programme.

At Cambridge I am indebted to various people in the Department of Geography: Mike Young, Lois Judge, and Ian Agnew in the drawing office; and Dennis Blackburn in the photographic department. He is to be congratulated for improving the appearance of my (often) poor-quality photographs which are included in this volume. The exceptions are the satellite photograph (Plate 2.2) and that of the city at night (Plate 2.1) taken by a Mexican friend and professional photographer, Nancy González Lanck. Thanks, too, to Jean Lucas, my secretary at Fitzwilliam, for putting up with the 'midden' that was my office during the latter stages of production of the manuscript.

I am also indebted to the large number of individuals who have assisted me at some point or other with my research: not least the householders, agency personnel and private architects and professionals whom I interviewed, sometimes more than once. In particular I should like to thank Arq. Javier Caraveo, one-time Director of Planning in the Federal District. Our many discussions always proved most illuminating and I hope that my interpretations about planning reflect creditably upon some of the major advances that his group managed to implement between 1980 and 1983. I should also like to thank two of his team, Arq. Carlos Tejeda and Arq. Jorge Gamboa (the planning chief in 1989), for the numerous conversations we have had about the city, its architecture and its politics. Among my UK colleagues I am most indebted to Alan Gilbert with whom I worked on the PIHLU project. Many of the arguments about land and servicing emerged jointly in our earlier work and I am grateful to him for allowing them to be reproduced and extended here.

The bulk of the writing of this volume was undertaken between January and April 1989 in California. My warmest thanks go to Prof. Wayne Cornelius, the Director of the Centre for US–Mexican Studies and to all his staff for making my stay at La Jolla so pleasant, stimulating and productive. My thanks go to other Visiting Fellows at the Centre who put up with my often apparently 'off-the-wall' questions about the city, which, interjected *a propos* of no particular conversation, must have struck them as odd at best and, at worst, extremely eccentric. It was fun being a part of that group, and I hope that some of the enjoyment has rubbed off on the text. Finally, thanks to my beach which was a source of stimulation and invigoration, and to Crockett and Tubbs, who, often twice a night, helped while away the hours before Victoria came into my life. To her, I dedicate this book.

Cambridge, November 1989

1
The paradox of dominance yet dependence: Mexico City's Mask of Janus

Cities within a global system

Urban development has traditionally been analysed at two levels (Johnston 1980; Badcock 1984). First, the role of urban centres within a wider urban system: their commercial and administrative functions as 'central places'; their functions as *entrepots* as new lands were colonised; their position within the settlement hierarchy, and in particular their position in relation to some notion of a rank-size rule of urban settlement. The second level of analysis has traditionally concerned the nature of the urban place itself: its land-use structure; the socio-economic attributes of city populations and their behaviour; residential structure and housing markets. Increasingly, too, interest has grown in the role of the local state in mediating the allocation of urban goods. While there was always implicit recognition that these two levels were inter-related, until the 1970s few analysts sought to explain that relationship. Changes and processes within the city were explained largely in relation to the qualities of the city itself, and not as part of the outcome of the operation of a wider logic of national and international processes that, to a greater or lesser extent, shaped city development.

These analytically limited and limiting notions began to change broadly from the 1970s onwards. As is so often the case, however, the 'new' approach overreacted and overstated the relationship. Dependency theory in its earlier formulations emphasised the conditioning effect of 'metropolitan' capitalist expansion in the core (principally Western Europe) upon the Third World which was cast as the 'periphery' (Gunder Frank 1967; Dos Santos 1970; Amin 1974; Wallerstein 1974). Primary products were extracted from the periphery and shipped to the core economies where surplus value was added as they were converted into manufactured goods for export or for local consumption. Because the periphery was 'dependent' and under metropolitan hegemony (often through colonialism), the terms of exchange were unfavourable to the newly penetrated countries. This led to them being actively underdeveloped. Today this account is viewed as both crude and inaccurate (Palma 1978; Roxborough 1979; Corbridge 1986): not least because it failed to explain why certain areas had developed quite successfully (Argentina for example); why certain areas remained locked into pre-capitalist forms of development; and why, if the periphery was subject to an overall conditioning relationship, the experiences of regions were often so different (Roberts 1978; Gilbert and Gugler 1982).

The fact that experiences in the periphery were so different offered an important clue in analysing 'dependent urbanisation' (Castells 1977). Certain sorts of product have a greater propensity to generate urban linkage effects. Temperate agriculture in Argentina for example and coffee production in the south of Brazil led to the development of a broader system of urban centres, and to a wider distribution of wealth between them. Conversely 'enclave' economies such as mining towns, most plantation economies and so on, generated few multiplier effects, and offered little opportunity for wider socio-economic mobility (Furtado 1971). An excellent example of the way in which different types of production systems may shape town development is provided by Balán (1982) for late-nineteenth-century Mendoza and Tucumán: two provinces at the periphery of Argentina. Mendoza's economy developed around wine production on small holdings while Tucumán produced sugar on plantations. Both provinces developed significantly during the period and their principal cities were prosperous and well serviced. But because Mendoza's productive base was oriented towards wine it generated numerous multiplier effects: corks, bottling plants, etc. This created a more diversified and dispersed settlement pattern than was the case in Tucumán, where the focus around plantations and sugar mills led to greater concentration, a restricted economic base, and greater inequality of income distribution.

Thus we have begun to recognise that while broad conditioning relationships imposed by international capitalism are important, it is their *engagement* with the local economic, social and political structures that is all important in determining the shape and nature of dependent urbanisation. For the researcher this is precisely what makes it interesting. As Harvey stated long ago (1973: 232) 'global metropolitanism is embedded in the circulation patterns of the global economy ... different city forms are contained within that economy'. Strangely, though, we have not come very far in our analysis of the relationship nor of different city forms. The focus of study has, quite correctly, been upon the changing nature and logic of capital accumulation processes internationally, and how this is restructuring relations of production on a *global* scale. Increasingly finance operations and, more importantly, production itself, is being put 'offshore' where tax restrictions are less onerous, and where labour is cheaper (Dicken 1986a; Sklair 1989; Herzog 1990). The deskilling of the production process has facilitated the use of labour (often female) in the Third World. The organisation of this process is vested in transnational corporations whose headquarters are in so-called 'World Cities'; their research and development operations are in removed high-amenity locations associated with major seats of learning or technological advance; while actual production is no longer wedded to skilled labour or specific materials supply, and may be located where labour is cheap and passive. As Harvey (1987; 1989) has argued, in terms of time, accessibility and costs of transfer of capital, information and goods, the world has shrunk as capital accumulation processes have become much more 'flexible', capable of switching sectorally and spatially as conditions demand (Martin 1987). This is the so-called New International Division of Labour (Henderson 1986).

Of course, not all cities and countries are locked equally into this arrangement. Certain nations – the Newly Industrialised Countries (NICs) – have successfully created export-oriented manufacturing industries around which they have developed rapidly. Others have not. Having spent two or three decades developing an industrial strategy constructed around import-substituting industrialisation (ISI) in order to reduce their dependence upon advanced capitalist economies, many countries have found it difficult, or have been unwilling, to adjust to export-oriented growth. In Latin America, Brazil, Mexico and to a lesser extent Argentina, have made the adjustment and achieved technological advance in different ways (Gwynne 1985). But the most successful examples remain the East Asian 'Gang of Four' (Singapore, Taiwan, Hong Kong and South Korea). Mexico's export growth has developed around certain investment sectors in which it has a comparative advantage (oil and petroleum-derived products) and around its export-processing zone along the border with the USA. These latter in-bond (assembly) industries have led to the establishment of over 1000 factories and 250,000 jobs. (Sklair 1988, 1989).

Although we now have a more accurate idea of what, precisely, is important in driving the settlement process internationally, few have studied the impact that these processes have upon Third World cities. Thus there is a danger of repeating some of the intellectual errors of the dependency school: we understand the conditioning process, so the outcomes are predictable. The aim must be to verify the relationship and, once again, to analyse how it engages with local structures. We must avoid general-isations such as those relating to World Cities (Friedmann and Wolff 1982), which suggest that certain large metropoli (e.g. Mexico City and São Paulo) fulfil control centre functions in the 'semi-periphery', similar to World Cities such as Los Angeles, New York, London, Frankfurt in the core. Neither Mexico City nor São Paulo exercise anything like the international or even sub-regional importance that World City status proposes. They will soon be the world's largest cities; but economically, financially, techno-logically and in terms of information processing, they are not among the most important.

The urban process

The second level of urban analysis concerns individual city structures. The question becomes one of explaining the changes that an individual city experiences. Most recent research has tended to emphasise as the *leitmotif* of city development its function either as a centre of production or as one of consumption. Obviously a city fulfils both functions, but it is a question of where the emphasis is placed. And in both cases the role of the state is a critically important determinant of city processes. Since this volume is specifically about Mexico City, I do not propose to address the debate head-on although some of my findings may relate to it tangentially. There are many other specialist texts which do justice to the topic (Castells 1977, 1979; Saunders 1979, 1986; Harvey 1985). My purpose in this volume is to analyse the way in which inequality is reproduced through existing city structures and through state action.

Castells' work has focused upon the city as a unit of consumption. For him, it is the way in which the city 'reproduces labour power', particularly through public and private investment in a broad range of services which he calls the 'means of collective consumption'. There are problems with this term as well as with his rather artificial separation of production and consumption functions (Harloe 1977; Pickvance 1976; Saunders 1979). But Castells' work was analytically attractive, especially in relation to the Third World, because it provided an alternative basis around which class consciousness might emerge, and class struggle might be organised. Classical theory of revolution, of course, was built upon an extensive industrial proletariat which did not exist in developing countries and was fast disappearing in advanced nations as well. He identified the provision of the 'means of collective consumption' (cf. the means of production) as the locus around which conflict would evolve, increasingly with the state cast in the position of protagonist responsible for providing the means of consumption (1979: 18). In effect this politicises the issue and brings to the forefront state intervention and response to social conflicts that arise.

Harvey's (1985) work, in contrast, emphasises the logic of capital accumulation processes by different income groups, and identifies different forms of urban development that result from fundamental contradictions arising in the process of capital accumulation, and in particular to over-accumulation crises. The point is that this leads to capital investment flowing out of the 'primary circuit' (of production) into alternative circuits of capital accumulation such as the secondary circuit, which includes the 'built environment for production'. This embraces infrastructure, transportation, investment in the provision of electric power, etc. Capital may also be invested in the 'built environment for consumption' which includes housing, pavements, parks, etc. Often investments fulfil both productive and consumption functions (Lojkine 1976; Saunders 1979, 1986). However, given the large-scale nature of many of these investments, their 'lumpy' nature, etc., there is a tendency for capitalists to underinvest

4

in the built environment for production and consumption. Instead it is the finance market and often the state which takes on investment in large-scale projects. This switch of resources requires a credit system to be created, controlled by financial and state institutions which play a mediating role between the primary and secondary circuits of capital accumulation (Harvey 1985). They play a crucial role in affecting the volume and direction of capital flows and cannot, therefore, be excluded from a study of urban development processes (see also Lamarche 1976). The tendency towards overaccumulation is a contradiction arising from the competitive nature of relations between members of the capitalist class, and it dictates a cyclical nature of capital flows into the secondary and tertiary circuits. These investment cycles are argued to have different 'wave' lengths or periodicity (Harvey 1985; Gottlieb 1976).

The shift or 'switching' of capital into the built environment leads to a 'displaced class struggle' (Harvey 1985) which Harvey sees as essential for social change and for resisting the 'violence' that will otherwise be visited upon working-class populations in cities. Thus, as with Castells, urban politics move to centre stage (Saunders 1979, 1986). However, while the potential for conflict exists, so too does the propensity for state intervention to defuse, coopt or ultimately repress working-class movements – as will be demonstrated throughout this book.

From 'Boom to bust': Mexico's recent economic development

In this section I want to sketch out the backcloth to Mexico's recent economic performance, to concentrate primarily upon the nature of economic structural change in recent decades and identify the objectives and outcomes of economic management since 1970. This will provide a context in which Mexico City's growth and predominance may be analysed.

Economic change before 1970: the years of the 'miracle'

The economic and social upheaval caused by the Mexican revolution during the second decade of the century gave rise to one of the most stable and arguably least oppressive societies in Latin America. Yet it is also one of the most unequal. Neither rapid economic growth between 1940 and 1970, nor enormous expansion in oil production during the late 1970s have significantly changed levels of income inequality, though both processes have generated major changes in the nature of economic activity.

In the short term the Revolution (1911–18) caused enormous disruption. Population declined; the traditional elites were overthrown and replaced by recently formed interest groups some of which were regionally based while others were tied to different sectors of economic activity. Finally, the break-up of agricultural estates led to a period of virtual anarchy in rural areas, causing production levels to fall. Except for manufacturing which recovered quite quickly, economic performance during the 1920s and 1930s was sluggish. This was partly an outcome of worldwide depression and the decline in export earnings from precious metals. It was also a result of inadequate foreign investment which had been discouraged by the radical stance taken by President Cárdenas (1934–40) after he nationalised oil production and actively pursued a programme of Agrarian Reform. As well as being a hero in his own time, Cárdenas' policies laid the foundations of much of Mexico's subsequent political and economic development.

Although the development of an industrial base during the *Porfiriato* (1876–1911) and the social and political transformations that evolved from the Revolution constitute the origins of the Mexican 'miracle', its fruition only came after 1940. Between 1940 and 1970 the Mexican economy grew at over 6 per cent annually and at more than 3 per cent annually per capita. In certain sectors such as manufacturing it was significantly higher. Hansen (1974) explains this phenomenal growth as being due to several factors. First, political stability was achieved during the 1930s and institutionalised in a single governing party (the PRI, discussed in Chapter 3). Second, public financial institutions such as the *Banco de México* and *Nacional Financiera* became the vehicles for large-scale state support and intervention in economic development. In the early period (1940–50) these institutions underwrote the development of basic industries, while later they directed investment to infrastructure such as electric power and railways. Other state interventions were also important and helped stimulate rural to urban migration – necessary to supply adequate cheap labour to the cities. Third, changes in the social and psychological make-up of the elite and the new opportunities for socio-economic mobility enhanced development.

How extensive was this development? In agriculture, production rates grew very fast at the outset but dropped back to average 4.3 per cent between 1950 and 1960 and 2 per cent in the last five years of the 1960s (Scott 1982: 77). By 1970 there were clear indications that agricultural production was in crisis. The production of certain staples was falling behind demand; guaranteed prices for basic foodstuffs had declined in real terms; and land was increasingly being turned over to export crops and to cattle rearing (Tello 1978: 15–20; Heath 1985). However, state response was ineffective since much of the assistance and the new techniques associated with the 'Green Revolution' favoured larger, more commercialised farming units (Cockcroft 1983: 165–73). Increased production levels were especially marked in the highly capitalised sectors of sugar, coffee, market gardening and cotton. The latter, alone, contributed 18 per cent of commodity earnings abroad. Yet despite the pressures working against them, small-scale peasant farmers still generated 40 per cent of the corn crop. Indeed, overall production on *ejidos* kept pace with that on private farms though the former concentrated much more upon the production of staples (Hansen 1974). Nevertheless the overall effect of agricultural development during this period was to reduce the opportunities and viability of the smallholder. Between 1950 and 1960 the level of landlessness rose from 2.3 millions to 3.3 millions (Hansen 1974: 81), and the proportion of the total labour force employed in agriculture declined from 65 per cent in 1940 to 39 per cent by 1970. Similarly its share in gross domestic product (GDP) declined from 23 per cent in 1950 to 16 per cent in 1960 to 11 per cent by 1970 (United Nations 1980).

It was in industrial development that the 'miracle' was most pronounced. Manufacturing grew at over 8 per cent annually (Hansen 1974: 41). Import-substituting industrialisation complemented investment in activities that produced goods for export. The state intervened to enhance Mexican competitiveness abroad by devaluing the *peso* in 1949 and 1954 and by holding down wage increases. Foreign investment in Mexican industries was stimulated by providing infrastructure, by tax incentives for new firms, by low rates of tax generally, and after 1965 by special concessions in the US–Mexican border zone which made it highly profitable for US companies to establish industries in that area using Mexican labour.

This very successful period of economic growth had widespread repercussions upon both the total population and its distribution. Total population increased rapidly from 19.6 million in 1940 to an estimated 81 million in 1987. Also, Mexico became primarily an urban country. The proportion of the national population living in urban areas (defined as more than 10 000 people) rose from 22 per cent in 1940 to 42.3 per cent in 1970, and today stands at around 55 per cent (Scott 1982: 53).

Yet, despite the impressive rates of economic growth recorded, the distribution of incomes has not altered significantly. Indeed, it appears that the early phase of rapid economic growth was achieved at the expense of growing income inequality. Measures of inequality show an increase during the 1950s when the position of the poorest income groups deteriorated (Makin 1984). In the 1960s the lowest 40 per cent of the economically active population earned only 11 per cent of the national income and there were pessimistic forecasts that this situation was unlikely to alter appreciably during the 1970s (Navarette 1970). In fact some recent progress has been made. The level of income inequality has declined (from a Gini coefficient of 0.551 in 1956 to 0.503 in 1977 (Makin 1984: his Table 2.6). With the single exception of the lowest paid 10 per cent, all income groups have improved their position in absolute terms. But, if the fruits of economic growth have trickled down to a limited extent, they have fallen mostly into the laps of the middle- and upper-middle-income groups. The Mexican 'miracle' appears to have resulted in a redistribution of incomes in favour of these middle-income groups at the expense of the top and bottom sectors. (Hansen 1974). Income distribution in Mexico remained one of the most unequal of all Latin American nations (Weisskoff and Figueroa 1976).

Moreover, by 1970 the high social costs associated with economic development were beginning to surface. Wage levels and employment conditions were worsening and the 1970 census revealed enormous levels of deprivation among large sectors of the population. There were also political consequences: growing alienation among the intelligentsia; increasing unrest in rural areas and the first signs of groundswell of public protest in low-income areas of the cities. In particular the disturbances of 1968 and 1971 were key signals which demanded adjustment to the policies that had previously sustained the so-called period of 'stable development' and heralded a period that was, perhaps optimistically, referred to as 'shared development' (Teichman 1988).

'Boom, bust and belt-tightening': instability and austerity

Economic management and crises 1970–88

In order to tackle some of these problems, incoming president Echeverría sought to assert the directive role of the state in the national economy and created or revitalised a large number of state enterprises in the fields of production, distribution and welfare (Tello 1978; Needler 1982; Goulet 1983). Public sector expenditure in social welfare increased significantly in real terms. Wages were increased, tax reforms were proposed as were other actions which sought to favour working classes at the expense of the private sector (Tello 1978). Inevitably many of these proposals encountered strong resistance from elite groups (Cockcroft 1983), but they failed, ultimately, not because of that opposition but rather as a result of a combination of national and international factors. The promise of gradual structural changes to the economy foundered, and the period emerged as one of disequilibrium and erratic economic expansion.

Although the overall economy continued to grow at a satisfactory rate during the 1970s (at an average of 5.9 per cent of GDP between 1971 and 1980) it has not been a smooth passage (Padilla Aragón 1981: 14). Whereas between 1963 and 1970 the growth of GDP per annum never fell below 6.3 per cent, the period 1971 to 1980 saw it fall below 6 per cent on several occasions (Table 1.1). Three 'depressions' figure prominently: the first began late in the administration of Díaz Ordaz and reached its worst point in 1971; the second began in 1973 but its impact did not really become discernable until the latter part of 1974 and culminated in a near 100 per cent devaluation of the *peso* just before Echeverría left office in 1976. The economy did not pick up again until López Portillo reflated in 1978 and thereby abandoned policies imposed by the IMF as conditions for their support. Unfortunately, the spurt of economic development in the late 1970s was short-lived and failed to touch, in any appreciable way, the underlying structure that had contributed to the earlier crisis. A third 'depression' emerged as the economy overheated, bringing about further devaluations and IMF intervention in 1982–3. During each crisis the GDP growth rate per capita dipped below 1 per cent (Table 1.1).

These crises are partly an outcome of the Mexican system of mandatory

Table 1.1 Growth, prices and purchasing power in Mexico since 1970

Year	Percentage increase in GDP over previous year[1]	Percentage GDP per capita (rate of development)[2]	Inflation: percentage increase in CPI[3]	Purchasing power over previous year[3] percentage variation for:	
				(a)	(b)
1970	6.9	3.5	7.0	10.8	2.7
1971	3.5	0.1	5.3	−5.1	−0.1
1972	7.9	5.0	5.0	12.6	0.5
1973	8.2	4.9	12.0	−6.2	−5.2
1974	6.3	2.8	23.8	9.9	−4.5
1975	3.0	2.4	15.2	0.9	1.2
1976	2.1	1.2	15.8	11.6	0.7
1977	3.4	0.5	28.9	−0.9	−0.8
1978	8.3	5.2	17.5	−3.4	−2.9
1979	9.2	6.2	18.2	−1.1	−1.1
1980	8.3	5.4	26.3	−6.6	−3.7
1981	7.9	5.1	28.5	2.3	1.9
1982	−0.6	−3.1	57.6	−1.9	−3.3
1983	−5.3	−4.8	101.7	ND	ND
1984	3.7	0.7	65.5	ND	ND
1985	2.7	0.3	57.7	ND	ND
1986	−3.1	−2.9	86.3	ND	ND
1987e	1.4	ND	131.8	ND	ND

Notes:
(a) minimum salary; (b) wages in manufacturing industry; CPI consumer price index
ND no data

(1) *Source:* GDP figures are calculations by the author based upon *IMF International Financial Statistics*, various volumes. 1987 estimates are from the Economist Intelligence Unit, *Country Report – Mexico*, No. 3, 1988.

(2) *Source:* Banco de México, *Indicadores Económicos 1965–1982*, August 1984.

(3) *Source:* Banco de México, *Cuaderno mensual, Indices de precios*, no. 75, July 1984. CPI calculations by author. Percentages show price rise over previous year.

change of government every six years and reflect a degree of heady largesse in matters of public policy during the final months of any administration. They are also an outcome of demands by the President-elect that the incumbent 'clean the slate' and carry out any measures that are likely to be unpopular (such as devaluation) before the new Executive takes over. This was a feature of the handover in both 1976 and 1982. Indeed some authors view this regular renewal as a positive advantage allowing a clean break to be made, and new commitments to be forged (Whitehead 1980; Purcell and Purcell 1980). When López Portillo took office he was able to appear as conciliator between the government and private sector and the simple fact of his accession did much to restore public confidence. President Salinas, too, after his narrow victory in the 1988 elections, has a clear mandate to undertake fresh initiatives to modernise the government party and to win back some of the electoral support that has gone over to the opposition (Cornelius 1989).

A recent view, with which I concur, is that all Presidents are committed to economic expansion from their fourth year onwards if not before (Whitehead 1984). Policies of economic austerity oblige the state to make deals with those social groups that are likely to suffer most and upon which, ultimately, they depend for their legitimacy (e.g. the unions, and the poor), but such agreements can only be expected to endure for two or three years, after which growing unrest demands some degree of reflation. Also, inter-ministerial competition associated with the struggle to win the nomination for the Presidential succession itself creates strong spending pressures which the incumbent is unable to prevent (Teichman 1988). By 1984 there were already signs of growing unrest and of unwillingness on the part of the trades unions to continue to cooperate. Thus it appeared that some degree of reflation was underway. However, this failed to materialise given, first, the intensity of the crisis; second, the lack of available funding for a reflationary programme; third, the further cut in oil prices and the second 'round' of austerity measures enacted in 1985–6; and fourth, the personal determination of President De la Madrid to 'break the mould' and to succeed where his predecessors had failed by applying a brake upon expenditure throughout his *sexenio* in office. Even the intense competition for the Government Party candidature in 1986–7 did not lead to any significant reflation.

But it would be wrong to suggest that these crises are merely a sexenial phenomenon: external and internal factors are also important. The inter-national recession and rising prices from 1973 onwards, a growing balance of payments deficit, inflation, and the transfer of capital out of the country were important factors which contributed to undermine the economic strategy of the Echeverría administration. Similarly the effects of inflation, over-extended public sector expenditure, and a growing balance of pay-ments deficit (partly induced by the enormous purchases of foreign techno-logy for the exploitation of oil resources and for industrialisation), led to spiralling indebtedness from 1978 onwards. When at the end of 1981 Mexico was obliged to cut the price of its oil by 8 dollars a barrel in line with other oil-producing countries, the country found itself suddenly broke. In effect the depressed price of oil meant a loss of 10 billion dollars in earnings during the first half of 1982 (Cockcroft 1983). Much of this anticipated revenue had already been earmarked and spent.

In part these crises reflect mismanagement, corrupt practices and bad luck. Inevitably, also, they are a consequence of Mexico's relationship with the USA and with other developed nations. The Mexican economy is not all its own. Despite a 'Mexicanisation' law which in the past was supposed to ensure that the majority of stock remained in the hands of Mexican nationals, in practice much of the investment came from outside and often constituted a controlling interest. The ratio of profits leaving the country through multinational corporations against new investments is very high, and leads to an overall 'decapitalisation' and 'dollarisation' of the economy (Cockcroft 1983). Many of the larger industrial enterprises are dominated directly or indirectly by the multinationals; basic foodstuffs have to be imported (despite attempts by the SAM and more recently PRONAL to encourage self-sufficiency), and imported goods far outweigh revenues from exports even taking into account the greatly increased revenues derived from petroleum. Finally, the most important sources of credit originate abroad. In 1982 the costs of debt servicing alone amounted to over one-half of the revenues derived from exports.

The deepening nature of this dependency relationship invariably works to the advantage of the external power, not simply in terms of growing access to a cheaper workforce that can be readily hired and fired according to the dictates of the originating economy, but also in the influence that can be exercised by the dominant power in negotiations in the area of foreign policy, and for the purchase of commodities such as oil, natural gas and technology. There is considerable evidence that, in exchange for credit, Mexico has been forced to provide the USA with greater quantities of oil and gas than it would have wished, and at prices preferential to the USA (Cockcroft 1983).

Since 1983 Mexico has struggled to work its way out of the economic crisis and while showing considerable success has found high US interest rates an unanticipated extra burden. Public spending has been cut, as has expenditure on imports, particularly in the area of capital goods which were reduced by 60 per cent (in value) in 1983 (*Comércio Exterior*) April 1984: 360). Attempts have been made to encourage foreign investment. Inflation, which was 102 per cent in 1983 was reduced to 66 per cent in 1984 and further (to 54 per cent) in 1985. Although it rose again dramatically (to 159 per cent) in 1987 there are recent signs that De la Madrid's economic reforms and 'Social Pact' with the private sector and with the unions have led to inflation rates of 51 per cent in 1988 and an estimated 18 per cent for 1989 (Duran 1988; Whitehead 1989, *Unomásuno* 19 December 1988). Wage hikes have been severely restrained: in 1983 alone their real value was eroded by an estimated 23 per cent and the 1984 real increases only kept up with inflation in that year.

Debts amounting to 23 billion dollars that were due to be repaid between August 1982 and December 1984 have been successfully rescheduled to provide four years' grace with repayments spread over a further four years (*Comércio Exterior* April 1984: 364). Also, longer-term rescheduling has been negotiated which effectively shifts the burden of repayment into the 1990s. However, early in 1989, debt renegotiation remained a key issue and government ministers were prevented from undertaking any actions that would require significant public expenditure – at least until successful renegotiation was achieved in July that year.

Opinions vary about the efficacy of De la Madrid's policies. Some criticise the lack of real economic growth and the entrenchment of an increasingly inflationary programme (Kouyoumdjian 1988). Others are rather more positive about the reforms and optimistic about the medium- and long-term benefits that will accrue, and which the Salinas administration is expected broadly to continue (Duran 1988).

The paradox of dominance yet dependence

Sectoral performance 1970–88

Since 1970 the several sectors of the economy have been affected in different ways. In terms of contribution to GDP and relative importance as an employer of the economically active population, agriculture has fared particularly badly although its decline began much earlier than the 1970 cut-off point considered here. The industrial sector, and in particular manufacturing, has grown sharply both in terms of its contribution to GDP (from 31 per cent for industry in 1965 to 40 per cent by 1983), as well as in employment opportunities that have been created. In recent years, of course, petroleum has reinforced the contribution that this sector makes to GDP though it generates relatively few jobs. Services and commerce have always been important, and since the 1960s have contributed over 50 per cent of GDP. However, its significance in absorbing labour has increased dramatically over the same period: from 27 per cent of the economically active population in 1960 to over 43 per cent today. Much of the growth observed in services has involved the creation of 'genuine' jobs in banking, large-scale commerce, etc. However it also includes the atomisation of jobs within the tertiary sector: in activities such as small family businesses, individuals stalls, lottery ticket sales and so on.

In manufacturing there has been a significant shift in emphasis and a concerted effort to move away from the United Nations ECLA-inspired models of import-substituting industrialisation which, it was widely recognised, had failed to generate sufficient jobs and was leading to an increase in dependence upon imported technology, capital and raw materials. Instead, investment has focused upon industries which utilise locally occurring natural resources, such as food processing, mining, and petroleum production and petrochemicals (Needler 1982). An attempt was also made to extend 'backward' industrial linkages by developing machine tools and the production of other capital goods, themselves often dependent upon steel. However, at least in the short term, this process has threatened to increase Mexican dependence since much of the 'seed' technology is developed outside the country (Cockcroft 1983). According to one source there was a nine-fold increase in production goods imports during the 1970s, which led to the dramatic rise in the public sector debt (ibid.).

The important point to recognise here is that, while overall economic expansion occurred during the 1970s, it has been a stop–start process and was mainly concentrated within the industrial sector. While this generated considerable employment, particularly in manufacturing, the largest growth area as far as jobs are concerned has been in the service sector. The expansion of the public bureaucracy during the 1960s and especially in the 1970s was another important feature of the changing structure throughout the period. Inevitably these processes have had major repercussions upon prospects for employment and wage levels both nationally as well as in Mexico City, points to which I return below.

The impact of oil production

Within this sharply contrasting economic performance, oil has been both a boon and a bane. While the rapid rise in known reserves and the dramatic increase in production allowed López Portillo to reflate the economy, it also led ultimately to economic collapse. Knowledge about the extent of known reserves was a carefully guarded secret from 1974 onwards. At the end of the Echeverría period reserves were set at 6 billion barrels; López Portillo uprated this estimate in 1978 to 20 billion, and again in 1979 to 40 billion (Whitehead 1980). In 1982 Mexico's reserves were set at 72 billion barrels and an eventual level of 250 billion barrels is not beyond the bounds of possibility. This would place Mexico not far behind Saudi Arabia in the oil-producing league (Cockcroft 1983).

At the outset of the boom in petroleum production the government expressed its firm intention to avoid squandering revenues from oil. It did not wish to encourage consumption of expensive consumer durables, nor was it prepared to bail-out the purchase of food imports on an ongoing basis. In the rhetoric of the day oil was a national patrimony to be shared by all and to be used to generate long-term development. This conflict between 'expansionists' and those who urged more caution became the locus around which intense inter-ministerial infighting occurred between 1978 and 1981 (Teichman 1988). Ultimately the forces of caution (these included De la Madrid as the then Minister of Programming and Budgeting) won-out and got the head of PEMEX (the state-run Petroleum Company) dismissed, but not before he had driven up production levels, contracted huge debts against future oil revenues, and silted-away a large fortune for himself and other cronies. Thus, the damage was done. Little wonder, perhaps, that De la Madrid, once he was President, 'went after' the ex-head and had him imprisoned for embezzlement.

The original idea was that no single country was to receive more than 50 per cent of total exports in an attempt to avoid the dangers associated with overdependence on a single source of foreign earnings. As a consequence a daily production limit was set of 1.5 million barrels throughout the 1980s (Cockcroft 1983). Yet this was later raised to 2.2 million barrels and production at the end of 1982 was scheduled to reach 2.7 million (Needler 1982). Work to expand port development to cope with much higher levels of oil production also suggested that in the future these production ceilings would count for little. Moreover, despite the guideline about a maximum level of exports to any single country, by 1981 more than four-fifths was going to the USA. The crux of the problem was that Mexico needed the money: the only way out of the spiralling indebtedness was to increase oil production. Also important, however, was external pressure from the USA to provide increasing amounts of oil and gas for its consumption, thereby allowing that country to conserve the rate at which it was obliged to exploit its own reserves. The substance of that pressure was the threat to withold financial credit.

The paradox of dominance yet dependence

Oil production also fuelled the crisis in another way. Inevitably, perhaps, almost all of the technology required to extract the resource had to be purchased from abroad. This meant that PEMEX was spending far more than the profits it was bringing in. By mid-1982 it had accumulated a foreign debt of $25 billion: one-third of the nation's total (see Whitehead 1980; Cockcroft 1983).

The problem of indebtedness

The absolute size of the public debt has grown inexorably since the mid-1970s and by 1982 had come to account for a large slice (around 46 per cent) of public expenditure. This rise reflects the growth of new credits, the effect of devaluations, and, more recently, high interest rates in the USA. By 1984 Mexico's foreign debt totalled 89 billion dollars which, along with Brazil, was the world's highest. More immediately the problem was one of servicing the debt and, when in 1983 De la Madrid announced that Mexico was going to find it difficult to meet even the interest payments, further interim credits were provided. Since then a large proportion of debt repayment has been rescheduled. Under López Portillo, from 1978 onwards, interest and debt repayments consumed over one-half of foreign exchange earnings (Padilla Aragón 1981). In 1984 this ratio had been reduced to 24 per cent (*The Sunday Times* 13 May 1984).

Some attempt has been made to raise revenues through taxation. Echeverría initiated higher rates of income tax and raised the efficiency with which they were collected. However, the relative contribution made by income tax compared with other forms of tax (oil, imports, etc.) fell from 51 per cent to 33 per cent between 1979 and 1981 (Padilla Aragón 1981). Moreover, López Portillo raised the thresholds upon which income tax was liable, and imposed value-added taxes so that the net effect of tax reform under his administration was to produce a more regressive structure (Needler 1982). Later, his successor increased further the rates of value-added tax and extended them to all but basic subsistence commodities.

The benefits of growth: employment and wages

The pattern of growth and contraction that I have described had an important impact upon access to employment, the opportunities for economic mobility and the value of real wages. But, as I have shown, this period also saw a shift in the structure of the Mexican economy, particularly in relation to the nature and scale of activities carried out within the industrial and service sectors. The imposition of austerity measures by the IMF seriously affected government expenditure and wage levels. The changing nature of employment and wages, therefore, were a response to all of these factors and are not simply an outcome of the rate of economic expansion. The important question to ask here is whether the poor benefited significantly from the changes induced since 1970 and from the oil bonanza. For several reasons the broad answer to this question is no. The Mexican workforce is increasingly vulnerable to international economic changes. The level of labour utilisation in Mexico is low compared with most other Latin American countries (around 27 per cent of the population), and has actually declined from 39 per cent at the beginning of the century. According to some authors this suits capital in so far as it represents a 'reserve army' of labour that may be maintained without cost and absorbed when required, as well as functioning to keep wage levels low, and to weaken attempts at labour mobilisation for improved conditions, etc. (Cockcroft 1983; but cf. Roberts 1978). Labour can be regularly hired and fired according to the amount of work available, or to ensure passivity of the workforce or to avoid contractual obligations required for 'permanent' employees. Workers are also arguably 'superexploited' not simply by being paid low wages but also by an increasing intensity of work and by an extension of the working day (Cockcroft 1983). Vulnerability is further heightened by the growing use of capital-intensive technology in industry that generates less employment per unit cost investment – arguably an undesirable trend given Mexico's youthful age structure and the estimated 800 000 new jobs required each year to cater for those entering the labour market for the first time, and to allow for the growing participation of women within the economy (Mexico, SPP 1983).

Vulnerability also arises from the fact that so much recent industrial investment comes from outside the country. Increasingly we may conceive of an international division of labour whereby transnational companies utilise the relatively cheap labour available in Mexico and effectively decide the workforce's livelihood. This is not a feature unique to Mexico alone; it is a familiar enough problem in the UK. But Mexican workers are more vulnerable than their British counterparts because the level of dependence upon external companies is greater and because their activities are often limited entirely to the assembly of imported goods. There is considerable truth in the maxim that when the USA sneezes, Mexico catches cold.

Unemployment

Unemployment has shown a clear tendency to increase during the periods of economic depression identified earlier. In both 1974–5 and 1982 many factories were closed down temporarily, others went bust as did many small-scale businesses. There are few good data available that describe 'unemployment' or underemployment at a national level though one estimate suggests that early in 1975 more than 4 million workers were affected (amounting to 25 per cent of the economically active population [Padilla Aragón 1981]). It is estimated that in 1984 approximately two in every five Mexicans did not have full-time employment. Between 1981 and

1983 the rate of 'urban unemployment' nationally rose from 4.2 per cent to 12.5 per cent.

There is some evidence to suggest that families today are consciously adopting a 'strategy' to maximise their employment opportunities. It has been argued that in rural areas many peasants have become 'proletarianised' and now work as waged labour on large-scale commercial farms but also utilise family labour in subsistence farming or in handicrafts to survive economically (Cockcroft 1983). Multiple earning strategies have long been utilised in the *maquiladora* industries in the north which employ a large female workforce. There are suggestions that similar patterns may be observed elsewhere and that they may have growing relevance for urban areas (Cockcroft 1983; Pommier 1982).

Neither should we assume that, given a choice, people automatically opt for employment in the 'formal' sector: an industrial job for example. Recent labour market studies in Guadalajara which has a tradition of 'outwork' in clothing and shoemaking suggest that some self-employment or employment in the 'informal sector' may maximise the household's earning power (Arias and Roberts 1985). Also, during periods of wage restraint informal-sector activities are not subject to the same restrictions as formal employment: prices and fees can be raised more readily to meet inflation. Although it might be sensible to have one household member employed in an industrial enterprise, thereby enabling the family to qualify for social security, it may be economically and socially more convenient for other household members to work 'casually' (González de la Rocha 1988).

Nevertheless, it does appear that during times of crisis when workers are shed from the industrial sector they seek employment in the tertiary sector. Indeed, if they are to work at all there is no other alternative. In Mexico City for example, tertiary-sector employment expanded between 1974 and 1978, not all of which can be explained by an expansion of civil service jobs (Pommier 1982).

Inflation and wages

The whole of the period 1970–88 is epitomised by rapid price inflation. Between 1971 and 1978 it averaged 15.2 per cent annually in contrast with 2.8 per cent between 1959 and 1970 (Padilla Aragón 1981). Since 1977 it has spiralled to 25 per cent per annum (1977–80) and to almost 100 per cent in 1982 and 1983. It declined in 1984 but overshot the 40 per cent target for that year. However, considerable success has been achieved through the 'Social Pact' in bringing down inflation from 159 per cent in 1987 to an estimated 19 per cent in 1989. But during the 1980s wages have not increased concomitantly. Although real wage levels were restored in 1974 to above their previous highest level, the purchasing power declined sharply after 1977 (Table 1.1; see also Bortz 1983). Maximum wage increments (*topes*) allowed for workers were negotiated by the government and the unions between 1977 and 1980 and again in 1983 but these fell far below price increases over the same period.

In Mexico the traditional means of protecting the value of real wages has been one of regular (usually annual) revision of the daily minimum wage. In times of rapid inflation or after a devaluation, minimum wages have been renegotiated but have usually resulted in an erosion of purchasing power. They take a month or two to introduce, while in contrast prices are raised overnight, bringing about short-term hardship. Since late 1982 there has been some call from organised labour for the introduction of a 'sliding scale' whereby wages are automatically adjusted every three months to take account of price increases (Bortz 1983; Garavita 1983). During the early months of 1983 the government was lukewarm in its response to the idea. Although it was never admitted publically, a sliding scale adjusted automatically every three months would have reduced the bargaining strength of the government in its relations with labour. Also, from the government point of view, faced with appeasing the IMF, a decline in real wages was both anti-inflationary and provided a windfall to capital whose production costs were thereby reduced. Nevertheless, as a concession to the unions, the Ministry of Labour agreed to allow the Minimum Salaries' Commission to meet 'as often as required'.

Therefore, in terms of changing access to employment opportunities, levels of full employment for both men and women, and the value of real wages, the impact of economic growth upon the wellbeing of the average Mexican worker has been extremely limited. Granted, during the buoyant periods employment has expanded but there has been little evidence of fundamental structural changes that will enhance future employment prospects. Quite the opposite: the industrial structure has become more dependent upon foreign technology and capital; it has become more capital intensive; and the level of indebtedness means that any freedom to manoeuvre that the government might have exercised will be severely curtailed. The first round in the battle to use oil resources to guarantee the country's future was lost resoundingly.

Mexico City's changing economic structure

The limits of Mexico City

Throughout this book by 'Mexico City' or the 'Metropolitan Area of Mexico City' I mean the contiguous built-up area shown in Figure 1.1. Thus I will not usually include municipalities whose urban areas are not contiguous (such as Teotihuacán to the north east of the city). For the time being these form part of a separate 'Metropolitan Zone' which is not quite the same as Metropolitan Area, although the two spatial entities are fast converging as the city continues to expand outwards. Thus the definition of

The paradox of dominance yet dependence

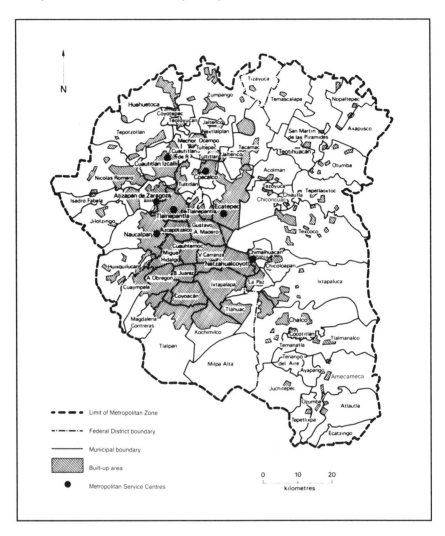

Figure 1.1 Political limits of Mexico City, the Federal District, and the 'Metropolitan Zone'

what constitutes Mexico City is not fixed. It cumulatively absorbs outlying political entities, as will be demonstrated in the following chapter.

Within Mexico City the 'Federal District' is a political unit created in 1928 which, as I shall describe in Chapter 3, enjoys a unique administrative status within the confederation of Mexican states. Internally it is divided into 16 political-administrative units called *delegaciones*, which are identified on Figure 1.1 and on most subsequent maps. Parts of Mexico City's built-up area extend outside the Federal District into the surrounding State of Mexico. Here, as in all states, municipalities form the political sub-units.

Autonomy of the municipality is an important element within the Mexican Constitution, although in practice it counts for little (Rodríguez 1987).

Occasional reference to the 'inner-city' or downtown area loosely refers to the four central *delegaciones* of Miguel Hidalgo, Benito Juárez, Cuauhtémoc and Venustiano Carranza. In the past this area was also often referred to as the 'City of Mexico' but in order to avoid confusion this study will not adopt the term.

The city's national dominance

The impact of national economic growth between 1930 and 1970 was felt disproportionately in the capital city. Indeed, public policy acted to further concentrate industrial production in Mexico City throughout this period. The city was especially favoured in its access to electricity generation, oil and other power sources and products for petrochemical industries, the provision of water and drainage facilities and, last but not least, was the focus of road investment programmes (Garza 1986). As a result of these state-led investment programmes the rate of return on industrial goods was systematically higher in Mexico City than elsewhere (ibid). However, Garza concludes that although industrial location in the Metropolitan Area offered many micro-economic advantages, it presented major obstacles and problems when viewed from a national perspective. Specifically, it generated all sorts of diseconomies for the city's population (pollution, long journeys to work, high costs of basic goods, etc.); and it also accentuated the regional inequalities that exist between the capital city and the provinces.

Mexico City, with slightly less than one-fifth of the national population always exercised a position of paramount importance in the national economy. The proportion of national GDP created within the city grew from 30.6 per cent in 1940 to 36 per cent by 1960 after which it roughly levelled off at between 37–38 per cent (Puente 1987). In certain sectors its national importance is even more pronounced: in transportation until 1980 for example. In services, too, around one-half of the total national product generated by the sector is created in the Metropolitan Area (Table 1.2). The same is true for manufacturing industries. Although slightly less than one-third of all industry production in 1980 took place in the city, this included 48 per cent of all manufacturing activities (Garza 1987). The decline in the proportion of total industrial production registered since 1960 (Table 1.2) reflects a rising importance of alternative industrial centres elsewhere in the country. But the predominance in manufacturing remains, and indeed, with the exception of the total wage bill 1970–80, this predominance appears to be increasing (Table 1.3).

Moreover, these high levels and steady increases since the 1930s are not only relative, but reflect, also, a dramatic absolute increase from a total city GDP of 7010 million (constant 1950) pesos in 1940 to 115 338 million pesos in 1980. In effect, city GDP has doubled in real terms every decade,

19

The paradox of dominance yet dependence

Table 1.2 Gross domestic product generated by Metropolitan Area of Mexico City, by sectors 1940–80

	Mexico City's gross domestic product in constant (1950) *pesos*				
	1940	1950	1960	1970	1980
Agriculture	30	28	37	54	105
Percentage of national product	0.6	0.3	0.3	0.3	0.4
Percentage of all sectors	0.4	0.2	0.1	0.1	0.1
Industry	2286	3378	10509	16086	34619
Percentage of national product	33.7	27.1	42.7	30.9	30.8
Percentage of all sectors	32.6	27.2	39.1	28.4	30.0
Transportation	576	1038	2184	2775	4788
Percentage of national product	66.6	62.2	60.0	58.1	34.4
Percentage of all sectors	8.2	8.4	8.1	4.9	4.2
Services	4118	7983	14128	37816	75826
Percentage of national product	40.9	46.0	44.0	49.0	50.5
Percentage of all sectors	58.8	64.2	57.2	66.6	65.7

Source: Sistema de cuentas de México. Producto interno bruto por entidad federerativa año 1980, Dirección General de Estadística, SPP.

Table 1.3 Evolution of Mexico City's manufacturing industry 1930–80

	1930	1940	1950	1960	1970	1980
Number of establishments (%)	6.8	8.7	20.0	29.9	27.9	29.5
People employed (%)	19.0	24.6	25.0	46.0	41.9	46.9
Total earnings (%)	32.9	36.7	44.1	41.1	51.3	48.0
Capital investment (%)	22.6	29.3	35.5	37.8	42.5	ND
Manufacturing contribution to GDP (%)	28.5	32.1	40.0	46.0	46.8	48.0

Source: Garza 1987: 101.

broadly paralleling national expansion. Inevitably this growth generated a huge demand for labour especially in manufacturing and in services, much of which was met, initially at least, through provincial-to-city migration (see Chapter 2).

Broadly, there has been a shift away from industrial and manufacturing production towards services since 1960 (Table 1.2) and this 'tertiarisation' of the city's economy has almost certainly intensified since 1975. In 1975 industry and services generated 30 per cent and 61 per cent of GDP respectively: by 1985 these proportions had declined to 26.5 per cent in the case of industry, and risen to 67 per cent in the case of services (Villegas 1988). A similar decline is observable in the case of people employed in industry which declined relatively from 43 per cent of the national total to 36.5 per cent between 1975 and 1985 (although the absolute numbers increased from 724 312 to 936 624).

The most important industrial activities undertaken in the city comprise: the manufacture of clothing, furniture (and repairs), publishing activities, production of rubber, plastic and metal goods as well as the assembly and repair of electrical goods. Also, the city generates a large number of transformation industries oriented towards the local market: consumer durables such as food, drinks, shoes, petrol and gas refining, etc. Only 35 per cent of those employed in industry produce goods which have no intrinsic orientation towards the local market (Camacho 1987). The important point to recognise is that most of this production is for a **national** and **local** market rather than oriented towards global markets. To the extent that Mexico exports, other areas are more important: such as the 'finishing off' in-bond assembly industries (*maquiladoras*) developed in the northern Mexico–US border zone (Herrera 1988; Sklair 1988). The location of the different types of industrial activity varies within the city. These features are examined in greater detail in Chapter 4, but briefly the Federal District and its inner areas are increasingly oriented towards non-durable consumer goods industries, while the outer areas and the metropolitan periphery are more directed towards capital goods and the production of consumer durables.

It seems inevitable that sooner or later there must be some relative decline in the importance of manufacturing industry in the Metropolitan Area, but unless existing decentralisation policies begin to take effect, perhaps along-side the initiatives set in train after the 1985 earthquakes, the absolute increases will continue (Garza 1986, 1987).

The changing nature of the urban labour market

Mexico City constitutes the largest single labour market in the world with over 7 million economically active people within it (Judisman 1988). According to one study approximately 37 per cent of those working in metropolitan areas in Mexico were classified as being in the 'informal' sector, which comprises those activities – usually small scale – which carry only small or minimum levels of capital investment and involve low levels of productivity. Moreover, wages are low and personnel engaged in the informal sector are usually not covered by social security or other forms of public welfare protection. In Mexico, self-employed workers may contribute into the social security system but, given the lower levels of benefits they receive, relatively few opt in. Since the 1970s general under-standing of the nature and organisation of the informal sector has tended to emphasise the importance of its close connectedness with, but domination by, the 'formal' sector (Bromley 1978). Even informal sector activities such as 'garbage-picking' are often tightly organised and closely tied into the formal sector in terms of the recycled inputs they provide on terms set by the latter (Birkbeck 1978; Castillo *et al.* 1987).

In Mexico City there is a clear trend of inter-related expansion and contraction of the two sectors, with the formal sector growing at the expense of the informal sector during times of economic growth and buoyancy (eg. 1978–81) and the latter picking up the slack in the labour market during the period 1983–7. The proportion of workers employed in the informal sector grew from a low of around 34 per cent in 1981 (when there was actually a labour shortage in unskilled labour for construction, cleaning services and even in some manufacturing industries) to almost 40 per cent in 1987 (Judisman 1988). This is a result of workers being shed from one sector to another: as well as a tendency for an increase in the participation rates of those members of a household who work (especially women) during periods of economic crisis and declining real-wage levels. Nationally the participation rates of the economically active population increased from 43.6 per cent to 51 per cent between 1970 and 1980. In Mexico City they have always been higher, but also show both a tendency to increase (47.6 per cent to 53 per cent) and to fluctuate between a low of around 53 per cent when times are hard and extra-income-earning activities of women, children and the elderly become especially essential to survival (de Oliveira and García 1987; Judisman 1988). The increased rates of economic participation have been especially noticeable in the State of Mexico municipalities between 1970 and 1980 for both men (70 per cent to 76 per cent) and women (18.6 per cent to 27.6 per cent) (de Oliveira and García 1987).

As well as more male and female workers entering the workforce, there have been important structural changes in Mexico City's labour market since the 1950s (Muñoz and de Oliveira 1976). Although the overall proportion of those employed in the tertiary sector has not changed greatly, the activities that these personnel fulfil have probably become more 'productive'. Although the data displayed in Table 1.4 at first glance suggest some decline in the importance of service jobs between 1970 and 1980 this is almost certainly due to the larger number in the 'unspecified' jobs category (de Oliveira and García 1987). Many of these workers are in the tertiary sector which the same authors argue continues to absorb around 50 per cent of the total economically active population (ibid.). The absolute expansion of jobs in the tertiary sector is not directly related to migration and a proliferation of urban 'marginality', nor does it demonstrate rising 'underemployment' (García, Muñoz and de Oliveira 1982). These are 'genuine' jobs, the creation of which is associated with rising tourism, and the expansion of service activities associated with industrial change and consumerism.

Within the tertiary sector, too, while female participation in the labour

Table 1.4 Economically active population in Mexico City, by principal
worktype and sex of employee 1970–80

	1970 Total	1970 Men	1970 Women	1980 Total	1980 Men	1980 Women
Professional	10.18	9.69	11.34	11.82	11.01	13.37
Bureaucrats/directors	5.14	6.04	3.07	2.11	2.70	0.99
Administrative personnel	11.59	12.85	22.56	17.01	14.31	22.20
Commerce and sales	11.03	11.18	10.67	10.18	10.36	9.83
Service workers	21.15	15.71	33.68	15.18	12.89	19.60
Agricultural workers	2.41	3.13	0.75	0.85	1.11	0.35
Workers and artisans	31.05	38.14	14.71	26.91	32.81	15.56
Unspecified	3.24	3.25	3.22	15.93	14.81	18.10

Source: de Oliveira and García 1987: 145.

market is increasing there also appears to be a segmentation process
operating once people are in employment. Patterns of wage inequality
between men and women, for example, do not appear to be the result of
prejudicial hiring and firing of women relative to men, but are associated
more with the allocation of tasks **once in employment**. Men are more likely
than women to be in the 'public space' where their access to tips and higher
wages rates is enhanced (Chant 1990).

During the 1970s employment and unemployment changes reflected
closely the national economic fortunes described earlier. Within the Federal
District the cycles of unemployment associated with economic decline are
quite clearly enunciated (Pommier 1982). Unemployment reached its height
in 1977 (at 8.4 per cent of the active population) and dropped regularly
thereafter to less than 5 per cent by mid-1980. It rose again in 1982 and
1983. Compared with men, female workers are particularly vulnerable to
unemployment, as are migrants and those workers entering the labour
market for the first time (Muñoz, de Oliveira and Stern 1977; Pommier
1982). Certain districts like Netzahualcóyotl have particularly high levels
of unemployment and underemployment. Although there has been an
important rise in unemployment and work was not easily come by during
1977–8 and 1982–3, the situation is almost certainly better in the capital
than elsewhere. Also the rate of female participation in the economy of the
Federal District is almost twice the national average (García *et al.* 1982). In
part this has come about by the expansion of *maquila*-type industries
established in Mexico City over the past decade.

Nevertheless, wages are not high. Despite the fact that the majority enjoy
regular employment, most are poorly paid. According to one sample, 41 per
cent of those employed earned the minimum wage or less while 60 per cent
earned less than twice the official minimum wage (Muñoz *et al.* 1977). The
minimum wage offers a subsistence income and in June 1984 stood at just
under 5 US dollars a day.

Getting by in Mexico City: survival strategies of the urban poor

At a national level access to social security coverage is unequally distributed both spatially and socially (Ward 1986). Although Mexico City residents fare much better than their provincial counterparts, there are important variations in access across the city – as I shall discuss in later chapters. Also, as I pointed out above, there are important temporal changes in the economic welfare of the city's population which lead to important shifts in economic participation rates, work strategies between sectors and so on. But on a day-to-day basis how do they survive? How do those without social security protection, for example, meet one-off payments such as the costs of a 'barefoot' midwife to attend the birth of their children? How can they afford to bury their dead? These may appear to be extreme examples but they are just a few of the problems that low-income people must regularly confront in Third World cities.

The strategies which poor people adopt to overcome these difficulties have been recognised implicitly for a long time but they have only recently become the subject of detailed study. Few low-income families possess sufficient savings upon which to draw in times of crisis. If hard cash is required and cannot be borrowed from friends or kin then the alternatives are the pawn shop (assuming that one has an object worth pawning), or loan sharks who charge very high rates of interest. Some households belong to an informal credit system in which an agreed amount is contributed weekly and each household takes turns to receive the pooled amount. In the event of an unexpected crisis suffered by one member, the group may allow that individual to swap their turn and take that week's savings.

Given a lack of savings and facing job loss or declining real wages people may respond in a variety of ways. First, they go without. Children drop out of school (or never go in the first place) and take on some sort of employment. People stay ill: stomach complaints go uninvestigated and untreated; minor treatable illnesses become chronic. Meat, if it ever figured in the weekly diet, disappears altogether and is replaced by cheaper but less nourishing substitutes. Likewise leisure pursuits that cost money are dropped. Finally, shelter costs are minimised: cheaper rented accommodation is sought; others squat and construct dwellings made from recycled throwaways. Those who have achieved some security of land holding and through self-help have improved their dwellings to a basic level must suspend consolidation and may even lose their plots of land through failing to meet repayments.

A second strategy involves adjustments at the household level. Nuclear households may be extended by the inclusion of brothers, sisters, in-laws, married children, etc. Extended family structures offer greater security in that they are likely to have more members engaged in paid employment, so if one person loses their job there is still some income from other sources. Extended family systems also have other advantages such as mutual child care which allows more adults to work outside the home (Chant 1985).

Multiple employment strategies in both nuclear and extended households frequently aim to ensure that members are represented in both the 'formal' and 'informal' sectors thereby enjoying the benefits of both. Having at least one member in the 'formal' sector will usually ensure special health care benefits for the whole family; having others in the 'informal' sector can mean higher earning capacity. During times of wage restraint those working in the public and private sectors may suffer an erosion of purchasing power, while self-employed workers in the informal sector can more readily raise their prices to match inflation (Arias and Roberts 1985).

Third, the poor may seek support from a wider social network that embraces kinsfolk, friends and neighbours. Individual circumstances vary of course, but these networks are often critically important sources of credit, food, child care, moral support, and accommodation (Lomnitz 1977). Networks may be formalised through godparent relationships (*compadrazgo*) created around a range of events such as confirmation or graduation as well as baptisms. Occasionally, economic obligations may be so onerous that better-off families whose support is constantly sought by kinsfolk are forced physically to remove themselves from the residential group in order to reduce the demands upon them (Kemper 1974).

Finally, an important source of welfare protection is patronage from one's employer. To some extent traditional relationships between workers and a patriarchical head of a family enterprise have disappeared as factories and stores get bigger and are run along corporate lines. However, many workers in small firms still go to their boss if they need financial assistance. Similarly, domestic servants and retainers frequently expect their employers to help them and their families in times of difficulty. Usually this involves a loan, cash handouts, medication and payment to visit a private doctor. Middle-class patronage of this nature is rarely analysed or taken into account. Yet it is important both in quantitative terms in the level of protection and assistance it offers, and ideological and political terms in so far as it reinforces the dependency of one social group upon another and sustains the continuance of discretionary patronage that pervades the social system in Latin America.

Decentralisation: attempts to redress Mexico City's predominance

Thus Mexico City presents a dual face. Internationally it is highly dependent, forms part of the global semi-periphery, and has relatively little clout. In some respects its impact and role within the international economy is less important than minor cities such as Santa Cruz in Bolivia, or Medellin in Colombia: centres of cocaine production and distribution.

Yet the paradox is that at a national level it is all powerful and all dominant. In 1989 its 19 million inhabitants comprised approximately one-fifth of the national population. The Urban Development Plan of 1978 highlighted the two extremes: Mexico City on the one hand; and on the other, some 95 000 settlements with less than 2500 inhabitants. In particular the aim has been to stimulate the growth of intermediate-sized urban centres within integrated functional systems (Mexico SAHOP 1978). Politically, the Federal District is the seat of government, and power is heavily centralised in the Executive and in Federal Agencies and Ministries. Mexico City has also enjoyed a privileged access to employment opportunities compared with most other urban centres. In 1980 the Federal District alone received 54 per cent of all private investment (Makin 1984). In terms of consumption of electricity, transport, water and public utilities those living in the city are heavily subsidised (Bazdresch 1986).

In the area of social welfare facilities the city does better than the provinces. The Federal District has three times as many doctors *per capita* than elsewhere. The number of people covered by some form of social security is twice as high as the national average. School facilities are better in the Federal District and children are not only more likely to attend school, but also to complete the various stages of schooling. Similarly the lion's share of investment resources for public housing have been directed towards the Metropolitan Area. Between 1963 and 1975 for example 58 per cent of the public housing units constructed for the poor and for lower-middle-income groups were built within the Metropolitan Area (Garza and Schteingart 1978).

Therefore it is not surprising that people still flock to the city (although migration has long since been displaced by natural increase as the primary determinant of growth). Nor is it surprising that relatively few people leave, despite the quality-of-life horror stories to which I alluded in the Preface.

Chilangos rule OK?

People born in the Federal District are known as *chilangos*. In Mexico the use of 'nicknames' for people is very common and rarely ill-intentioned or taken badly. However, for many in the provinces the term *chilango* is increasingly associated with antipathy and resentment. As a Federation, Mexico has, until recently, looked to different states for its national leaders, and although the centre benefited more than anywhere else, so, too, did those regions from which top leaders and camp followers were drawn. Part of the problem today is the emergence of a new, more technocratic elite educated (if not born) in the capital and whose origins and loyalties are less regionally oriented. Moreover, the Federal District is beginning to export people as a result of public-sector efforts at decentralisation to provincial towns and as middle-class intellectuals decide that the diseconomies of the city no longer offer professional and personal attractions as they did in the past. But the resentment traditionally felt in the provinces about Mexico City's preferential treatment is nothing compared with tension and anger expressed today against many *chilangos* who are perceived to be taking housing and jobs which ought, by rights, to be destined for local people.

They are also accused of driving up land and housing prices, and generally acting with arrogance and a lack of sensitivity. 'Sé patriota – mata un chilango' (Be patriotic – kill a *chilango*) is a sad, but not uncommon, slogan found in provincial cities.

Decentralisation programmes

In addition to arguments relating to greater equity and a reduction in regional disparities there are various other reasons why decentralisation programmes have figured prominently in government rhetoric in recent years. The need to contain the growth of Mexico City and to deflect migration to alternative 'growth poles' was one motive; as was the desire to move towards a more 'log normal' distribution of urban population another (Mexico SAHOP 1978). Better utilisation of national resources and the industrial development of petrochemicals together with the need to stimulate growth in towns and cities throughout the territory informed the Industrial Secretariat's Development Plan of 1979. Politically, too, in the provinces where the government Party (the PRI) had traditionally been very strong several major cities were captured by the right wing opposition party (PAN) and the image of the PRI had become rather tarnished. By the late late 1970s and early 1980s there was a perceived need among government supporters for the centre to assist the 'periphery' in its efforts to restore legitimacy to state and municipal governments and to reinforce support for the party apparatus.

The most strenuous efforts at decentralisation were made between 1982 and 1988 under the De la Madrid administration. But the concept of decentralisation may cover many meanings. Where it embraces some **devolution** then it may involve a genuine shift in power and autonomy to peripheral regions. However, **deconcentration** may achieve some shift in resources, people and plant, but it does not, necessarily, invoke a shift in the spatial locus of power. It may simply transfer specific faculties to a subordinate person or administrative entity (Rodríguez 1987). The central superior body retains the possibility of control. Genuine devolution of power in Mexico has been resisted and the main purpose and effects of De la Madrid's decentralisation policies were 'the establishment of a system which is decentralised administratively but remains centralised politically' (ibid.). Although the new legislation reasserting the principle of municipal autonomy and freedom offered potential powers of devolution to the grassroots, in practice the initiative was 'hijacked' by state governors who appropriated the power and resources intended ostensibly for the municipality (Rodríguez 1987). Thus, although there was some slight reaccommodation in the political centre of gravity towards the states, this did not go far enough, nor did it percolate down to the municipal level.

Some decentralisation of public administration was achieved during the 1980s. The public health system was decentralised, as were several 'light-weight' government departments and institutes (Jeanetti Davila 1986;

27

Beltran and Pórtilla 1986). But the lack of full political commitment to decentralisation was laid bare by the government's response to the earthquake in 1985. The worst damage was sustained in the inner-city of the capital, and large-scale financing was generated from national fiscal resources as well as from loans through the World Bank. Instead of using these resources to undertake reconstruction outside Mexico City and to relocate those people who had lost their homes, the government opted for the politically less contentious strategy of rehousing the population *in situ*. Moreover, the financial terms on which rehousing low-income households was undertaken represented another major subsidy. In real terms cost recovery was minimal on the fiscal resources. The opportunity to use those funds as 'seed' capital for a national housing programme was given up – for political reasons.

It seems unlikely, therefore, that Mexico City's national predominance will change very much during the remainder of this century. Even if some relative shifts in power, resources and population were to take place it would be illusory to believe that this would significantly change or improve conditions in the capital. Mexico City will continue to grow – albeit a little more slowly. Thus we need to examine how far the city can accommodate future expansion, and develop systems of political management that will determine whether it survives, thrives or falls apart. This is the subject of the following chapters.

2
Urban growth and the appropriation of space: from plaza to suburb to megacity

Introduction: the growth of la region más transparente

La region más transparente is the title of a novel about Mexico City written by the contemporary Mexican author Carlos Fuentes. Usually translated as 'Where the air is clear' it describes a clarity and sharpness of light in the Central Valley that was truly remarkable – at least until the early 1960s. Since that time, clear days, when as a daily feature of the landscape one can see 50 kilometres to the distant snowcapped volcanos of Popocátepetl and Iztaccíhuatl, have become so rare that they are something of a novelty worthy of comment and photographs in the following day's newspapers.

In 1989 Mexico City with over 19 million inhabitants is the third largest city in the world after New York/Jersey and Tokyo/Yokohama. Unlike its two slightly larger counterparts, however, it is a single city rather than two or more large urban centres which merge into a single metropolitan area (Hauser in Brambila 1987). Also, it is growing much faster than its developed nation counterparts and by the turn of the century Mexico City and São Paulo will be the world's first and second largest cities respectively. But league tables based upon city size do not mean very much. More important are the processes and dynamics of city growth and the effects that these have upon the life chances of its citizens. In the previous chapter I examined Mexico City's role in the national and international division of labour and spelt out the changing nature of job and income-earning opportunities for the city's population. I want now to describe the impact that some of these economic processes have had upon city growth. Specifically, I want to exemplify how social inequality is embedded within the spatial structure of the city. Later chapters in this book will address the extent to which these inequalities are changing in ways that are socially progressive or regressive.

My focus in this book is unashamedly contemporary, but it is important to recognise that Mexico City is not only the largest single urban area on the continent but is also one of the oldest. Located in an upland basin some 7000 feet above sea level the Spanish *conquistadores* built their colonial city upon the ruins of Tenochtitlán – the capital of Moctezuma's Aztec Empire. Indeed this was the final phase (albeit one of the most splendid) of several periods of urban or ceremonial-centre development in the Central Valley which has left pyramids in Cuicuilco (now adjacent to the southern peripheral motorway) dating from 400BC, and at Teotihuacán (some 30 kms to the north-east) which flourished around 300AD (Hardoy 1967). In the final chapter of this book I will return to describe briefly the city's early history. Here I wish only to note the important Pre-Columbian origins and to encourage the interested reader to explore that history with others more competent than I (Sanders, Parsons and Santley 1979; Duran 1967; Calnek 1975, 1976).

Nor do I wish to dwell upon Mexico City's development during the colonial period when it flourished as the political and economic centre for New Spain ruled by proxy through a series of viceroys until independence early in the nineteenth century. Thereafter the city was the seat of power for a series of rulers with often dubious and spurious legitimacy such as the self-imposed 'Emperor' Iturbide 1822–4; the Archduke Maximilian imposed by a French expeditionary force in 1863; and a series of elected presidents the most notable of whom was Benito Juárez whose death in 1872 heralded the rise to supreme power of the dictator Porfirio Díaz. The latter ruled Mexico with an iron hand between 1876–1910 before himself being displaced by the Revolution (Kandell 1988; Lombardo 1987). From the outset, the colonial city was laid out on a grid-iron pattern as prescribed by the Spanish monarchy and later embodied in the Laws of the Indies established by Philip II in 1573 (Stanislawski 1947). The central plaza was the seat of the principal Council buildings, the Treasury, and the Cathedral, while the rich lived in large residences on the main streets running east and north. Once established the colonial city expanded relatively little between 1700 and the mid-nineteenth century covering an area of approximately 6–10 km^2 (Morales 1987, Connolly 1988). It was not until the stability and economic growth of the *Porfiriato* that physical city expansion began in earnest.

From the very earliest settlement to the present day the site has been an impressive one. The Central Valley is surrounded by volcanic mountains, two of which rise 10–12,000 feet above the valley floor. Much of the area was a saline inland lake and even during Aztec times fresh water had to be brought to the city by aqueduct. Today, most of the lake is gone and once marshy land is covered by a swathe of low-income settlements. Although smog and pollution restrict visibility across the city, on days that are clear or at night when driving down from mountain passes on the Toluca or Cuernavaca high roads, the sight is spectacular and awesome. I can think of no other place in the world where so much humanity is laid-out and visible to the naked eye (Plates 2.1 and 2.2).

Plate 2.1 View north across Mexico City from the southern slopes of Ajusco (Photo by courtesy of Nancy González Lanck)

Plate 2.2   Satellite photograph of the Metropolitan Area

City demography since the Revolution

The years after the Revolution saw a sharp rise in the City's population as stability began to draw back many of those who had fled the strife and as camp followers joined the principal protagonists of those vying for power. Between 1921 and 1930 the population of the central city grew from 615 000 to over 1 million (Negrete and Salazar 1987). Once the traumas of Revolution were over the city grew steadily and the pace quickened with industrialisation from the 1930s onwards. The population of the 'urban area of Mexico City' grew by 4 per cent per annum during the 1930s and rose to over 6 per cent between 1940–50. Since that time annual growth rates have been around 5.5 per cent – approximately doubling the population every twelve to thirteen years. In 1989 the population of the Metropolitan Area is over 19 million people and although current estimates suggest a continuing slowdown in growth rates (due in large part to the national decline in rates of natural increase) there is little doubt that Mexico City's population in the year 2000 will be around 26 million inhabitants (Delgado 1988).

The dynamics of city growth derive from provincial migration and from natural increase. The latter has been most important and although birth rates are lower in the Metropolitan Area than generally apply elsewhere in Mexico, they remain high. Crude birth rates for the city have declined from 44.7/000 inhabitants in 1950–60 to 37/000 1970–80. Death rates have declined from 12.9/000 to 7.3/000 during the same period (Partida 1987). Mortality and morbidity rates for the city appear higher than for many areas of Mexico, but this may reflect more assiduous reporting and the higher level of treatment available in the capital (Fox 1972). Migration is also an important factor although its relative weight is often overstated. During the early decades of the city's growth, when the demand from industry for labour was high, migration flows accounted for around 60 per cent of population expansion, with the remainder the result of natural increase (Unikel 1972). But, in the absence of a sharp decline in the birth rate achieved nationally or locally, natural increase quickly took over as the principal component of city growth. The initial in-migration of young adults accentuates those cohorts about to embark upon the family-building stages of their life cycles. For example, at the Metropolitan level decennial rates of annual natural increase declined from 3.18 per cent to 2.97 per cent between 1950–60 and 1970–80 respectively; while the proportion attributed to migration fell from 1.66 per cent to 1.09 per cent. Indeed, as I will explain later, some downtown areas of the Federal District have been losing population through out-migration to the suburbs. Never-theless, cityward migration added an estimated 38 per cent to the city's net population between 1950 and 1980 (Partida 1987a). In 1978 the Metropolitan Area's growth rate was 4.45 per cent per annum comprising 2.30 per cent natural increase and 2.15 per cent migration (Stolarski 1982). According to the National Population Commission (CONAPO) the aim was to reduce this to 3.51 per cent by 1982 and to 1.64 per cent by the year 2000 with most of the decline relating to natural increase.

Province-to-city migrants do not usually move much further than they have to in order to satisfy the original reasons for their move (Cornelius 1975; Gilbert and Ward 1986). In Mexico City by far the largest proportion came from adjacent states or from those that were relatively near (Ward 1976a; Stern 1977: 126). During the earlier stages of out-movement from villages and towns there is evidence that migrants are 'positively selected' from among their home population and tend to be slightly better-off, better educated and more venturesome than those who stay (Balan et al. 1973; Kemper 1974, 1976). Combined with ready access to work in the expanding industrial base during the 1950s–70s it is not surprising that one observes few economic or housing-improvement differences between city-born people and migrants, even where lower education opportunities in rural areas have led to significantly lower levels of schooling (Gilbert and Ward 1986).

Thus at least until the mid- to late-1970s, when access to job opportunities and land markets began to tighten, migrants to Mexico City do not appear to have been disadvantaged relative to city-born inhabitants. Nor is there a general tradition in Mexico City of migrants from particular regions or villages concentrating themselves spatially and almost exclusively in one or two neighbourhoods, although some anthropological studies of specific groups do give a contrary view (Lomnitz 1977; Butterworth 1972; Orellana 1973). Although kin and *paisanos* (people from the same village) are very important in providing orientation and assistance to newly arrived migrants, the large size of most Mexico City neighbourhoods and the sorting processes associated with selection of permanent residence make unlikely the local dominance of migrants from a single region. However, information flows and antecedent kin contacts do lead to some minor (but not dominant) concentration in particular settlements. **Within** settlements or tenements, however, some spatial clustering and concentration may be observed.

Spatially this population growth has led to a 'wave' of rapid population expansion moving outwards, first through the DF and then into the surrounding State of Mexico (Table 2.1). The central area of the city absorbed most of the population increase until rapid suburbanisation processes began to take over during the 1940s. Thereafter many city centre residents began to move out to the intermediate ring *delegaciones* (boroughs), several of which tripled or quadrupled their population between 1940 and 1950 and doubled it during the 1950s (see Figure 2.1). A ban imposed in 1954 upon the authorisation of low-income sub-divisions in the DF also led to some premature movement into adjacent State of Mexico municipalities of Netzahualcóyotl and Naucalpan where the law did not apply. This process was accentuated later once the wave spread out further into other municipalities during the 1960s and 1970s. In addition to those municipalities already mentioned, Tlalnepantla and Ecatepec

Table 2.1 Mexico City's population growth 1940–80 for different 'rings' of expansion

	Total population (millions) and decenniel growth rates								
	1940		1950		1960		1970		1980
	%		%		%		%		
Metropolitan Area	1.64	6.7	3.14	5.6	5.4	5.5	9.2	4.6	14.4
Percentage in DF	107[1]		103[1]		96		80		64
Central city area	1.44	4.5	2.2	2.3	2.8	0.6	2.7	−1.1	2.7
First 'ring' areas[2]	0.18	15.8	0.8	10.2	2.2	8.3	4.9	4.6	7.6
Second 'ring' areas[3]	0.01	—	0.05	—	0.4	14.2	1.3	9.6	3.3
Third 'ring' areas[4]	—	—	—	—	—	—	0.01	—	0.8

Source: Adapted from Negrete and Salazar 1987: 128.

(1) 1940 and 1950 figures exceed 100% because some population centres within the Federal District were located outside the built-up area of Mexico City.
(2) Includes the following *delegaciones/municipios*: Alvaro Obregon, Azcapotzalco, Coyoacan, Gustavo Madero, Iztacalco, Iztapalapa, Cuajimalpa, Naucalpan, Netzahualcóyotl.
(3) Includes the following *delegaciones/municipios*: Magdalena Contreras, Tlalpan, Xochimilco, Tlahuac, Tlalnepantla, Chimalhuacan, Ecatepec, Atizapán, Coacalco, Huixquilucan, La Paz, Tultitlán, Atenco, Cuautitlán Izcalli.
(4) Includes the following *delegaciones/municipios*: Milpa Alta; Cuautitlán de Romero Rubio, Chalco, Chiautla, Chicoloapan, Chiconcuac, Ixtapaluca, Nicolas Romero, Tecamac, Texcoco.

expanded greatly at this time as did some southern *delegaciones* of the Federal District. Since the 1980s the 'wave' of growth has run into the more distant municipalities of Cuautitlán, Tecamac and Chalco: today's rapid-growth areas. It is predicted that the population of Tecamac will grow from around 156 000 in 1987 to over 1 million by the turn of the century (Delgado 1988).

The physical expansion of the built-up area

Until just before the latter part of the nineteenth century Mexico City was confined to what is often referred to as the First Quarter (*Primer Cuadro*) comprising an area of about 20 km² centred around the Zocalo or main plaza (Morales 1987). In Chapter 7, I analyse the architectural influences and urban investment interests which shaped the beginnings of the move outwards on the part of the elite, and only brief mention will be made here. Traditionally, the elite lived in and around the city centre in large palaces and residences close to the prestigious main square and its municipal and ecclesiastical buildings (Scobie 1974; Schnore 1966). The poor lived in precarious hovels and tenements well away from these streets, but remained

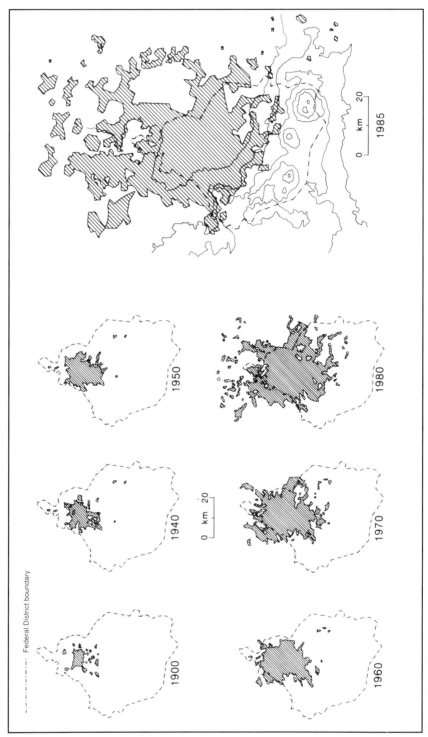

Figure 2.1 The physical expansion of the Metropolitan Area 1900–1985

within walking distance of their place of work. Transport to the outlying townships was by private or public carriage but there was no daily commuting (Vidrio 1987).

In Mexico City, as elsewhere in Latin America, the movement of the elite out of the city centre was predicated upon a changing social base in which displays of status through housing and consumption were fast becoming a substitute for status ascribed through birth. A new political elite, economic mobility, and an emerging class of *nouveau riche* and middle classes led to property development in the physically most attractive areas of the (then) periphery. This was to the south and west, down the Paseo del la Reforma – the Mexican equivalent of Paris' Champs Elysees – which had been redesigned as a splendid boulevard around the turn of the century to link the President's (then) official residence (Chapultepec Castle) and his workplace at the National Palace in the Zocalo. Congestion in the city centre was becoming problematic, as was the fear of exposure to dangerous diseases. Many wealthy elites already had 'summer houses' in outlying *pueblos* such as Tacubaya, Mixcoac and Coyoacan. During the earlier period only they could afford private horse-drawn transport, but the improved roads facilitated greater and more continued use of these residences.

Animal drawn trams existed in the late nineteenth century and were gradually replaced by electric trams from 1900 onwards. These new trams, combined with two 'suburban' railway lines to Tacubaya and Villa Guadalupe respectively allowed the rich and middle classes to move outwards, as well as the expansion north and east of working class barrio districts (Vidrio 1987). As the rich moved out so their residences were turned over to alternative land uses, either for commercial purposes or subdivided as tenement accommodation for working-class families. If colonial mansions were not available for conversion to single room accommodation for low-income households then they were purpose-built (Plates 2.3, 2.4). Once set in train, the process whereby properties were evacuated by the wealthy and 'invaded' by the poor intensified, and accelerated further land-use changes, rising densities, greater congestion and insalubrity.

During the 1930s and 1940s expansion took place in all directions but most markedly in ribbon-type development towards the south, some of which began to incorporate the nearest *pueblos* along the newly extended main roads of Insurgentes and Calzada Tlalpan. Subsequently the interstitial areas were also in-filled (Figure 2.1). From the 1940s all social classes were engaged in land acquisition processes, usually in different directions. The appropriation of space and the segregation between social groups intensified. Broadly speaking the better-off groups moved west and south; while the poor moved east and north. During the 1950s large tracts of urban land began to be privatised for conversion to residential subdivisions. Later chapters of this book will take up the rationale for these processes, but this privatisation of space was often achieved illegally through the improper disestablishment of *ejidal* land (held under use-rights and in common by

Plate 2.3 Classic *vecindad* comprising colonial building subdivided to form low-income tenement accommodation

Plate 2.4   Purpose-built *vecindad*, downtown Mexico City

specified residents of agrarian communities) which was subsequently converted to elite and upper-income estates. Alternatively *ejidatarios* sold off
parcels of land to low-income households (Varley 1987). At the other
extreme real estate developers privatised government lands which were
ceded for agricultural improvement purposes only to convert and sell these
areas as unserviced plots to the poor. Private landlords in the east of the city
also saw the opportunity to capitalise on poor-quality land holdings by
selling off plots with minimum capital investment. Settlements such as
Ramos Millán and Aeropuerto in the east of the DF were laid out (if not
occupied) during the early 1950s before the ban was introduced in 1954
prohibiting any further residential subdivisions. Thus the ban, although
enforced, was not terribly effective because many large settlements had been
established if not populated before it was imposed. Elsewhere, landlords
struck informal deals with households and, in exchange for some payment,
turned a blind eye to occupation of parcels of their land. However, an
important feature of the ban was that it stimulated the supply of plots in the
State of Mexico (where the ban did not apply), and by 1960 residential
expansion into Naucalpan, Netzahualcóyotl and Ecatepec was well under
way (Figure 2.1). Between 1940 and 1970 the built-up area of the city grew
almost seven times from 117.5 km^2 to 746.4 km^2, and the population
increased concomitantly (Delgado 1988).

Since the 1970s the Metropolitan Area has grown rapidly and by 1980 it
covered over 1000 km^2 extending significantly into the State of Mexico
where some 36 per cent of the total population now lived. In 1989 the built-
up area extended over approximately 1250 km^2 and the current 'frontiers'
of physical expansion have spread into the south eastern municipality of
Chalco where *ejidal* lands are being alienated alongside the motorway to
Puebla; to the north into Tecamac; and into several municipalities in the
north west and west. In the Federal District opportunities for physical
growth are more restricted by the lack of suitable available land and the
tight controls exercised by the urban authorities over its alienation. The
principal zones of conflict are the southern mountain slopes of the Ajusco
and the rich agricultural lands around Xochimilco in the south east. Further
out the *delegaciones* of Tláhuac and Milpa Alta are beginning to grow
appreciably and are expected to double their populations between 1980 and
2000 (Partida 1987b). Elsewhere in the DF much of the population growth
is being absorbed through increasing densities on existing plots.

Population densities in Mexico City

Crude population densities are high in Mexico City relative to other World
Cities, being slightly higher than Tokyo, double that of Metropolitan New
York, triple that of Paris and four times that of London (Connolly 1988a:
70). Compared with other major Latin American cities densities are at least
double those of São Paulo and Buenos Aires, and roughly similar to the very
topographically constrained Caracas. Only the Asian cities of Bombay,

Calcutta and Hong Kong appear to have higher densities (ibid). Moreover, some areas of the city have extremely high densities: the central area for example. But also some of the older 'consolidated' low-income irregular settlements have densities of over 400 people per hectare (Connolly 1988a). Once all plots are occupied in irregular settlements, densities rise as young households have children, and as other families are accommodated on plots either in formal rental tenements developed by small-scale landlords, or as kinsfolk and/or grown-up children double-up on plots living independently in a 'compound' type of arrangement (Ward 1976a; Lomnitz 1977).

Until the early 1950s population densities in Mexico City corresponded with the normal bell-shaped curve distribution usually associated with western 'developed' city structures (Connolly 1988a). Densities were high in the city centre (around 800 inhabitants per hectare) and declined outwards giving an average of 133 in 1940. Significantly, however, these densities and the nature of the curve have changed since that time. First, overall densities declined to 104 in 1960, before rising again to 122 in 1970 and 148 in 1981 since when it has dropped back a little to 139 per hectare. In particular there has been a sharp difference between the density changes experienced in the DF and the State of Mexico. In the Federal District average densities rose steadily from 127 to 172 between 1960 and 1981. In the State of Mexico where recently established settlements lead to much lower densities these, too, have fluctuated. They increased from 23 per hectare in 1960 to 135 by 1975, but have since fallen back to 121 and 112 in 1981 and 1983 respectively (Connolly 1988a: 81). A second major change is that the top of the 'bell-shaped curve' began to cave-in as central downtown densities fell from 800 to 550 by 1970 (ibid.: 83). This was a result of the absolute decline in cheap rental accommodation opportunities and low profitability of housing investments in the city centre since the 1940s. These densities will almost certainly have declined further as a result of the extensive damage caused in the downtown area by the 1985 earthquake, despite intensive reconstruction and *in situ* housing redevelopment that has taken place (Mexico RHP 1988).

This structure and these fluctuations may be explained primarily by the dynamics of city area expansion which are themselves informed by opportunities for finance capital to invest profitably in the built environment; by public policies to facilitate such profit-taking, and by the agents involved in promoting land sales. This is not the moment to analyse these factors in detail, but the overall production of irregular settlement led to the rapid areal expansion of the built-up area as people moved out of renting into illegal 'ownership'. Thus overall densities declined sharply from 134 persons per hectare in 1940 to 104 persons per hectare in 1960, and were especially low in the sparsely populated and newly created sub-divisions of the State of Mexico (Connolly 1988a). Since then, as noted above, densities have increased owing to a slow-down in the rate at which new land is being alienated illegally for 'ownership' at the periphery, and the greater difficulty that families who rent are experiencing in gaining access to a plot of land in a convenient location and at a price they can afford (Ward 1986). Densities have also fluctuated according to the effectiveness of state efforts to control irregular settlement expansion on either side of the Federal District boundary, and as a result of pressures from petroleum boom-induced finance capital searching for suitable investment outlets in urban development and redevelopment (Ward 1986; Connolly 1988a).

Housing markets and intra-urban mobility

Housing production in Mexico City

City expansion and the dynamics of housing markets are closely linked but the relationship between the two remains poorly understood. Much of the following analysis seeks to identify the processes and the functioning of the (largely) low-income housing system and the considerations that intervene to determine people's moves. For Mexico City there is a lot written about the mechanisms of land development for housing, the agents engaged in the process, the housing needs and strategies of different groups, and the appropriateness and effectiveness of public policies. We know a considerable amount about the nature of some of the interventions within the housing production, circulation and distribution processes depicted in Figure 2.2. But we know precious little about how and **why** the whole processes operate over time (Drakakis-Smith 1981; Burgess 1982, 1990). In Mexico City, at least, little work has successfully explained the dynamics of housing production and the rationale underpinning investment behaviour in the built environment for production and consumption. Some authors have analysed certain aspects which impinge upon housing production, such as the construction materials industry (Ball and Connolly 1987). Others have tried to relate housing development to broader structural conditions but have done so in ways which fail to develop the analysis in sufficient detail (COPEVI 1978); or their interpretations are wedded to a particular ideological position and therefore fail to tackle evidence which is counterfactual (Legoretta 1983; Pradilla 1988).

Indeed, a weakness within my own work has been the tendency to focus upon certain patterns of consumption and distribution that have emerged at different times rather than addressing head-on the dynamics of different types of housing production process and their significance within wider processes of capital accumulation (Gilbert and Ward 1982a; Ward 1986, 1990). Although I have recently begun to address these questions I have deliberately chosen to do so in cities other than the capital (Ward 1989a). Mexico City is probably too large, too complicated and too fast changing for these issues to be explored in sufficient depth as to afford satisfactory explanations – and certainly to cope with the complexity hinted at in Figure 2.2.

In Mexico City, housing is provided either through the public or private

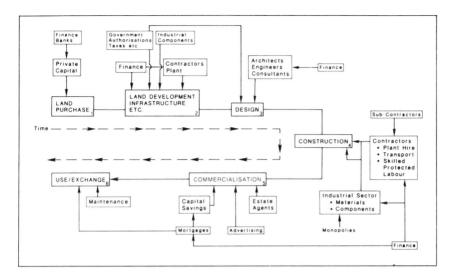

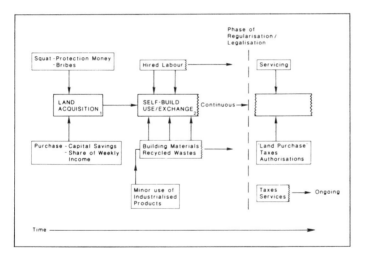

Figure 2.2 Modes of housing production: the 'industrialised' mode (above) and the 'petty-commodity' (self-help) mode (below)

housing markets. The latter includes both formal and informal systems of supply. Public housing intervention has changed in nature and has increased dramatically in recent years (Garza and Schteingart 1978; Ward 1990). Both qualitatively and quantitatively it has become more responsive to different sets of needs and income groups. Until the Housing Finance Programme (PFV) came on-line in the mid-1960s (financed through Alliance for Progress 'seed' capital) housing production had been built solely for specific social security affiliates, often for rent, and much of it in the Metropolitan Area. Subsequently the PFV generated so-called 'social

Urban growth and the appropriation of space

Plate 2.5 'Social interest' housing: Vicente Guerrero project, Federal District

44

Plate 2.6 Government resettlement housing project: Ejército de Oriente, Federal District

interest' housing which, in fact, came to house lower-middle-income groups who could afford the mortgage repayments. Alternatively the same groups 'raided' housing allocated to low-income groups reaccommodated from squatter areas and tenements elsewhere in the city but who could ill afford the transportation and other costs associated with the new housing locations (e.g. Vicente Guerrero, Plate 2.5). Only a few 'minimalist' dwellings which were insufficiently attractive to middle-income groups came to serve exclusively low-income populations, usually relocated from tenement or inner-city shantytown sites (e.g. Ejército de Oriente Plate 2.6). Recently, the housing funds (FOVI and FOGA) have raised their profile of financing middle-income housing provision in the city and elsewhere.

In the 1970s various housing agencies were deliberately created to raise the national profile of housing production and to ensure that housing policy genuinely met with the needs of low-income populations. The creation of INFONAVIT in 1973 for blue collar workers in formal employment raised production dramatically, such that during its first three years the agency generated as many dwellings as the entire state sector had achieved during the previous four decades. Middle-income state employees' needs were met in part by a special fund established for them (FOVISSSTE). Even so, these two funds only met an estimated 11.3 per cent of total annual demand between 1973 and 1980 (González Rubí 1984). Between 1981 and 1983 a large Popular Housing Trust Fund (FONHAPO) was developed to support housing production for those people earning up to or around 2.5 minimum wages and who were not in formal employment or eligible through INFONAVIT. Thus state housing production has become increasingly significant although it still falls far short of annual total demand (Ward 1990). Moreover, much of the housing production today is oriented towards support for self-help housing processes, especially through FONHAPO. Both INFONAVIT and FOVISSSTE have been especially active in the Metropolitan Area, while FONHAPO has had greater impact outside the city where housing costs are much lower, and where it has been able to produce housing at prices affordable to the poor.

Given the limited extent to which demand has been met through the state sector, housing production in Mexico is largely private. Middle-income and upper-middle-income groups seek housing through formal and (usually) legal supply systems; while the poor acquire land illegally and self-build (Connolly 1982). A large proportion of the population (around 44 per cent nationally in 1980) rent dwellings, yet until recently there has been little research into this important minority, and even less consideration of how public policy should address the rental sector (Gilbert and Varley 1990; Coulomb 1989).

Thus much of the supply of housing for low-income groups in Mexico City is privately produced and illegal (COPEVI 1977a; Ward 1976b). Rental tenements (*vecindades*) may comprise old vacated elite residences in which a household occupies a single room and shares toilet and washing facilities which are located in the patio area (Plate 2.3). A single tenement may house several dozen families. Some large *vecindades* were purpose-built during the first four decades, but the physical arrangement is broadly similar (Plate 2.4). Located in and around the inner-city, many of these tenements had their rents 'frozen' in the 1940s. This led to a withdrawal of investment in rental housing by landlords and greater population stability among many working-class households in the central city area who continued to enjoy the pre-1940s rent levels. By the 1970s many buildings had become dangerously dilapidated and there was an absolute decline in the downtown rental housing stock as buildings collapsed (COPEVI 1977a). To compensate, some landlords developed temporary shackyard accommodation on plots around the city centre – the so-called 'lost cities' (*ciudades perdidas*) – the rents of which were not frozen and, although low, represented a high return on the minimal investment made in provisional shacks with limited or non-existent services (Plate 2.7). The most rapidly expanding rental accommodations, however, are the new tenements (*vecindades nuevas*) located in the older irregular settlements. Developed by petty landlords, these tenements are much smaller than their precursors and usually house between five and fifteen families (Plate 2.8). Overall these rental housing systems accommodate around 35–40 per cent of the city's population (Turner *et al.* 1972; Ward 1976b).

Irregular settlements in Mexico City comprise squatter settlements where households capture land through well-orchestrated invasions that involve large numbers of families. Although in Mexico City several famous invasion settlements exist in the south of the city this mode of acquisition tends to be the exception rather than the rule. Illegal subdivision of land for sale – by landlords, real estate companies or *ejidatarios* and/or their representatives – is a much safer, if more expensive means to acquire a plot. They are illegal because servicing norms are not met, or because authorisation of sale and transfer of title is not forthcoming or sought by the developers. Whichever mechanism of land development is adopted, the outcome is broadly the same: unserviced plots (usually around 200 m^2) upon which households take primary responsibility for dwelling construction and management (Connolly 1982). As we observed earlier, rapid expansion of these neighbourhoods occurred during the 1950s–60s, since which time the pace of formation has slowed. An estimated 50–60 per cent of the city's population live in settlements which began through one or other of these land alienation processes, although *post hoc* legalisation and servicing combined with on-site dwelling consolidation and improvement have often dramatically changed the legal and physical status of the neighbourhood (Plates 2.9 and 2.10; see also Chapter 7). Those settlements established in the early period of expansion have long since been engulfed and incorporated to form the spatial 'intermediate ring' of the city, and their densities have increased in the manner described earlier in this chapter.

Plate 2.7 *Ciudad perdida* ('lost city') shantytown

Plate 2.8 Purpose-built *vecindad nueva*: new tenements in older irregular settlements

Plate 2.9 Early phase of consolidation and development in irregular settlement (*colonias populares*) of Mexico City

Urban growth and the appropriation of space

Plate 2.10 Later phase of consolidation and development of formerly irregular settlement showing impact of self-build and service installation

51

Urban growth and the appropriation of space

Intra-city migration patterns in Mexico City: flight to the suburbs?

Explanations about why and how people migrate around Mexico City owe much to the work of John Turner whose seminal paper in 1968 offered the first general model to explain low-income migration patterns in Latin American cities. Residential location was determined essentially by three variables: (1) tenure – specifically the choice between renting and owner-ship; (2) location – proximity to unskilled employment opportunities mainly located in the central city; and (3) shelter – an individual's priority for modern standard shelter. Recent migrant arrivals ('bridgeheaders') favoured cheap rental accommodation in the central city, from which they could search for work, and had a low preference for ownership or high-quality accommodation. However, gradual integration into the employment market, greater urban familiarity, and growing family size would affect these priorities. The established migrant would now be in a position to become a 'consolidator': an (illegal) owner in the urban periphery. Such 'ownership' offered space for expansion and the possibility to extend a dwelling through self-help. The theory suggested, therefore, that most low-income migrants would live first as renters in the inner-city and later move as owners to the peripheral low-income settlements. From his work in Lima and Mexico City, however, Turner recognised that this two-stage (province to city centre to city periphery) model was liable to become distorted in large cities as the opportunities for cheap rental accommodation dried-up, and where previously formed irregular settlements had become integrated into the urban fabric. Residents in this consolidated 'intermediate' ring were now prepared to rent rooms to 'bridgeheaders' or to help their recently arrived friends and kin by offering them temporary shared accommodation. In Mexico City this was exacerbated by the rent controls imposed upon many *vecindades* which slowed down the throughflow of migrants. Thus a 'breakdown' in the classic pattern was proposed with new migrants arriving to the intermediate ring, or indeed, direct into the periphery (Turner 1968a). In turn, these migrants later moved to the expanding current periphery following the same priorities of former 'consolidators' (Brown 1972).

By the end of the 1960s, evidence from numerous Latin American cities had provided support for Turner's hypothesis, and the classic 'two-stage' model had become 'widely accepted' (Morse 1971: 22). However, there are several problems with the theory. First, as with all behavioural models it tends to emphasise housing preferences of residents and their ability to exercise a **choice** between options. But are the preferences exogenously determined or are they a response to the housing environment? Second there was growing evidence during the 1970s that challenged the Turneresque pattern (Vaughn and Feindt 1973; Vernez 1973; Brown 1972). Indeed my own survey of mover trajectories into squatter settlements in Mexico City also pointed to a 'breakdown' in Turner's classic two-stage pattern. Although many residents of irregular settlements during the 1940s and 1950s had begun their urban lives in inner-city tenements, a substantial proportion had not, but had moved direct to the periphery (Ward 1976c; Lomnitz 1977). Moreover, residents in newly formed settlements created during the late 1960s and early 1970s had rarely lived in the inner-city tenements. Rather, they had either rented or shared lots with relatives and friends in the intermediate ring or current periphery (Ward 1976c).

As part of a larger study concerned with government intervention in the housing and land markets in Bogotá, Valencia and Mexico City, the intra-city trajectories of residents in six irregular settlements in Mexico City were analysed (Gilbert and Ward 1982b). Very few migrants to the city moved directly into these settlements. Although most of them received assistance from antecedent kinsfolk and/or friends, only 33 per cent lived with kin for more than one year after arrival. 45 per cent rented accommodation (Gilbert and Ward 1982b). In terms of location of 'bridgehead' residence, there appears to have been a clear shift away from the traditional city centre, initially towards the older working-class areas to the north and east, and subsequently to the more dispersed areas of irregular settlement that emerged during the 1950s and 1960s (Figure 2.3). These data suggest that even in the earlier periods irregular settlement attracted many more migrants than is implicit in the Turner model – a conclusion supported by my data for Sector Popular settlement founded in 1947, to which a substantial minority of migrants arrived direct without any stopover in the downtown district (Ward 1976c). It is also apparent that some of the old *pueblo* cores that had been absorbed by the city's growth now fulfilled the role of reception centres for incoming migrants. These areas offer many of the advantages of the city centre, and suggest the need for a further modification in the original Turner model.

Turning to examine the mobility patterns for all residents (i.e. migrants and city born) it is apparent in Mexico City that the last settlement of residence before moving to the current home was located relatively nearby (Figure 2.4). This feature is most apparent in the newly created settlements such as Liberales and Santo Domingo. Only in the two oldest settlements (Isidro Fabela and El Sol) did many come from further afield – in part inevitable given the fact that at the time of formation their highly peripheral location was always going to draw residents from further-flung districts. The siphoning-off of residents from nearby arises because most information about housing opportunities comes from family and friends living locally (Jackson 1973; Gilbert and Ward 1982b). Moreover, in Mexico City the illegal settlement process leaves 'owners' vulnerable if they fail to occupy their plot immediately. There is always the threat that someone else may usurp the plot and this makes for more rapid settlement; and it also means that residents living nearby can best maintain surveillance over their plots. In Santo Domingo for example, a large minority (approximately two-fifths) had been sharing (*arrimados*) with parents or kin in surrounding squatter areas. When the invasion took place they were well placed to join-in, always with the proviso that they could return to their kinsfolk if the invasion was repressed. Many, too, could continue living with kin, maintaining a single

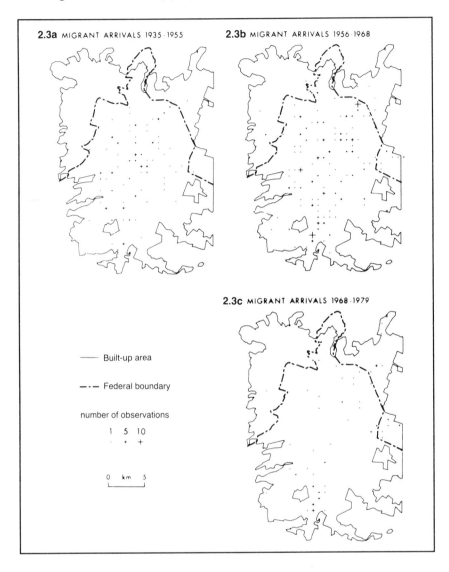

Figure 2.3 a-c The changing locations of migrant arrivals to Mexico City since 1935 (built-up area as at 1980)

member of the family on the plot to 'guard' over it and to warn off would-be usurpers (Ward 1976a).

In our comparative analysis of patterns of residential movement in the three Latin American cities we concluded that such patterns were more a product of constraints imposed by the land and housing markets than the outcome of migrant choice (Gilbert and Ward 1982b). Access to land

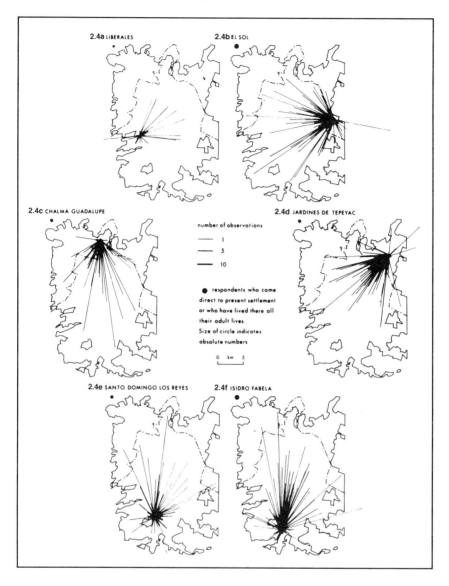

Figure 2.4 a-f Location of last place of residence before moving to one of six irregular settlements surveyed in 1978–9

ownership appears to be critical. Where land is freely available at not especially distant locations (as in Valencia), then 'bridgeheaders' often moved direct to the periphery as owners. Why rent when one can just as easily own? In places like Mexico City where the supply of land is more limited and often risky to capture, then migrants and city born are obliged to rent or to share with kin for long periods. State intervention, too, may also have a critical effect on the housing and land markets. Legalisation of plots, service provision, and tougher controls imposed against the formation of new settlements are likely to drive-up land prices and reduce the supply of plots. This, in turn, will intensify the pressures of non-ownership and prolong residence either as renters or sharers. Also, rent controls and a lack of direct state support has supressed the rental housing market and accentuated the propensity for many households to subdivide and share their plots with kinsfolk. Finally, the physical fabric of the city and rate of growth are likely to affect residential patterns. The large size of Mexico City now means that people tend to relate to a sector of the city rather than to the overall area. Moreover the existence of subcentres – whose functions resemble the central core – offers opportunities within the urban fabric that will further shape people's mobility patterns.

The appropriation of space in the Metropolitan Area

Residential segregation in relation to positive and negative externalities

During its conversion from plaza through suburb to megacity Mexico City has become spatially more differentiated and more segregated. The city's land-use pattern will be analysed in greater depth in Chapter 4, but a brief glance at Figure 4.1 (p. 95) shows that most of the built-up area comprises residential land-use, and that the largest industrial sites are located in the north east (in the State of Mexico) and north west (DF and State of Mexico). These locations, together with the unsuitability for urbanisation of the eastern ex-lake-bed areas, determined that the cheapest end of the land market would be to the east and to the north. Indeed, the first waves of wealthy suburbanites moved west and south towards areas with the greater positive externalities (woodland, fresh water, low [dust] contamination, existing road access and the small extra-urban townships and services these offered). Thus a broad pattern of social differentiation was entrained between south and west (richer) and north and east (poorer).

The 1950s ban on new subdivisions in the Federal District did not greatly disturb these directional trends. Although some new upper-middle-income residential estates were established in Naucalpan and a large number of low-income subdivisions were created in various municipalities of the State of Mexico, within the Federal District the existing divide remained even though both rich and poor had to adopt illegal methods of land appropriation. I will return to discuss these mechanisms later, but suffice to note here that different pretexts were to disestablish *ejidal* land. The rich used the mechanism of *permuta* (exchange); while the poor invaded or purchased direct from *ejidatarios* (Varley 1985a, 1987). The point is that not even the 'monopoly' control of *ejidal* lands by *ejidatarios* disrupted the pattern that had been established. This 'sifting' of the allocation of residential space

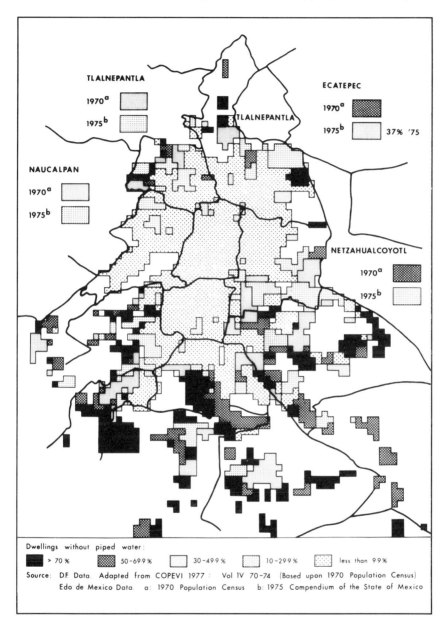

Figure 2.5   Distribution of piped water supply to households in Mexico City

continued until the early 1970s when political conditions facilitated several large-scale low-income invasions of *ejidal* lands in the south of the Federal District.

Some would argue that today the whole of the Metropolitan Area constitutes a negative externality, such is the generalised way in which everyone is affected by the problems associated with living in conditions of high levels of atmospheric contamination, the lack of adequate servicing for many, small amounts of green space, long journeys to work and so on. The existence of and factors shaping these problems will be analysed in the following chapters, but although everyone suffers they do not do so in equal measure. If one fills in the shading for the municipalities in the State of Mexico as indicated on Figure 2.5 then the east and north have the lowest levels of servicing and, although water and drainage networks have been extended to these areas, the levels of relative deprivation remain much higher than elsewhere in the city. Levels of overcrowding, dwellings constructed with inadequate or provisional building materials, and without proper toilet facilities reiterate the same pattern (Puente 1987). Parkland is at a premium in the city and is preferentially distributed to the west and south. Chapultepec Park may be intensively used by lower-income groups at weekends, but during the week it is the preserve of the better-off who use it for recreation, jogging, and as general exercise 'work-out' area.

Contamination, however, is less respectful of such socially differentiated spatial nuances. Air pollution occurs because of the frequent temperature inversions, a large number and wide distribution of sources of contamination, and the complexities of regional air flows within the Central Valley (Jáuregui 1987: 38). Vehicular emissions generate the largest source of contamination and are concentrated where the traffic is greatest: in the downtown area. Photochemical smog, which may form after several hours on sunny days, affects most severely the south west of the city, being transported across it by the breezes which usually come from the north east in the afternoon (Jáuregui 1973). These same winds bring dust and particle-born diseases from the poor eastern suburbs and are distributed throughout the city without regard to the social status of neighbourhoods (Fox 1972). The *tolvaneras* (localised dust storms) which are most common during the hot dry season (March–May) affect mostly those areas where they are generated: the eastern settlements on the ex-lake-bed (Jáuregui 1969). Isolines showing the concentration of sulphur dioxide are highest in the city centre extending north westwards across the Vallejo industrial zone into Naucalpan and Tlanepantla. A second 'outlier' hovers over the north eastern industrial district of Xalostoc. Thus everyone in the city suffers the effects of air pollution although the periodicity and source of contamination may vary across social areas.

Changing patterns of social segregation

It would be misleading to suggest that social segregation did not exist in pre-industrial or pre-revolutionary Mexico City. Although rich and poor resided in close proximity, they did not live cheek-by-jowl. The poor lived apart in discrete *barrio* areas at the then northern and eastern edges of what came to be the *Primer Cuadro* (Lombardo 1987; Morales 1987). Suburbanisation reproduced social segregation over a much larger area. But an important question is whether, once entrained, the process has become self-perpetuating; or whether there are other processes of social and spatial integration at work.

The existing pattern of social segregation is readily demonstrated by the distribution of population according to income levels (Figure 2.6). The highest income areas of Jardines de San Angel, Las Lomas (de Chapultepec, de Reforma and de Tecamachalco) are all clearly differentiated as are the more numerous second category of areas such as Napoles, Polanco, Satélite, etc. In contrast, the poorest areas are to be found in the eastern and northern peripheries. The mixture of socio-economic groups in the inner-city generates lower-to-intermediate areas of income distribution, but there is also evidence that low-income groups living in and around the city centre are significantly better off than their counterparts who live at the periphery (Valencia 1965; Brown 1972; Mexico RHP 1986).

This spatial distribution may be depicted as a series of zones, sectors, and nucleii which form the broad pattern of the city's ecology (Figure 2.7). Poorer areas have developed as a series of concentric zones in the east and north. As one moves outwards, so the settlements become poorer and more recently established. Hence their level of physical integration is lower (measured in terms of levels of urban infrastructure, residential consolidation, population densities, etc.). Generally speaking these zones expand through new housing production at the periphery with increasing densities in the inner and intermediate zones. Those groups in the upper-income bands also provide a *leitmotif* for urban expansion, creating new areas of exclusivity in which symbols of wealth and 'cachet' may be displayed. However, the desirability for clearly defined neighbourhoods which may be protected against encroachment from other groups has led to the emergence of wedge-shaped sectors following the contours of the land and using natural barriers as divides (Figure 2.7). Some 'elite' residential development is also occurring through the gentrification and infilling in the more attractive ex-pueblo cores such as San Angel and Tlalpan. In the past some formerly exclusive elite areas have moved slightly downmarket as upper-middle-income groups 'filtered' into residences and plots that were vacated by their would-be peers who have moved out to more recently developed and ever more 'exclusive' areas (Johnston 1973; Ward 1976a).

The spatial locations for residence of middle-income groups are, therefore, determined either by their willingness to filter into these vacated residences or, more usually, through residence in suburban estates developed specifically

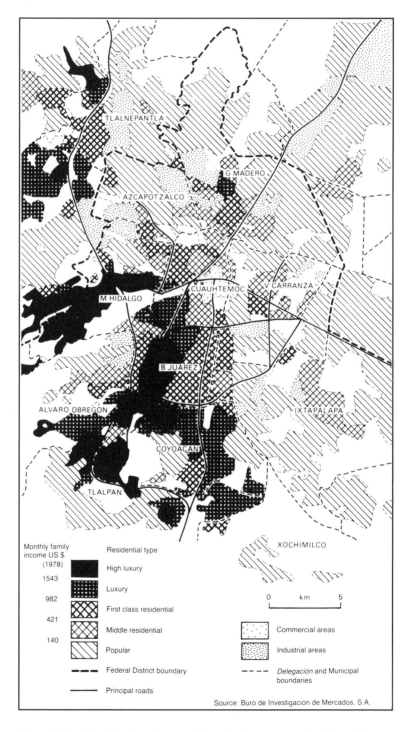

Figure 2.6   Distribution of population by income and residential type

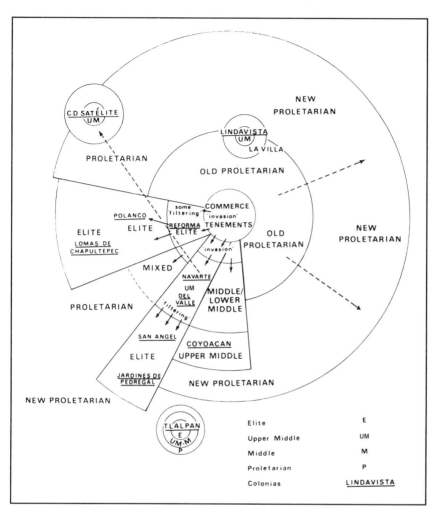

Figure 2.7 Diagrammatic representation of 'ecological' areas of Mexico City

to meet their needs. Colonia Del Valle in the centre-south of the city, Satélite and Echegary in the north east are good examples. These, too, may be subject to subsequent 'filtering' processes. Parts of Polanco have moved downmarket two categories from elite to middle-income during the past thirty years. Elite areas and upper-income areas developed during the first decade of the century (e.g. Roma Norte) have long since been subject to 'invasion' processes whereby commercial redevelopment pressures have led to changing land-uses from single-family residences to shops, offices, and multifamily poor or middle-income housing.

However, the largest ecological areas are occupied by the poor. As already noted these are in eastern zones of the city, but also the poor have occasionally managed to drive a wedge between social classes in the south and west of the city. The ability to capture these areas relates to the specificities of original land tenure and/or political period in which neighbourhoods were created, but the effect since 1970 has been to insert the poor into some western and southern areas of the city, thereby breaking-up the middle-income economic homogeneity of these districts.

A systematic attempt to analyse these processes of social differentiation was made using census data and factor analysis of some 18 variables (subsequently reduced to 7: Ruvacalva and Schteingart 1985, 1987). Two broad factors of differentiation emerged: (a) 'urban consolidation' associated with variables such as levels of home ownership; dwellings with water service; persons per room; and (b) 'socio-economic development' associated with the proportion of economically active persons; proportion with primary education; proportion earning more than six times the minimum salary. Between them these two 'factors' explained almost three-quarters of the total variation, with urban consolidation emerging as the most important way of differentiating socio-spatial patterns in the city. Unfortunately in their analysis the data were aggregated and displayed at the level of *delegación* and municipality so that the resulting patterns are rather generalised (Ruvacalva and Schteingart 1987). The factor 'urban consolidation' shows sharp differentiation between the high levels in the three western downtown *delegaciones* of Miguel Hidalgo, Cuauhtemoc and Benito Juárez but is lower across a broad west–east divide. Factor 2 (socioeconomic development) shows even more clearly the sharp divide between western political entities and those of the north and especially the eastern municipalities. More significant, perhaps, was the finding that up until 1970 there was a tendency towards greater polarisation between social areas, but that the evolution of the urban area during the 1970s and 1980s has begun to reverse this process. In particular they note a tendency for the position of middle-income groups to improve between 1970 and 1980 at the expense of the upper-income and lower-income groups. They conclude that there has been 'a decline in the spatial and social differences, despite the fact that extreme disparities remain for important indicators between the zones' (Ruvacalva and Schteingart 1987: 114).

This conclusion is important because it underlines the fact that conditions in Mexico City may not be deteriorating inevitably and inexhorably in the manner often claimed by Marxist theorists. In making this point I am not seeking to extenuate the existence of the clear disparities that exist. Nor am I suggesting that, left to its own devices and market mechanisms, these spatial inequalities will gradually be resolved. But it does underscore the need to take account both of the complexities of the processes involved in the evolution of the Metropolitan Area, and the fact that as the city develops it also makes adjustments that may **raise** people's life chances and reduce the more onerous aspects of city life. The remaining chapters in this book will examine specifically the ways in which the city is reproduced, and the impact that these processes may have upon the physical patterns of social inequality depicted above.

3
The politics of city management: defending the high ground

It is not only the economic, demographic and physical space of the city that has undergone profound changes during the 1970s and 1980s. The political space of city governance has expanded too. Moreover, since the government sustained major electoral losses in the city in 1988, and then in July 1989 for the first time lost a State Governorship, it has found its legitimacy and hegemony seriously undermined. Thus the political and managerial structures of the state are currently undergoing what will probably prove to be the most important phase of its development since the existing arrangement was established in Mexico City in 1928. This chapter aims to explain why, and to analyse how city management is a key mechanism through which many of the patterns of social inequality described in Chapter 2 are reproduced.

But before we are able to turn to look at Mexico City specifically the reader will need to be briefed on the national political structure and its recent dynamics. This is necessary because the economic and demographic importance of the Metropolitan Area in national life is reinforced by the heavy centralisation of federal government in the capital. City politics are, to a significant extent, national politics. Moreover, national politics are in a state of flux. Broadly, the political and governmental structures have progressively drawn apart in recent years so that the careers and personnel overlap less and less. In particular the government is manned increasingly by technocrats rather than by 'old style' politicians (Cornelius et al. 1989). Yet the Mexican government faces a paradox. On the one hand it must continue this process, isolating the so-called 'dinosaurs' from the political process; while on the other hand it must seek to repair some of the damage caused by the growing division between governmental and party-political apparata. Although not the Salinas administration's (1988–94) preferred path, it has nevertheless to find a way of modernising the PRI, thereby restoring its legitimacy and ability to deliver electoral success – all without the opposition parties' legitimately crying 'foul!'. Below I exemplify and explain this process at both national and city level.

The national political structure: who governs in Mexico?

On paper the Mexican government resembles closely that of the United States. It has a presidential system, three autonomous branches of government comprising the Executive, Legislative and the Judicial (Cornelius and Craig 1988). The Federation contains 31 states and a single Federal District. With the exception of the latter, each state has constitutional autonomy, as do individual municipalities within each state. Elected officials govern at both levels. Despite this federalist structure and the principle of 'municipal freedom' enshrined in the Constitution, in practice autonomy has traditionally been heavily constrained by centralism – both political and governmental. Central government controls the purse-strings and most developmental activity is undertaken through the ministerial or parastatal agencies. As Fagen and Tuohy (1972) poetically report from the state governor's perspective 'the central government screws me; so I screw the municipality'. Although the De la Madrid government in 1986 sought to give greater effective power to the municipal level, this has been resisted by state governors reluctant to sacrifice any of their power (Rodríguez 1987). Political centralism remains entrenched, too, so that in practice those allowed to 'run' for local and district elections are handpicked by higher-ups within the PRI-government apparatus described below (Cornelius and Craig 1988).

Since the 1930s Mexico has been dominated by a single party, which has evolved through several stages from its early origins as the National Revolutionary Party (PNR), to become the Mexican Revolutionary Party (PRM) under President Cárdenas and finally in 1945 to emerge in its definitive form as the Institutionalised Revolutionary Party (PRI). During the metamorphosis the Party shed much of the influence of the military that had been influential in the post-revolutionary decade (1910–20) and took on-board a greater representation of labour, subsequently broadened to include middle-income and 'popular' groups. It has been described as 'a party of consensus, moderation and stability' (Needler 1982: 29). The significance is that since its formation it has always been the governing party. The President is a PRI 'candidate' and, at least up until the dramatic 1988 July elections, always won an overwhelming proportion of the vote. Nor had the PRI ever conceded the loss of a State Governorship until July 1989 when the National Action Party took Baja California Norte adjacent to the north west US border. Similarly PRI senators and deputies dominate almost all elections for the legislature. The PRI colours and the national flag are one and the same. Little wonder, therefore, that the popular impression is that the PRI is, in effect, the government.

While this impression is deliberately fostered by the PRI, it is, I believe, a false one. It is important at least for the purpose of analysis to draw a careful distinction between the Party political apparatus and the government bureaucracy, (and in particular the Executive wing of government). Although there is some occasional overlap, they are usually quite distinct in terms of personnel, career tracks, functions, and access to resources. In the following sections I examine the importance of political parties in general, and the PRI in particular, in exercising influence over decision making and the allocation of resources for social welfare provision. A key question to be resolved at this point is whether political parties in Mexico provide effective channels for influencing decision making.

Party politics in Mexico: the growth of genuine opposition?

The Mexican political system is generally considered to be authoritarian. It displays a low level of political mobilisation, and limited pluralism in which the contest for power is restricted to supporters of the regime. The latter possesses a 'mentality' rather than a clear ideology (Smith 1979: 53; see also Needler 1982). Inevitably, in a system such as this, considerable importance is placed upon election results as a source of legitimacy for the governing elite.

Until 1988 when its proportion of the presidential vote fell to fractionally over 50 per cent, the PRI had been accustomed to receive overwhelming electoral support: almost always more than 75 per cent of the turnout at presidential elections (Smith 1979; Cockcroft 1983). Despite this fact a dilemma faced by the PRI is how to retain absolute control and sustain existing levels of support while at the same time stimulate sufficient interest among the opposition in competitive electoral politics. This has been resolved on the one hand by ensuring support from the grassroots through its tripartite structure (see below) and by rigging the ballot-box. On the other hand, while competitive party politics has been narrowly circumscribed, the presence and activity of opposition parties has been carefully sustained and sometimes sponsored by the PRI. Indeed, the greatest threat to the PRI's cultivation of a democratic facade used to be posed by abstentions (González Casanova 1970). If the PRI is considered to occupy the middle-left ground of the political spectrum in Mexico then the only concerted opposition, at least until recently, has been provided by the right-wing National Action Party (PAN). Established to combat the left-wing tendencies adopted by President Cárdenas (1934–40), the PAN attracts support from conservative business circles, provinical and large-city middle classes, and from the Catholic Church (Cockcroft 1983: 305). Although it rarely won more than 15 per cent of the vote it regularly took a few electoral districts by majority vote. Very occasionally these included large cities such as Ciudad Juárez and Chihuahua. Its strongholds are located primarily in the north of the country and in Merida in the Yucatán. As already noted, the PAN achieved a major breakthrough in June 1989 when it became the first opposition party to win a State Governorship: in Baja California Norte. Previous elections in *Panista* strongholds have almost certainly been rigged in favour of the PRI but an important element in the Salinas administration's 'democratisation' project is greater respect for electoral results even if this means that the PRI must concede certain losses. How far this will continue is an open question.

However, in the past, the opposition in Mexico has been stage-managed by the PRI (González Casanova 1970) such that by the late 1960s the need to revitalise the political structure and to restore the legitimacy of the governing elite was widely felt. Political reforms were initiated in 1973 and extended further in 1977. Two important changes were introduced. First, the reforms provided for the registration of a host of new parties, most of which were left-wing. The most important among these were the Mexican Communist Party (PCM), the Socialist Workers' Party (PST) and the Mexican Workers' Party (PMT). On the right, and far more populist than the PAN, is the Mexican Democratic Party (PDM) with a regional stronghold in Guanajuato. Secondly, the size of Congress was increased, and one-quarter of the 400 seats were given to opposition parties to be allocated on the basis of proportional representation of the votes received.

These initiatives had an important effect upon the political process. In 1982, 50 of the opposition seats went to the PAN, while the remainder were shared between the PDM (12), PST (11), PPS (10), and the PSUM (a PCM-led coalition of several left-wing parties, [17]). While the PRI's pre-eminence was assured and a clear majority in the Congress was guaranteed, there was now greater incentive for opposition parties to participate in elections. Their representation in the Chamber of Deputies sharpened the level of debate and criticism of government policy. Although a carefully controlled minority they provided an important channel for registering political dissent. Whether or not this ultimately made any appreciable difference to the position of working-class Mexicans is open to question. However, the *apertura democrática* initiated by President Echeverría and extended by López Portillo, represented a significant step in opening political franchise and expression in Mexico. But we should recognise that its purpose was not one of reducing the authority and role of the PRI but rather to enhance and sustain it.

This arrangement changed as a result of the 1988 elections. Here is not the place for a full chronology of events leading up to the elections, but the bare 'facts' begin with the failure in 1986 of the PRI to resolve and manage the democratic current that had emerged among certain senior members of the Party. Several of these individuals had held high office in the government, came from the political left, and were disillusioned with the inability of the Party to respond adequately to contemporary pressures and social needs. They were also dissatisfied with the '*dedazo*' system of nomination for high office, which in one or two cases probably presented a frustration to personal ambitions (Cornelius *et al.* 1989). Ordinarily, one would have expected the PRI to 'accommodate' this position within its ranks.

In retrospect I am sure that the failure to do so is deeply regretted. However, after much debate and acrimony, several key figures in the *corriente* withdrew from the Party late in 1987, and Cuauhtemoc Cárdenas (son of the former President and himself recently a State Governor) launched himself as candidate for the presidency. Ultimately supported by the majority of the opposition parties of the left, his Democratic Front ran a close second to Salinas.

The election results were a huge embarrassment for the PRI, in part because they did so badly; in part because of the doubts that surrounded the way in which the results were published. The delay (of almost one week) before full results were announced fuelled rumours that the PRI had actually lost the election. The results, when they came, declared that Salinas (PRI) had gained 50.36 per cent of the vote; Cárdenas (Democratic Front) 31.12 per cent; and Clouthier (PAN) 17.07 per cent. There seems little doubt that the bare 50 per cent majority over the opposition was contrived (Barberán *et al.* 1988). In Congress the failure to put up single opposition candidates meant that the PRI swept the board by 249 seats to 51 on the seats allocated by absolute majority. However, as was noted above, a large number of seats are also allocated according to proportional representation and this has meant that the PRI only has an overall majority of 15 or 16 seats in the Legislature. Opposition (*Frente*) senators won in one of the 31 states and in the Federal District. It seems unlikely that PRI or government initiated legislation will enjoy an easy ride from now on. Constitutional reforms in particular, requiring as they do a two-thirds majority, are likely to be blocked by the opposition.

The PRI

Given the prominance of the official party it is necessary to examine the extent to which it wields influence over policy making. The Party is built around three sectors: the National Confederation of Farmworkers (CNC); a labour sector (CTM), and a socially heterogeneous Confederation of 'Popular' Organizatons (CNOP) comprising middle-class professions such as teachers as well as local organisations representing low-income settlements, trade unions etc. Each of these sectors represents a solid grassroots organised on a strictly hierarchical basis, with minimal horizontal linkage either between sectors or individual federations. Thus all party or federation bosses look upwards for their orders and often compete openly against those on a similar level to themselves (Schers 1972; Eckstein 1977). Although they are all within the same umbrella organisation (the PRI), this hierarchical structure offers enormous scope for political manipulation from above. Up-and-coming party militants can be set against one another; those who show particular promise may be promoted and lifted into a bigger pond; those who become too powerful can be frozen out and isolated (Schers 1972; Smith 1979).

The politics of city management

The incorporation of this mass base of grassroots support into the governining party might lead one to believe that the structure provides the means whereby working-class interests are represented upwards through the executive committee of each sector to the PRI executive and thence to shape directly government policy. However, this 'aggregate interest model' (Scott 1964; Huntingdon 1968) does not seem to apply. In fact the Party has minimal power over decision making and only limited access to resources (Padgett 1966; Hansen 1974; Eckstein 1977; Smith 1979). The PRI's role is principally to provide a career structure for up-and-coming politicians; to conciliate the negotiation of jobs (i.e. patronage) given the high turnover of electoral posts every three and six years; and finally to ensure the legitimacy of the government by mobilising support at the polls. Indeed I believe that one can go further to argue that the PRI's function to the state is to provide political and social control (Hansen 1974; Eckstein 1977). This is achieved by concentrating power in the hands of a few sector bosses at the top, by controlling the selection of personnel, by the cooption of leaders and organisations, and by the manipulation of factions within the PRI.

For electoral purposes the PRI is organised at four levels into sectional, municipal, state and national committees. Deputies elected to the Legislature have little or no local responsibility to their constituents. The national President, State Governors and Municipal Presidents are 'unveiled' and only then does the PRI step in to run their election campaigns. As we shall observe below, selection to 'run' for these executive posts is not a preserve of the PRI. Although some municipal Presidents and even Governors may have held previous elective offices or positions within the Party apparatus, they are equally likely to come from a career track outside it. Generally speaking the higher the post the less likely it is that the individual has been directly dependent in the past upon PRI patronage for a job. Since 1970 no national president had run for electoral office prior to being chosen as candidate (Smith 1989).

Nor in the past has the fact that these elected government officials depend upon the PRI for stage-managing their electoral campaigns usually shaped their subsequent behaviour in allocating resources preferentially to PRI constituents. This is for two reasons. First, the individual is aware that he/she must serve primarily as a government functionary and any Party allegiance should be placed after other considerations. Primarily he/she will be judged on ability to pacify all interest groups and to minimise outpourings of public dissent or upwellings of unrest. If favours are solicited by a party official they will be met only in so far as the personal weight and influence of the PRI member making the request demands it, and the extent to which the individual executive officer feels that his/her future career may be firmly located within the Party political apparatus. Second, resources at the disposal of State Governors and especially Municipal Presidents are very limited. Funds remain firmly in the hand of federal government and its agencies. It is to them that elected officials look and not to the PRI which has no ready access to or influence over federal expenditure. The irony is that as part and parcel of its normal endeavours to coopt and integrate local groups the PRI deliberately encourages the impression that it has this special access and influence. Yet, in fact, close association and integration under the Party's umbrella is likely to reduce the probability of a group getting what it wants simply because, once coopted, it becomes subject to PRI orthodoxy which seeks to reduce the level of demand made upon the system (Eckstein 1977; Cornelius 1975).

In future as electoral districts become more hotly contested by the new political parties, and as the state continues to demand that the PRI deliver the vote on behalf of the government and executive officers, it seems likely that the pressure for preferential treatment of groups affiliated to the official Party will grow. There is a basic and growing contradiction, therefore, between the state's desire for *apertura política* which requires that the PRI should not be seen to have privileged access to resources, and the ability of the Party to guarantee future support without being granted greater opportunities for exercising patronage.

The government and the executive

If the official party has relatively little influence over national policy, we may ask how policy is determined. To evaluate this question we must look briefly, first, at the structure of government and, second, at the way in which different groups articulate their interests and the factors that determine their success.

In Mexico the President holds office for a non-renewable six-year term and appoints cabinet members and many other high-level offices according to a wide range of criteria. People are selected for their personal loyalty and past support. The President must also aim to reconcile a wide range of interest groups and seek to ensure that all are included in his cabinet (Needler 1982). However, to balance this and to keep a cross check on the actions of ministers he will often appoint his own people to sub-ministerial posts. Until restrictions were imposed in 1983, nepotism and sinecures for relatives and friends were widespread. Increasingly, though, appointees must be professionally competent. Important jobs require sensitive handling and banana skins must be carefully avoided.

Differences in ideology do not usually form the basis that determines the constitution of different 'groups' in Mexican politics (although they may be tied to specific vested interests; Cockcroft 1983). Rather, groups are organised into 'leader-follower' alliances sometimes called *camarillas* (Grindle 1977; Cornelius and Craig 1988). These may be best envisaged as teams which form around a particular person and as that individual moves between different posts in government so, too, does his team. This explains why the same people may appear in such unlikely consecutive positions as the Subsistence Foods Enterprise (CONASUPO), the Ministry of Health and Welfare, and the State of Mexico Government (Grindle 1977). Each *camarilla* actually comprises a series of layers with 'leaders' and sub-teams at each level. Ultimately however, they lead to the same top politician. Occasionally, *camarillas* overlap leading upwards to two influential leaders. In such a case a close alliance would usually exist between the two, and the sharing out of jobs and placement of personnel may be done by agreement. In these cases working for one boss after previously working for the other is acceptable. Otherwise transfer across groups is not tolerated and among the 'rules' of behaviour the greatest breach is disloyalty (Smith 1979; Grindle 1977). Political 'nous' in Mexico is the ability to recognise and predict the implications of any single action upon competing *camarillas*.

Over the past two decades an important shift has taken place in the type of person who gains top public office. Gone are the old-style politicians from provincial and often military backgrounds (Needler 1982). While the ruling elite continue to be drawn from among wealthy well-known family names, they are increasingly likely to be from the central regions of the country and from the Federal District in particular. Increasingly too, they are 'technocrats', though clearly if they are to advance significantly they must also show political acumen (Cornelius *et al.* 1989). Most will have gone through the National University (UNAM) and the Colégio de México; some will have taught there. While Law used to be the most popular form of professional training this has widened to encompass engineering, architecture and economics, usually supplemented by post-graduate experience abroad (Needler 1982).

Compared with the USA, the Mexican bureaucracy is vast and has expanded considerably since 1970. In 1975 it comprised 18 ministries, 123 decentralised agencies, 292 public enterprises, 187 official commissions and 160 development trusts (Grindle 1977: 3). Since that date attempts have been made to reduce the overall number and to coordinate more closely their activities by making them responsible to 'heads of sectors'. But in several ways a distended bureaucracy may be highly functional to the state. By providing jobs it facilitates the circulation of patronage. It creates opportunities for manipulation by the Executive: personnel posing a threat can be 'frozen-out' or their authority undermined by the creation of a duplicate agency; support can be bestowed upon certain agencies and subtly withdrawn from others. Also, an intricate bureaucracy with ample red tape slows down the outflow of resources while at the same time creating an appearance of being 'busy' and overworked.

Another feature of government is the way in which the six-year cycle creates an important dynamic of its own. Broadly the first year to eighteen months comprise the coordination of teams, establishing new policies and often disassociating oneself from those of one's predecessor, and securing adequate finance to carry through one's programmes (Grindle 1977). The latter constitutes years three, four and five after which people begin to look around and get close to those who are likely to figure prominently in the forthcoming administration. Once one of the existing cabinet has been named as the new candidate (in effect President elect), then all bets are off.

Those overly associated with the 'losers' are said to be 'burned' (*quemado*), and know that they will not figure significantly in the next government. Although it would be incorrect to suggest that during the last year the President is a lame duck, within government agencies and ministries few new actions are undertaken and most work concentrates on completing projects already underway.

Policy making: who rules?

We have observed that public policy in Mexico does not emerge from within the ranks of the official party, nor from the Legislature. Neither is it the product of a clear ideological stance. Mexico watchers tend to have their own particular analogy that best describes the nature of the political process. Some see it as a card game in which different interests participate – occasionally winning a little, sometimes losing, but never destroying everything by kicking over the table (Needler 1982). Others see it as 'marriage', governed and delimited by certain rules yet actually worked out on a day-to-day basis of negotiation (Purcell and Purcell 1980). In fact it is very difficult to say precisely how policy is formulated as discussions take place behind closed doors 'beyond the purview of the general public and the rank-and-file adherents of the official party' (Grindle 1977).

The political system may be envisaged as a delicate balancing act involving all elite interests incorporated into a 'political bargain' which is constantly renewed in day-to-day action (Purcell and Purcell 1980). It is 'inclusionary' in so far as all groups or interests are represented, though inevitably any sharp change in policy will advance certain interests at the expense of others. The adverse effects of such action are usually minimised, and a tacitly agreed aim is to avoid the existence of outright 'winners' and 'losers'. However, every administration creates certain imbalances and the expectancy is that these will be redressed in the following administration. This helps explain the tendency demonstrated in Figure 3.1 for a pendulum-type shift back-and-forth between 'activist' to 'consolidatory' presidents (Purcell and Purcell 1980: 222; Cornelius and Craig 1988). The critical task of the President is to strike and maintain that balance within his administration (Smith 1979).

Key groups incorporated into the governing elite are, of course, the leaders of the CTM, CNC and CNOP; they are likely to be accorded significance but not predominance. The coalition can ill afford to alienate the *campesino* sector or organised labour, but the degree to which the Executive is prepared to support actively the interests of these groups depends upon the balance of forces within the coalition at any point in time (Purcell and Purcell 1980). Also closely involved is the private sector. Opinions differ about the degree to which it actually forms part of the governing bloc and most analysts see a clear separation between government and business interests (Needler 1982; Smith 1979: 214; but cf.

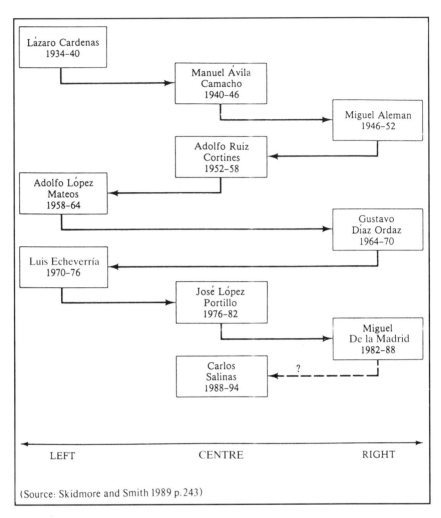

Figure 3.1 'Pendulum politics' in Mexico: swings between 'activist' and 'consolidatory' presidents, 1934 to present day

Cockcroft 1983: 210). However, there are several state/corporatist entities such as the Confederation of Chambers of Industry (CONCAMIN) and of Commerce (CONCANACO) which are designed to directly inform government decisions. Equally there are numerous other independent 'voices' such as the Employer's Confederation (COPARMEX) and that of manufacturing industries (CANACINTRA). Undoubtedly soundings are taken from these groups but policy is essentially decided within the Executive: the President, his private office, and others whom he sees fit to involve (Teichman 1988). While decisions may be taken that hurt certain interests the 'bargain' demands acquiesence on the understanding that imbalances will eventually be redressed. If any group breaks this agreement, then they are likely to be 'disciplined' in one of several ways that are open to the government (Purcell and Purcell 1980).

Government without democracy in Mexico City: defending the high ground

The structure of government in the Metropolitan Area

The Federal District (DF) has existed as a special political entity within the Federation since August 1928 when it lost its status as a state and series of municipalities. It then became a special political entity divided into a central department comprising a number of quarters (*cuarteles*) and thirteen *delegaciones*. There were two principal reasons for the change. First, the municipalities were in major financial difficulty and incapable of delivering essential services. Second, intense political in-fighting among fledgling political parties during the Carranza period was being played out through the local *ayuntamientos* even where these parties all supported the President. These troubles continued through the 1920s until Obregon, as part of his election campaign, embraced the proposal to create a special district. In a single move he sought to marginalise the (then) Labour Party's strength in the municipalities and to create a less anarchic structure capable of improved city management (Meyer 1987). In 1970 the *cuarteles* were reconstituted as *delegaciones* to make a total of sixteen that exist today. But the original reconfiguration was more political than spatial; a special district, as the seat of federal powers, belonged to the nation as a whole. Instead of locally elected representatives running City Hall, the Mayor (*Regente*) is a Presidential appointee, as are the sixteen local mayors (*Delegados*), although in practice many are usually nominated by the *Regente* for confirmation by the Executive.

The argument has always been that the national President is, in effect, also elected as Governor of the Federal District. Given his other duties, he delegates these responsibilities to the *Regente* and to the local mayors. The administrative and political structures of the Federal District are portrayed in Figure 3.2. The National Congress is charged with legislative functions both for the nation and for the Federal District. An additional 'tier' has recently been created (the Federal District *Asamblea de Representantes*) comprising elected party-political representatives. Its functions are vague, but in practice it appears to be acting as an important 'watchdog' assembly on City Hall expenditures and policy (Figure 3.2). Since 1977 the DF has also created a hierarchically ordered neighbourhood consultative structure on civic matters organised at the levels of *delegación* (the '*Juntas de Vecinos*') and Federal District (the Consultative Council).

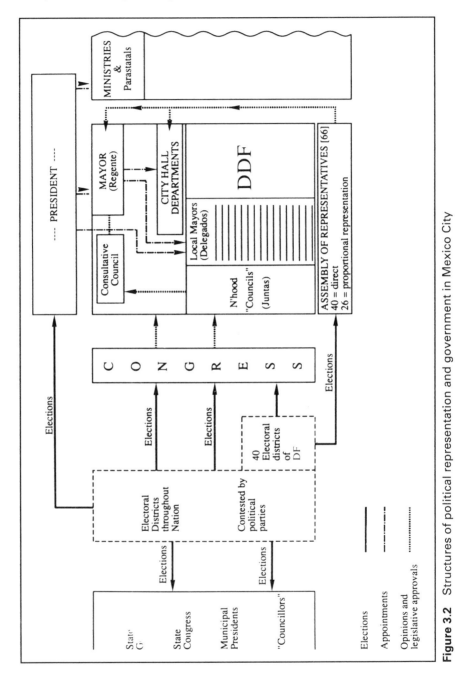

Figure 3.2 Structures of political representation and government in Mexico City

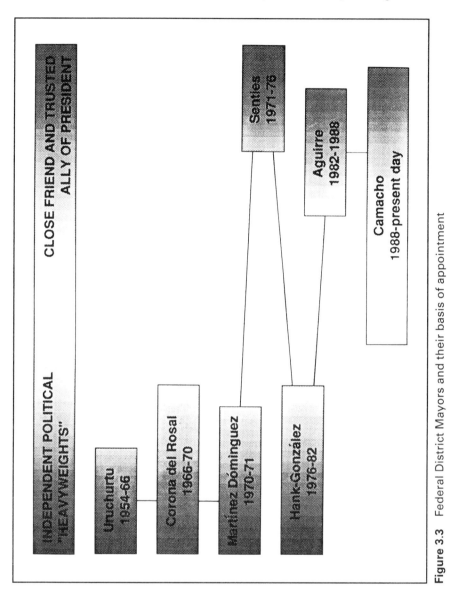

Figure 3.3 Federal District Mayors and their basis of appointment

Once appointed, the Mayor brings in his own staffers to key posts within City Hall (the Federal District Department, DDF). He holds a high-ranking cabinet office and his influence has grown as a result of the economic predominance of the Federal District within the national economy, its role as the political centre, and its spotlighted position on the national, and sometimes international, centre-stage. The large population, too, must be kept sweet, for this is the President's backyard and he can ill afford to be embarrassed by it. Therefore the city receives a disproportionate share of national resources and its citizens have preferential access to housing, urban services, heavily subsidised transportation, and so on. Traditionally, therefore, city governments have bought 'social peace' and wellbeing and passed on the costs to the nation at large. In addition, the President is likely to appoint to the Mayor's Office either a political heavyweight (since 1954 good examples are Mayors Uruchurtu, Corona del Rosal and Hank González) who can be relied upon not to screw-up (Figure 3.3). Alternatively, he will appoint a malleable but close ally from his own political group whom he trusts implicitly and through whom he can intervene directly if required (e.g. Mayors Sentiés and Aguirre).

Past mayors: rulers from elsewhere

Until Camacho took office in 1988 no previously appointed mayor was a native of the Federal District: all came from the provinces. Since the 1950s only one person has held the office of Mayor across *sexenios* – Ernesto Uruchurtu – who held office consecutively under three different Presidents (cf. Figures 3.1 and 3.3), largely because his firm control over city affairs and administration won him the confidence of successive executives. However, rapid city growth, the increasing complexity of city affairs, and his eventual loss of control over illegal settlement developments in the south of the city demonstrated that his policies had outgrown their usefulness and he was forced to resign in 1966. Alfonso Corona del Rosal who succeeded him had close links with the National Confederation of Popular Organisations (CNOP) and he mobilised clientelist links with local groups in order to win support and head-off social unrest (Cornelius 1975). A possible nominee for the presidential candidature in 1970, he has subsequently been 'out' of formal office although he continues to hold considerable influence as an 'elder statesman' within the Party.

The maintenance of social peace in the city is the primary political task of the mayor. When street rioting broke out in 1971 for example, Mayor Martínez Domínguez was held responsible and was sacked. In his place Echeverría appointed a close personal friend Octavio Sentiés and, more than any other President, he intervened directly in city affairs often over the head of the *Regente* (Ward 1981a). This pattern changed when Carlos Hank González was appointed Mayor by López Portillo in 1976 (Figure 3.3). Hank González had a considerable power base of his own but was ultimately ineligible for the Presidency because his parents were not born in Mexico. A political heavyweight, he was also perceived to have done a good job in the sphere of urban development while Governor of the State of Mexico (1969–75) which surrounds the Federal District. He knew, intimately, the problems of the low-income areas of city, and knew how to handle them. His specific interests, however, focused upon major urban development projects which would push contracts and resources towards his political backers. In large part because of this and because Hank González left the Federal District Department bankrupt and heavily in debt, Ramon Aguirre (an accountant) was charged with stabilising city finances by his close friend President De la Madrid. He lacked the clarity of political purpose of his predecessor, but muddled through and was one of the six 'pre-candidates' identified by De la Madrid in 1986–7 for possible adoption as Party presidential nominee.

The latest mayor is Manuel Camacho, a trusted friend of Salinas for whom he has worked for many years. A former academic and 'technocrat' he is very capable and is widely respected. The losses sustained by the PRI in the Federal District in the Presidential and congressional elections would have been important considerations in his appointment to that particular job. If anyone can successfully 'manage' city affairs it is probably Camacho. While his position derives, first and foremost, from his closeness to Salinas, he has developed some considerable political 'weight' in his own right in recent years (Figure 3.3). He was Underminister and Minister of SPP and SEDUE respectively and in the latter position oversaw what was ultimately a very successful earthquake reconstruction programme 1986–7. Before he became Mayor, Salinas made him Secretary General of the PRI (in executive terms the key post) charged with restoring international legitimacy so badly tarnished by the 1988 election results. Traditionally the Federal District has not presented a good springboard to the Presidency, but provided he does a reasonable job he is likely to be one of a small number of front-runners for 1994.

Outside the Federal District, in the surrounding State of Mexico, the local populace elects its Governor and Municipal Presidents who thereafter exercise executive authority for six and three years respectively. However, the actual candidates are usually selected by the President, Governor, organised (compliant) labour groups, and the PRI itself. The PRI orchestrates the election on behalf of candidates who emerge from this non-democratic process which takes place behind closed doors (Cornelius and Craig 1988). None the less the electorate can demonstrate their dissatisfaction with those proffered candidates by abstaining or by voting for the opposition. There are also local elections for the state legislature and for the equivalent of councillors in the municipality. At the settlement level there is the opportunity to vote on two tickets, although this is patchier in its operationalisation. The first ticket is for settlement representatives on neighbourhood development issues; the other is to select a handful of local residents to act with the authority of the Municipal President and to see that law and order are effected and represented within the settlement. Although this arrangement embodies the principles of municipal autonomy, these principles are seriously undermined by centralised or state control exercised over scarce resources (Fagen and Tuohy 1972; Rodríguez 1987).

Apart from Mayor Hank González, there has been no tradition of movement of executive offices from the State of Mexico to the Federal District. By and large, *camarillas*, career trajectories, and unwillingness to concede political power, have conspired to accentuate the split between the two political entities – a point to which I return later.

Políticos and técnicos

Earlier in this chapter I argued that administrations in recent years have become increasingly technocratic. This has been particularly true of the Executive and with one or two notable exceptions (such as Agrarian Reform), it applies to most ministries and parastatal agencies as well. But individual bureaucracies differ in the extent to which they are guided by 'technical' or 'partisan political' rationality (Gilbert and Ward 1985). This spectrum of rationality embodies parameters of bureaucracy autonomy from day-to-day partisan political interference; stability of personnel and budgets; accountability of performance; and 'objectivity' of decision making according to established criteria and procedures. Generally speaking the more critical an area of sectoral activity is to economic production or to strategically important activities, then the more likely it is to be towards the 'technical' end of the spectrum. By and large, ministries and federal agencies will be less subject to partisan political pressures than those whose responsibilities are explicitly spatial in character (Governors, Municipal Presidents, state agencies, and local decentralised branch offices of national ministries).

But which type of rationality applies in the Metropolitan Area? The short answer is both. Officers whose brief is to manage and maintain social peace in spatial entities such as *delegaciones* and municipalities are more likely to make decisions based upon political criteria (i.e. who might benefit or suffer given a particular action). Generally, however, their control over resources is limited and they must approach centralised departments for assistance. Other officers in charge of sectoral programmes are more likely to be oriented towards establishing norms and criteria of management that can be implemented as widely as resources will allow.

The Mayor and State Governor respectively set out the policies to be followed. Each also exercises an overall watching brief through control over extra-budgetary or centralised resources and can respond discretionally to competing demands. Hence the Mayor and State Governor, ultimately, must respond more to political influences than to technical ones, no matter what their personal background. Not only do these pressures vary in space, but also in time. Changing economic conditions, social unrest and class

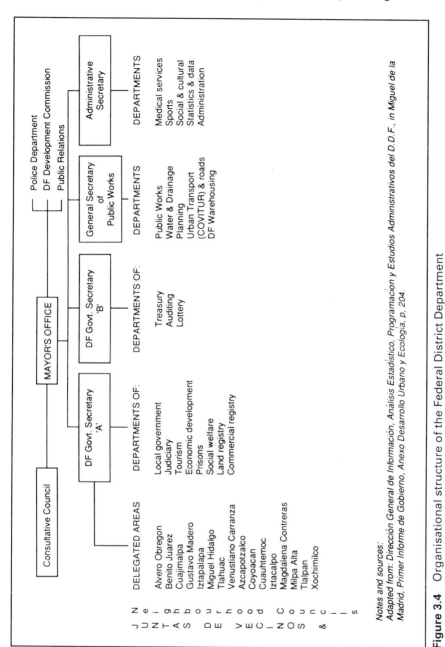

Figure 3.4 Organisational structure of the Federal District Department

Notes and sources:
Adapted from: Dirección General de Información, Análisis Estadístico, Programación y Estudios Administrativos del D.D.F., in Miguel de la
Madrid, Primer Informe de Gobierno, Anexo Desarrollo Urbano y Ecología, p. 204.

Table 3.1 Total DDF expenditure and proportional allocation to certain specified areas

Year	DDF expenditure actual	constant 1978 (pesos) (billions)[1]	Public debt (%)	Public works (%)	Water and drainage (%)	COVITUR (%)	Delegaciones (%)	Planning department (%)
1971	4.4	13.1	12.3	9.7	20.0	ND	ND	1.7
1973	11.7	29.2	8.3	8.1	17.2	ND	5.2	3.3
1975	15.4	26.9	21.9	8.0	7.6	ND	6.0	1.1
1977	20.6	24.2	9.1 (24)[2]	4.0	5.0	ND	11.0	1.1
1979	50.4	42.7	15.3	17.9	9.6	10.3	9.9	1.1
1981	108.4	56.5	14.7 (23)	13.0	7.2	29.2	9.1	0.8
1982	222.6	73.9	32.8	4.6	3.7	22.2	7.6	0.2
1983	274.6	44.8	12.2 (48)	4.8	6.0	25.3	12.1	0.8
1984	498.6	49.2	12.2 (21)	6.4	7.7	13.3	15.9	0.3
1986	1086.2	36.5	10.2 (31)	4.7	9.1	13.1	17.9	0.9

Source: Cuenta Pública del DDF, 1970–87.

ND No data available.

(1) billion = 1 thousand million.
(2) Figures in brackets indicate debt budget allocations in specified years – probably a more realistic indication of its actual importance and size in any one year. In effect the depressed actual expenditure on debt raises the apparent allocation to other areas.

struggle, the political orientations of those in authority, and one's own predilection will shape the nature of the decision-making environment.

From central government's viewpoint good city management in the Metropolitan Area requires that social unrest be contained and appeased. This may be achieved through political mediation as well as through successful and efficient systems of delivery of public goods (Ward 1986). Depending upon individual career tracks if party-political and/or personal ambitions can be advanced at the same time, so much the better. But this is secondary. Although future advancement is always uncertain, loss of political control and weak management ability will almost certainly lead to removal. Nevertheless several areas of the Federal District Department structure are more overtly political than others. The post of Government Secretary 'A' is an especially critical one – in effect the Mayor's right hand. Note in Figure 3.4 that the *delegados* (i.e. the decentralised political officers) are under this individual, as are other key organs of state control (Judiciary, social welfare, land and commercial registries). Public security and the police are controlled directly by the Mayor, while big-spending technical departments are coordinated under a single Secretary of Public Works.

Within the budgets accorded to different departments, certain technical agencies stand out (Table 3.1). These are invariably those public enterprises engaged in large-scale 'lumpy' activities such as power and water supply systems. These are big-spending departments essential to both production and consumption. Always likely to be important, their budgetary priority will vary according to the particular policy emphasis of different adminis-trations: sometimes deep drainage (early 1970s); sometimes urban high-ways (1979–81); at other times Metro extensions (1981–3). Although the rate and order of introduction of local services such as domestic water and electricity to specified communities may be prone to some political interference by *delegados*, the procurement of water and power, together with the construction of drainage works are usually governed by relatively technical procedures.

The loss of municipality and the lack of local democracy

An important feature arising from the special status of the Federal District is the structure of policital representation of Mexico City's citizens – or, stated more accurately, the **lack** of representation. Few places in the democratic world have less local democracy than Mexico City. This is the 'high ground' that City Hall authorities have sought to defend for so long. My sense is that today alternative claims to the high ground may be beginning to break through those defences.

Mexico City: an opposition electoral heartland?

Certainly had Mexico City citizens the opportunity to elect local government officials then at least part of the City Hall administration (probably
one or two *delegaciones*) would have been delivered into the hands of the
opposition parties. This would especially have been the case in the 1988
presidential elections when Salinas (PRI) did very badly in the Metropolitan
Area taking only 27 per cent of the vote in the Federal District compared
with 49 per cent for Cárdenas and his *Frente*. (Results in the State of Mexico
were almost identical.) The argument no longer holds true that the national
President is also the voters' choice for the 'governorship' of the Federal
District.

The spatial distribution of broad electoral strengths throughout the
Metropolitan Area for each of the three main candidates is displayed in
Figure 3.5. Cárdenas swept the board in the DF and predominated in all but
a handful of districts such as the downtown areas (1 and 16) where
Clouthier (PAN) came out on top. Cárdenas was especially strong in the
low-income irregular settlement areas of Netzahualcóyotl, Ecatepec and
Chalco. This association between income and voting behaviour may be
observed most sharply in Naucalpan in the north west of the Metropolitan
Area where in electoral districts 20, 19 and 7 (largely working-class areas)
Cárdenas took 60 per cent, 43 per cent and 47 per cent of the vote
respectively; while in district 18, which is broadly congruent with the upper-
middle-income district of Ciudad Satélite, his share of the vote fell to 24 per
cent with Clouthier (PAN) runaway winner at 50 per cent. In the past, too,
the PAN's strength has been distributed in the middle-class and often small-
scale business districts of the city such as in Juárez and Miguel Hidalgo
delegaciones. The distribution of support for Cárdenas particularly
emphasises the erosion of the PRI vote in the *colonias populares* where until
a decade or so ago the Popular Organisations Confederation (CNOP) had
usually managed to cultivate strong electoral support through clientelism,
negotiation, cooptation and, sometimes, through repression (Gilbert and
Ward 1985).

The congressional election results for the 40 electoral districts in the
Federal District also saw a decline in the PRI's share of the total vote from
56 per cent in 1976, to 43 per cent in 1985 and to only 31 per cent in 1988.
But the failure of the Democratic Front to form a coalition, or to agree on
common candidates, meant that the opposition vote was split several ways
and the PRI took most of the districts by majority. Had the same four
parties who supported a single presidential candidate (PPS, PMS, PFCRN,
PARM) also agreed single candidates for the congressional districts, they
would have swept the board with 37 of the 40 electoral areas, with the PAN
taking the other three (*Proceso*, 18 July 1988). The performance of each of
the four main parties relative to its own average is mapped for electoral
districts of the Metropolitan Area (Figure 3.6). It shows those areas in
which respective parties did particularly well or particularly badly. The

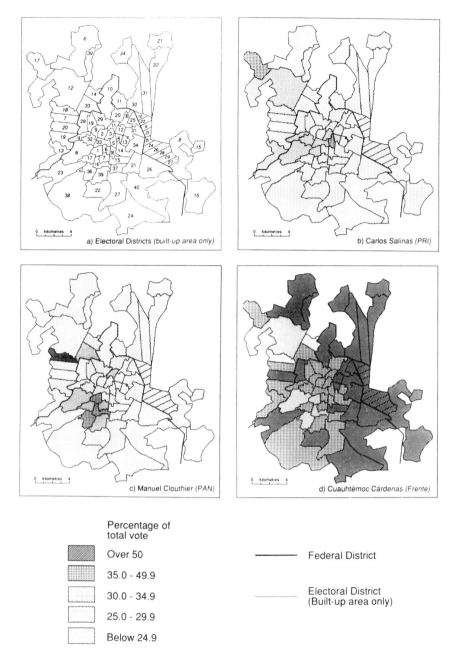

Percentage of
total vote

Over 50   ———— Federal District

35.0 - 49.9

30.0 - 34.9   ———— Electoral District
(Built-up area only)

25.0 - 29.9

Below 24.9

Figure 3.5 a-d Voting patterns in July 1988 presidential elections, by candidate for the Metropolitan Area

(Numbers on Box 3.5a are those for electoral districts in the DF and in the State of Mexico – hence the occasional duplication.)

83

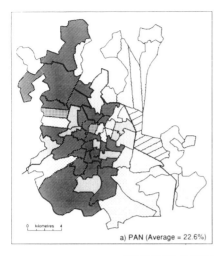

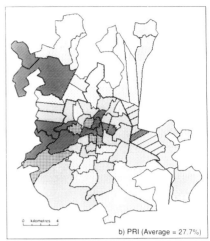

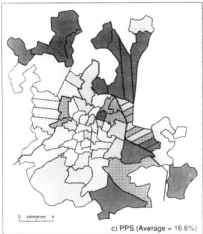

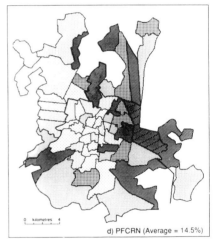

Percentage variation around
average vote for each Party

more than 3.1% above average

1.51% - 3.0% above average

within 1.5% either side of average

1.51% - 3.0% below average

more than 3.1% below average

PAN   Partido de Accion Nacional

PRI   Partido Revolucionario Institucional

PPS   Partido Popular Socialista

PFCRN   Partido del Frente Cardenista
        de Reconstruccion

*Note: averages calculated for DF and Metropolitan Area Districts.
Data are only for those Parties scoring 10% of total vote.*

Figure 3.6 a-d   Voting patterns in July 1988 federal elections, by political
party for the Metropolitan Area

84

pattern identified above of PAN strength in the west-inner areas of the DF and of the left opposition's strength in the periphery are brought into sharp relief in this figure. Moreover, as a further indication of the opposition stronghold that the Federal District presents this was one of two entities where the Democratic Front won the Senatorship elections. Finally, in the newly created Representative Assembly of the Federal District, the PRI took 24 districts; the PAN 13 and the *Frente* 3. A further 26 seats are allocated by proportional representation such that the combined opposition has almost equal voting weight to the PRI.

However, as I have already pointed out, the idea that the opposition parties might exercise real power and some direct control over the disbursement of resources in the national capital has proven an anathema to successive governments. To do so would signal the effective loss of social control over the population. Therefore citizens of the Federal District have been ruled by the President through delegated authority. Thus huge city resources are disbursed by unelected nominees and officials of whom few people will have heard before their being appointed. This situation has not passed uncontested. For many years opposition parties and the PRI have demanded greater democracy in the Federal District on two fronts. First, demands for an elected local congress with powers and responsibilities for the Federal District had virtually won all-party support by the end of the *Consulta Popular* in 1984. A second demand, with no overall consensus, was the call for direct elections for the *Regente* and *delegados*. Generally, members of the PRI were circumspect, knowing that their masters had some misgivings, while opposition parties were more openly in favour. But even the PRI wanted more direct and preferential access to policy making and resource allocation through its local district secretaries, and through local CNOP channels. For many years now the PRI has looked askance at the unwillingness of many City Hall officials to provide their representatives with privileged access to services, land entitlement, and so on (Ward 1981a). These are sought in order to reinforce the legitimacy and influence of local *priísta* leaders, and as sources of patronage in order to secure the vote on behalf of PRI candidates at elections. Opposition parties are also acutely aware that, in most cases, the majority of their support comes from residents in the Metropolitan Area, and are frustrated in their efforts to exercise any power on behalf of their would-be constituents.

'Adequate representative structures already exist'

For as long as possible the government has resisted calls to democratise the Federal District and reinstitute its municipal status, creating alternative structures which embodied locally elected representatives who enjoy no executive authority. As the saying goes: '*El PRI quiere cambiar todo para que nada cambie*' (the PRI wants to change everything so that nothing actually changes). Since 1929 the Federal District has had 'Consultative

Councils' comprising representatives from local enterprises, interest groups, lobbies, residents assocations, and so on. Regular (weekly) meetings, to be chaired by the Mayor or his appointee, would allow the Consultative Councils to express an opinion over servicing needs and public works.

In 1970 a new Organic Law of the Federal District retained the Council but extended it through local *juntas de vecinos* made up of representatives from different neighbourhoods. The *delegación* president sits on the Federal District Consultative Council. Although in place from 1970, the structure was not activated until considerably later. Instead, then-President Luis Echeverría (for it bore his *imprimata* more than that of Mayor Sentiés) used traditional patterns of patron-clientelism in order to achieve social and electoral control over low-income neighbourhoods (Cornelius 1975; Ward 1981a).

It was Mayor Hank González who began to use the *juntas de vecinos* structures, partly because he recognised that they provided both a mechanism for deflecting responsibility (and *bronca*) away from himself and onto his local *delegados*, but more importantly as a means of meeting criticism that the Federal District was fundamentally undemocratic and unrepresentative. What better than direct civic elections for block, neighbourhood, *delegación* and citywide representatives? Although the first 'round' of *junta* representatives was largely drummed up by local *delegados* in 1977–8, Mayor Hank González expended an inordinate amount of effort to ensure that elections in 1980 were highly publicised; that there was a large turnout; and subsequently that the *juntas* should be made to work (Ward 1981a; see also Jiménez 1988). This was not because Hank González believed in local democracy and elected officials: it was precisely because he didn't. The aim was that citizens would be satisfied with the opportunities for local representation that were now in place (Ramírez Saíz 1983; Cisneros Sosa 1983). Or so he hoped.

However, the creation of the *juntas* structure neither produced greater local democracy nor allayed demands for an elected local congress and for elected officials and chief administrators. Although there are signs that the *juntas* played some role in determining the prioritisation of settlement servicing programmes (Ward 1981a; but cf. Jiménez 1988), there is little evidence that this continued once Hank González left office. From 1983 onward their role diminished to that of an instrument of local control exercised by *delegados*. Increasingly, too, they were hijacked by middle-class representatives the individual fortunes of whom were closely tied to patronage received from the *delegado* (Jiménez 1989; see also Aguilar Martínez 1988). Demands for an elected congress arose once again during the 1982 federal elections (*Proceso* 14 May 1982). The nationwide *Consulta Popular* initiated by President Miguel De la Madrid in 1983 also fueled similar demands from opposition parties as well as from the PRI (*El Día* June 1984). Mayor Aguirre's response was that these proposals would be studied carefully by the Federal District Department and recommendations would be put to the plenary sessions of the *Consulta*.

This led subsequently to another arrangement purported to extend democracy and representation to the local populace. This was a compromise arrangement announced by the DDF Government Secretary for a local assembly with responsibilities for creating '*bandos*', setting-up local regulations, monitoring local authorities and so on (*Gaceta Oficial* 25 February 1988). Created through the elections on 6 July 1988, the Representative Assembly of the DF is, in my view, the latest in a long line of government initiatives to head off demands for a full democratisation of the Federal District and its administrative structure.

Demands for an elected mayor and local authorities have been circumvented – for the time being at least. Yet there are few cities in the world in which residents have so little say over who governs them, and over local urban policies and expenditures. Other special districts – for example, Washington DC and Bogotá DE – embody greater local democracy and enjoy direct elections of local urban authorities. I have argued that this is not an historical accident; it is the outcome of the fear among the revolutionary elite that the city would fall apart without discretionary controls exercised by the President and delegated through the *Regente*. They are also worried by the possible political effects of two powerful figures – both elected – with differing views and policies. The backyard is too big, too important, and too close to home to be entrusted to the opposition or to other factions within the same party.

Direction elections for DDF officials: the arguments for and against

But is it? Are residents of Mexico City's Federal District destined to be governed by non-elected officials in the medium to long term? Before seeking an answer to this question let me review the arguments for and against direct elections. One argument in favour of an elected Mayor is that the failure to have elected officials is likely to appear increasingly anomalous and unsustainable in the face of the current government's drive to democratise the Party, the unions, and the nation as a whole. In particular the argument that the President is elected by Federal District residents as the *de facto* Governor no longer stands up. As I have demonstrated, in the 1988 elections President Salinas lost the Federal District by a very large margin to Cárdenas.

Second, a growing recognition that it is probably impossible to govern the city successfully – or at least in a way that will satisfy the majority – may convince the PRI and government that they have little to lose. If the problems of Mexico City are insoluble, then, in a no-win situation, why not let in the opposition to make a hash of things? The government of Mexico City is not a zero sum game for the PRI (at least not as long as it controls the overall purse strings through Congress). The checks-and-balances system, although it has never really had to be used in the past, could quite easily tie the hands of opposition local government officials. In the United Kingdom

87

the Conservative Thatcher government demonstrated that by witholding central funding it could squeeze Labour-controlled councils whose spending policies it did not like.

A third factor in support of locally elected congress and officials is that Mexico may look seriously at other large metropolitan city experiences (London, Paris, Rome, etc.) where the opposition dominate (or have dominated) a city's administration without posing an unacceptable threat. Moreover, the existence of opposition local mayors in the backyard need not pose an insuperable problem for reasons that I have just pointed out. Indeed, the distribution of the population across two political entities and among a large number of *delegaciones* and municipalities provides ample scope for the central government to head off any across-the-board political protest before it gets out of hand. Besides, a growing proportion (around 40 per cent) of the population **already** live outside the DF boundaries where they exercise their constitutional rights, apparently without posing an unacceptable threat. As long as there were no single politico-adminstrative entity for the Metropolitan Area, this overall political control would not be threatened.

Viewed from these perspectives it is perhaps difficult to understand why the opposition is so eager to assert the principles of local representation and to demand that top officials be elected to City Hall – and also to understand why the government should contrive so hard to resist such moves. But there are good reasons. First, there are technical arguments relating to the location of federal buildings and institutions which have a national role and belong, therefore, to the nation rather than to a single entity. However, although this argument is invariably rehearsed by officials, it is beginning to sound lame and unconvincing. These technical constraints are not insuperable: it would be possible, for example, to create a special district for, say, the *primer cuadro* and for other specified plots, blocks, or even urban corridors which were considered to be federal in nature.

Second, what if control of the DF **is** a zero sum game and advancement for the opposition will be at a concomitant loss to the PRI? No-one can be sure. Third, perhaps the danger is not the opposition at all, but the PRI itself? If we assume a situation where the National President and the *Regente* were both elected by popular national and local vote respectively, it would be extremely difficult for the former to constrain the latter through budgetary controls in Congress. Consider, for the sake of argument, a shift back to PRI electoral dominance in which it holds overall national power **and** either a majority or an effective working minority in the Federal District headed by an elected Mayor of its choosing. In this situation one would have two very powerful elected political heavyweights operating in the same entity. This could cause huge political imbalance and potential for conflict. As a diluted example one need only look at the situation which already applies in the State of Mexico, where the Governor is appointed by the outgoing Executive a full year before the new President takes office. As a result, relations between the State of Mexico Governor and the President have often been uneasy and coordination between the two entities has traditionally been poor. The political instability would be magnified were the *Regente* to have a popularly elected mandate **independent** of the President's. Indeed, it would be very difficult for him to be controlled, and, ultimately, dismissed.

Fourth, it would be a major symbolic victory for the opposition, heralding – or accelerating – the beginning of the end for the PRI. Domino effect, slippery slope, thin end of the wedge: none of these metaphors does justice to the insecurity that the governing party would feel were it to lose executive control of the Federal District. A fifth reason relates to what I perceive as the personal ambition of the incumbent Mayor. If he proceeds cautiously Manuel Camacho is almost certain to be among the front-runners for the PRI presidential nomination for election in 1994. Any presidential ambitions he may entertain would probably be killed were he to take constitutional steps to 'deliver' executive authority for the Federal District – or some parts of it – into the hands of the opposition parties.

Obviously, therefore, there are strong arguments and counter-arguments on both sides. But there is no strong reason why the issues of the creation of a local congress and that of a locally elected executive should stand or fall together. They could easily be separated and I expect this to prove a politically prudent and expedient option. On balance, I think there is likely to be a gradual evolution of the democratisation of the Federal District in the direction of a local congress. Once the Representative Assembly has been observed to work without significantly interrupting city management, then resistance to an elected local congress will probably decline. However, one should not expect the concession to come automatically or easily. It will form the substance of future negotiations between the government and the opposition. But I do not expect any movement towards direct elections of the local executive (Mayor or *delegados*). Appointed officers may well find themselves subject to greater controls and monitoring by elected representa-tives, but direct executive authority in the hands of elected politicians is unlikely to happen.

Conclusion: change to effect no change

In this chapter I have identified the political rationale underpinning city management, particularly that of the Federal District Department. I have expressed the view that the content of the political project of recent governments has not been fundamentally one of democratisation, nor of improved social justice, nor of decentralisation and the reduction of centre–province imbalances. Rather the project is one of sustained social control and a halt to further deterioration in living conditions (Ward 1986). In Mexico City the power structure that has evolved is one of control, not one of development.

In my view a development-oriented power structure would have to implement two fundamental changes. First, the city would have to be conceived and managed as a single entity (albeit subdivided into appropriate administrative areas and not, as at present, divided in two). This is important not simply in order to achieve coordination between spatial entities – although this would help – but in order to allow the city to confront crucial issues and implement key policy initiatives. For example: whether and where to grow; who pays (local citizens or the nation and in what proportion); and what priority to accord various urban development goals? To tackle these questions, a second fundamental change is required: empowerment through democracy and full representation. Only a city administration elected on a political programme and charged with carrying it through has any possibility of approaching a development-based strategy. In order to tackle Mexico City's problems strong political will is required built around a firm agenda of action, and ultimately only elected politicians have the mandate to carry through policies upon which they are placed in office. If those policies are not implemented or prove inadequate, then at the next opportunity the electorate in a pluralist society may judge that administration accordingly.

Existing government structures are fundamentally structures of non-empowerment. They are anti-democratic and oriented towards sustaining social control in the hope that technical solutions, more efficient management, and occasional political compromise will allow the city to muddle through – as it probably will. If they think the city is about to fall apart, doomwatchers, revolutionaries, and bleeding-heart liberals will all be disappointed. It has survived thus far despite intense pressure and entrenched social inequality. It will survive for a lot longer. But it will not thrive. Some minor improvements may be achieved: through more progressive systems of local taxation and consumption charges; through administrative reorganisation; and through reducing losses from corruption, task duplication, etc. However, such improvements will not lead to any substantial change. Nor will they begin to redress the existing inequalities and antagonisms between capital city and the nation. These are likely to intensify so long as the Metropolitan Area continues to receive the lion's share of resources and to be heavily subsidised from fiscal resources. If fully representational structures emerge, then they will have to confront this antagonism and the inevitable outcome will be declining levels of subsidy and less preferential treatment. To keep existing levels of services in operation, a drastic revision of local taxation will be required by the newly mandated political local authority. And no matter how progressive these systems of taxation, all of Mexico City's population will end up paying more. The often forgotten bottom line is that fuller representation and democracy will be at substantial costs to city residents in terms of the taxes and local rating payments that they are obliged to pay. In clamouring for full representation, citizens must also ask themselves if they are prepared to pay the price of local democracy.

I have identified some of the pressures for democratisation in the Federal District. But the level at which these debates are being conducted and the content of the debate (elected congress and/or elected officials), although potentially important, are a far cry from what democratisation is all about. The latter is about popular participation in political and civic affairs. It is about experimenting with new opportunities for organisation and expression. It is about exploring new forms of leadership and representation. Ultimately it is about different power structures which are less hierarchical and less vertical. Of course, this is precisely what makes it unacceptable to the PRI. By and large, social movements in Mexico City have not really threatened, in Castells' (1977: 263) terms, to achieve a 'qualitatively new effect in power relations'. Most organisations have been successfully managed by government and by the PRI through time-worn mechanisms of clientelism, cooptation, divide-and-rule, and repression. On the very few occasions where horizontal solidarity has been forged and large numbers of people have mobilised, the government has been quick to strike a deal.

The changes that I have identified do chart some movement towards better city management. Moreover, the current period is one of further important potential changes and opportunities. But it seems likely that these will be too slow, too narrow, and too carefully moderated and constrained by the state. As such, one cannot be optimistic about significant progress to overcome spatial and social inequality in Mexico City. For that to happen the philosophy and politics of City administration have to change, and that is unlikely.

4
Urban land use and transportation

There is probably not a large city in the world where residents do not complain about a traffic problem. In the United Kingdom weather forecasters and transport planners must vie with each other for the position of the professional most often cursed by the general public. Weather forecasting does not really figure in a Mexican's daily life. Given the season, the weather is fairly predictable. More of a problem, perhaps, is the fact that transport planners do not count for much either. Although expenditure upon city transportation investment can be very high (Table 3.1), transport planners themselves do not carry much political clout. Thus in Mexico City the roots of the problem relate to the fact that transportation policy has been subject to sharp breaks in continuity associated with presidential cycles; has overly favoured the better-off economic groups who use private transport; and has wavered in its commitment towards what is considered the most appropriate form of public transport. Overall, though, I believe that the 'problem' in so far as Mexico City is concerned, is frequently overstated and exaggerated. Yes, the City does have major traffic problems and in particular can be vexatious if one expects to drive solo across its extent during peak times of the day. But this represents a distance of over 40–50 kilometres and most people are more circumspect in their needs and daily mobility; or at least have become so in the past two decades as the city has grown.

This chapter analyses the structure and nature of transportation systems in Mexico City, their evolution and politics. It is about the way in which people gain physical access to what I will broadly term urban 'satisfiers': work, markets, friends and entertainment centres, schools and other social service facilities. In a later chapter I analyse how in Mexico 'access' is often stratified socially and economically and I show how this can reproduce existing patterns of inequality within society. Here, however, my concern is to identiy how people's physical access to urban satisfiers is changing over time; at what cost; and whether the daily journeys that people undertake are becoming easier or more difficult. An answer to these questions requires that we look first at the city's land-use structure and how people relate to it. Only then can we begin to evaluate the efficacy of the changing nature of transport provision and the service it offers.

Land use and access in Mexico City

In Chapter 2, I described the physical and population dynamics of growth throughout the Metropolitan Area. I identified, also, the continuing spatial segregation among economic groups which in large part relates to the expansion and production of different housing opportunities within the city. In terms of proximity to externalities, the rich and better-off economic groups bid for serviced land with pleasant views, near to would-be peers and socially 'chic' service and commercial centres, and avoid negative externalities such as heavily polluted areas, noxious industrial plants and areas lacking social *cachet*. The converse applies to the poor who, with the exception of occasional privileged (illegal) access to some *ejidal* lands, are usually obliged to seek residence in poorly serviced lands with high negative externalities, that are undesirable to everyone else.

But there is also the argument that the poor do exercise real choice about where they live. They make important locational trade-offs at different 'stages' of their urban and residential experience in order to maximise proximity to certain crucial 'satisfiers': cheap markets, sources of unskilled employment, and low-cost rental (tenement) accommodation (Turner 1968a). For a recently arrived migrant creating a 'bridgehead' in the city it is the city centre that offers optimum access to these opportunities. In Chapter 2, I challenged several of these assumptions and showed how patterns had never fully conformed to the Turner model, and I suggested that, even where there was some resemblance in the past, these patterns have changed significantly in recent decades. One important reason has been the gradual absorption of many formerly outlying towns into the built-up area. For example, in order of absorption from the 1920s onwards: Tacuba, Azcaptotzalco, Tacubaya, Tlalnepantla, Tepeyac/La Villa, Mixcoac, Ixtapalapa, Coyoacan, San Angel, Ecatepec, Contreras and Tlalpan. Today, too, urban expansion at the periphery of the Metropolitan Area is often incorporating well-established *pueblo* cores (moving clockwise and starting in the north: Tepotzotlán, Coacalco, Chiconcuac, Chalco and Milpa Alta – see Figure 1.1). These old town centres are important because they offer a large number of land-use and service functions that were, until they were absorbed, exclusively found in the old historic core of the city. Cheap retail markets are an integral element in these centres as are many unskilled employment opportunities, services such as public baths, schools, shops, parks, entertainments, and often political/administrative functions as well (*delegación* or municipal offices for example). Although some of the large homes in and around such centres have been 'gentrified' (especially those in the south), they may also offer low-income *vecindad* or *'ciudad perdida'*-type accommodation for renters.

The important point to recognise here is that, as the city has expanded in size and areal extent, its functions have evolved to create a variety of spatially decentralised areas within the Metropolitan Area. Therefore, the majority of the population no longer relate to the old historic core of Mexico City for their day-to-day services and needs. Instead, they go to the nearest local sub-centre. The functionality of these 'cities-within-the-city' was recognised by planners during the 1970s and several existing *pueblo* cores were scheduled for 'consolidation' as 'Metropolitan Urban Centres' within the Urban Development Plan (see Figure 4.1 and Chapter 5). Where no such centre existed (e.g. Pantitlán and Netzahualcóyotl), then a new one was created.

Although small pockets of industrial development are spread throughout most of the Metropolitan Area, a few of the major industrial districts may be identified here. First, before the 1950s industry developed in two principal sites: north of the rail heads in Cuauhtemoc and into Azcapotzalco; and down the western edge of the (then) city limits focusing upon gravel and sand extraction and latterly cement and other mineral works. Since the 1950s there has been some new expansion of light industries in the east of the Federal District in Ixtapalapa, but the major industrial area of note remains Azcapotzalco.

A rather disingenuous attempt was made during the late 1950s to encourage industrial development elsewhere in the national territory and to reduce excessive concentration in the capital. It was disingenuous because no attempt was made to include the surrounding municipalities as part of the industrial exclusion zone (Lavell 1973; Unikel and Lavell 1979). Faced with controls imposed inside the Federal District, industry (like new residential development banned by Uruchurtu), established itself on the other side of the DF boundary in Naucalpan, Tlalnepantla, Ecatepec, and more recently still in Tultitlán and Cuautitlán.

As we observed in Chapter 1, the Metropolitan Area retains a disproportionately high share of the nation's industrial product and employment, and while this proportion has declined significantly since 1975, in absolute terms it has increased. It has also shifted its location somewhat. There are two key sectors of industrial land use running outwards from the centre towards the north east and north west respectively (Figure 4.1). Between 1960 and 1980 there has been an overall movement of industrial establishments from the centre to the periphery with the central *delegaciones* losing relative importance to Azcapotzalco (up to 1970), and to Tlalnepantla, Naucalpan and Ecatepec (up to 1975); and since that time outwards still further to Cuautitlán Izcalli and Cuautitlán de Romero Rubio (Garza 1978: 102–7). The central city area today predominates in activities which require less space (foodstuffs, drinks, shoes, printing); while the first 'ring' (see pp. 35–6) concentrates upon capital and intermediate goods and consumer durables, where greater space was required (Villegas 1988).

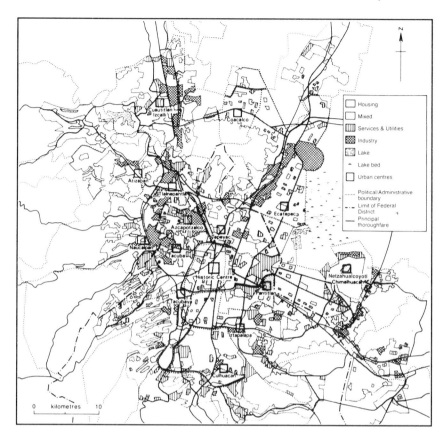

Figure 4.1 Principal land uses and urban 'centres' in the Metropolitan Area

Between 1975 and 1985 the second 'ring' has been the most dynamic, and covers a diverse range of production of industrial goods (ibid.).

This spatial distribution of service and industrial functions thus sets the pattern of daily journeys to work for many: just over 50 per cent of all daily journeys undertaken. Next come journeys to school (around 35 per cent, which is particularly high in Mexico given the youthful age structure of the population). Shopping and recreational trips cover around 8 per cent each (Lizt Mendoza 1988: 228). The means whereby people make these journeys are shown in Table 4.1. City and suburban bus services taken together have always been most important, but the Metro has become increasingly important in recent years. Given the poor standard of driving, the widespread existence of potholes, and occasional uncovered manhole, few people risk riding on two wheels. The industrial areas are closely served by working-class districts, many of which were irregular settlements

Urban land use and transportation

Table 4.1 Types of daily journeys undertaken in the Metropolitan Area of Mexico City, 1983

Means of transport	Total number of journeys	Percentage of vehicular journeys
1. Metro[1]	6 515 616	29.08
2. On foot[2]	6,104 626	—
3. City bus[3]	6 821 759	25.98
4. Private car	4 267 815	19.04
5. Suburban bus	3 147 929	14.04
6. Collective taxi	1 838 715	8.20
7. Trolley-bus	280 614	1.25
8. School bus	191 612	0.85
9. Ordinary taxi	154 802	0.69
10. Bicycle	90 929	0.41
11. Tram	59 035	0.26
12. Lorry	29 158	0.13
13. Motorcycle	15 498	0.07
TOTAL	28 518 208	100.00

Source: Adapted from Lizt Mendoza (1988: 226)
(1) Includes changing lines within the system
(2) Journeys of more than 500 metres or of 5 minutes' duration
(3) Includes routes operated by the State of Mexico Transport Commission (COTREM)

established during the 1950s and 1960s to accommodate the workforce that fuelled Mexico's economic miracle. For those living nearby, transport was not a major problem. However, for the 600 000 plus people in 1970 who lived in Netzahualcóyotl in the east, travel to work for many meant a 1–2 hour one-way journey to the factories in the north. Those working in services had a slightly shorter, but no less exhausting, journey to the city centre.

The problem was that Netzahualcóyotl at that time had very few urban 'satisfiers' of its own and enjoyed limited infrastructure with streets that were often impassable during the rainy season. Thus many people had a long walk through muddy streets to a paved street; long queues; an extremely uncomfortable journey by bus to the Federal District boundary where a break in journey to Metro and/or another bus(es) was undertaken (Navarro Benítez 1988a). Although transportation costs were subsidised and fares were often charged at a flat rate, outside the Federal District they were higher. The flat rate system led companies to run shorter routes thereby making frequent changes obligatory. For those coming in from far afield during the 1960s and early 1970s transport costs could be significant, although I doubt if these costs came near to 25 per cent of the basic minimum salary as some authors suggest (Navarro Benítez 1988b). My own data collected in 1979 suggest that working-class populations spent less than 10 per cent of the daily minimum wage on transport and most workers earned considerably more than the minimum (see Table 4.2). Thus public transport costs in Mexico City are financially affordable to the majority of users. It is the social and emotional costs of daily travel which are more burdensome, together with the time lost from other activities and the lengthening of the working day. Nevertheless, although travel conditions have improved markedly in the past decade, for those living in the distant periphery on the high roads to Puebla, Pachuca and Querétaro respectively, daily travel into town remains onerous. To the extent that an estimated 75 per cent of users of the collective transport system are male these costs fall disproportionately on their shoulders. But some 46 per cent of observed mobility is also around the home and these 'costs' fall more heavily upon women and children. There is, therefore, a gender division of transportation in Mexico City that has yet to be studied.

Although users of private cars do not suffer the same physical discomforts their journey, too, can be onerous. Distances are considerable from the more remote residential districts in the south and north west and, at peak periods or after a storm, traffic moves slowly even on the orbital and interior urban freeways. Contemporary isochrone diagrams suggest around 30 minutes' driving time from the western Federal District boundary to the city centre (Domínguez 1987). In addition to the service functions provided by the old *pueblo* cores and other urban 'centres', large hyper-market shopping malls have been established alongside the *periférico* on its northern and southern sections. Access is designed almost exclusively for private transport and these developments cater for the middle-class and upper-income groups.

Later in this chapter I will analyse in detail the nature and evolution of the transportation system. Here I want to suggest that average journey times for most Mexico City residents have not increased greatly in recent years. This is likely to prove a contentious point as most people believe otherwise. But it is important to recognise that the extent and efficiency of the transportation system have improved notably. Also important is the emergence of multicentred land-use functions alluded to earlier. Most people's daily needs are met within the broad sector in which they live. Their search for employment and accommodation tends to revolve around existing social networks and most people relate to one broad zone, or more usually to a single sector of the city (Jackson 1973). Education, shopping and other needs are also met locally – often through the cities-within-the-city structure outlined earlier. Since 1975 there has also been a notable improvement in the spatial distribution of industrial activities in the Metropolitan Area (Villegas 1988). The industrial structure has become more diversified over time, has generated a growing number of jobs in absolute terms, and spatially the locations of employment have moved outwards with the most rapid growth in the second 'ring' (ibid.). The importance of this decentralisation of 'satisfiers' through the changing nature of land uses should not be underestimated.

In a major study conducted in 1983 which examined the journeys of a very

Table 4.2 Journey-to-work time and costs experienced by heads of households in peripheral irregular settlements of Mexico City, 1979

	Isidro Fabela (%)	El Sol (%)	Santo Domingo (%)	Jardines de Tepeyac (%)	Liberales (%)	Chalma (%)	Total (%)	Total number
Principal mode of transport								
on foot	15	5	13	12	13	4	11	(50)
bus	44	51	42	65	25	79	51	(235)
pesero & bus[1]	13	4	12	1	4	2	7	(31)
Metro & other[2]	3	25	14	5	36	7	13	(62)
other[3]	25	15	18	17	23	9	18	(84)
Total number	*(100)*	*(78)*	*(90)*	*(83)*	*(53)*	*(58)*		*(462)*
Time taken in return journey								
1 hour or less	52	19	50	33	51	33	40	(178)
61–120 min	29	32	29	36	39	45	34	(151)
over 121 min	19	49	21	31	10	22	26	(116)
Total number	*(94)*	*(79)*	*(88)*	*(75)*	*(51)*	*(58)*		*(445)*
Average time of return journey (min)	86	141	93	116	78	108	104	
Average cost of return journey (pesos)[4]	$12	$10	$12	$10	$11	$9	$11	

Source: Settlement Survey, PIHLU study; see Gilbert and Ward (1985).

(1)   Includes a small number who only took *peseros* (collective taxies). This proportion will have increased somewhat during the last decade as the *pesero* network has expanded, and as it has become better organised and more integrated to complement Metro routes.

(2)   Metro, or a combination of Metro and other modes of transportation. (Liberales is near to Observatorio Metro Station.)

(3)   Includes private car and other unidentified combinations.

(4)   The average daily minimum wage in Mexico City early in 1979 was 138 pesos. Most heads of households earned a little more: around 15 per cent above the minimum on average (Gilbert and Ward 1985: 106–7). Late in 1978 the dollar rate of exchange was 22.8 pesos.

large sample of people for the Metropolitan Area it was found that the average journey was 52 minutes (Lizt 1988). This includes 21 per cent of journeys undertaken on foot (Table 4.1). Remarkably, working in 1979 among households in six peripheral irregular settlements of Mexico City where travel times could be expected to be much higher, I found that the average **round trip** journey to work for household heads was 104 minutes: identical to Lizt's findings. Moreover, in the three different-sized cities in which we worked, size of city and journey time to work did not increase in a broadly linear fashion. Rather, for those travelling the longest distances, travel times tended to level off at around the 60–80 minute threshold (Gilbert and Ward 1982b; and Table 4.2). In smaller cities people might well travel right across town or to the city centre: but in large metropolitan areas they keep to one broad area or sector. Less than one-quarter of workers from the surveyed irregular settlements in Mexico City spent more than two hours travelling to and from their workplace (Table 4.2). Inevitably, longer journeys were suffered by those living in the most peripheral and isolated settlements (El Sol and Jardines), but communications to these settlements have improved considerably since the survey was undertaken. Note, also, the way in which flat rate and subsidised rate and subsidised fares override any significant time (distance)/cost relationship (Table 4.2).

Despite Mexico City's enormous population it does not sprawl over anything like the same extent as many other modern world cities. Population densities are high and a relatively small proportion of the city comprises green spaces in the form of parks and gardens. In 1978 the Federal District had only 2.3 m^2 of green space per inhabitant (5.2 m^2 in the Metropolitan Area as a whole), compared with the 16 m^2 norm established by the World Health Organisation and 9 m^2 recommended by international standards (Guevara and Moreno 1987). Despite these already high densities, considerable opportunities were identified for further increases on 'inefficiently' used space within the city: an estimated 19 per cent of all plots being estimated as 'vacant'. Planning policy since the early 1980s has sought to encourage the conversion of vacant plots into active use.

Within the Federal District, land available for future development is almost entirely located in the south. However, a growing ecological awareness among state and society at large has identified this region as one which must be preserved as agricultural and conservation areas. Their importance is highlighted both in the need for reoxygenation of the highly polluted atmosphere, and as one of the principal areas for replenishment of the city's natural groundwater acquifers (ibid.). Some 70 per cent of the city's water supply comes from Central Valley groundwater sources and without adequate replenishment the problems of depletion, lowering water table, and drying out of the anhydrous clays of the old lake bed area, will lead to further problems of building subsidence.

Changing patterns of land use and capital accumulation in Mexico City

The changing pattern of economic activity in Mexico City was discussed earlier in Chapter 1. Specifically, I noted the shift towards a more tertiary-based urban economy, especially in the Federal District. There has been a decline in the role of the central city area as an industrial centre, and those functions which remain are oriented towards non-durable consumer goods such as shoes and clothes, printing and, lately, some textiles. The first and second 'rings' are more oriented towards capital and intermediate goods and consumer durables (Villegas 1988). Nevertheless the central city area retains considerable importance as an area of industrial production, although it remains unclear how much this was permanently affected by the 1985 earthquake. Some estimates suggest that as many as 18 per cent of establishments in the *delegación* Cuauhtemoc suffered extensive damage, especially the small and middle-sized clothing workshops (Garza 1986).

Other factors also intervene to change the pattern of land uses. The earthquake threatened to redefine much of the central city, but the early decision to rehouse low-income families on the same sites as their collapsed or demolished tenements has meant that the land use has remained the same, even though the buildings have changed. Elsewhere in the downtown area however, land has often been converted to open space or remains vacant – usually where there were once public buildings or private hotels and shops. On prime sites throughout the city one might also expect strong redevelopment pressures from commerce to clear away dilapidated residential properties and to initiate changes to more 'efficient' and profitable activities. In the early 1970s South Insurgentes Street between Colonia Napoles and San Angel comprised large residential homes built during the 1940s and early 1950s. Today almost all these residences have been demolished and adjacent plots merged in order to construct new offices and shops. Indeed, for Mexico City's Planning Department one of the most politically sensitive areas and questions is in Polanco – a formerly exclusive residential district – in which there are strong pressures for commercial redevelopment of land to which residents are strongly opposed. They fear an erosion of the area's residential functions and a decline in residential land values.

Research elsewhere has also begun to emphasise the existence of these redevelopment pressures from large-scale commerce. Inner-city shanty-towns have been identified as especially vulnerable in Rio de Janeiro and in Bangkok to name but two cities (Perlman 1976; Boonyabancha 1983). Indeed, contemporary World Bank philosophy explicitly seeks to 'assist selectively in subdivision of new land, particularly for the benefit of poor urban households displaced from central city locations by expansions in commercial uses of land' (Linn 1983: 182). The logic of capital accumulation processes demand the penetration and commodification of formerly illegal or informal land-use functions and their displacement to make way for more profitable investment opportunities.

Thus a particularly important question relates to the fate of the population who have traditionally lived in the inner-city. To what extent are residential areas in Mexico City being turned over to more commercial activities? Are the poorest groups most vulnerable to these pressures and, if so, to what extent is there a selective displacement of these groups from the city centre? Certainly displacement of these groups is frequently argued to be a consequence of redevelopment. One study drew attention to the rising pressure upon classic tenements (the *vecindades*):

> (the) continued existence of the central low-priced rented stock is threatened by the substitution of original proprietors by more dynamic property capital (which is) acquiring *vecindades* and vacant lots, sometimes without developing these locations immediately, and in other cases constructing middle-price range condominiums. (COPEVI 1977a: 43–4)

There is further evidence to support these arguments of displacement although it usually relates to large-scale one-off redevelopment projects (Batley 1982; Suárez Pareyón 1978). For example in São Paulo an extension to the Metro led to a total redevelopment of a working-class neighbourhood and to the expulsion of low-income families and traditional economic activities from the area:

> redevelopment shifts gains from tenants and small owners back to creditors, to the recipients of large scale reorganized land and to those who are able to meet conditions of the extended credit based land, housing and consumer goods markets. Expulsion is thus related to accumulation. (Batley 1982: 261).

Although this proposition invites agreement there are signs that these processes are far from inevitable. The extension of the Metro into working-class areas of Bras in São Paulo undoubtedly displaced large numbers of the local population yet the 70 metre swathe of vacant land cleared either side of the actual railway has not been redeveloped or commercialised. This is probably due to sharp reductions in the investment opportunities for finance and other capital during the recent economic crisis, and to a 'switch' to alternative and more profitable forms of investment elsewhere (see also Benton (1986) on Montevideo). A similar feature may be observed around the old wholesale market area of Mexico City, the surrounding blocks of which are not being 'gentrified' as might have been anticipated. However, there seems little doubt that during those periods when large-scale investment in urban redevelopment is profitable this leads to population displacement similar to that experienced at Covent Garden and elsewhere (Burgess 1978).

Nor were inner-city rental shackyards systematically turned over to private commercial development during the 1970s – despite their having been scheduled by the government for removal. These *ciudades perdidas* (lost cities) were prime sites for commercial redevelopment given their location in and around the city centre of Mexico City. Detailed information was gathered about these sites in the early 1970s (Ward 1976b). In 1982 all but one of those locations with an original area of 0.5–1.0 hectare (or 50–99 familes) – i.e. of a suitable size for redevelopment – were revisited and detailed land-use maps were drawn. This provided a sample of 75 separate sites. Ten of the 75 sites were listed in 1973 as having been eradicated, yet in our 1982 survey six of the ten still had shanties upon them (Ward and Melligan 1985). The widespread presence of dwellings on the majority of sites suggested that removal and redevelopment had had little impact. Only thirteen sites had little or no residential functions and here we may assume that major clearance has occurred. A further 21 sites had between 15 per cent and 65 per cent of their area inhabited and these were defined as of 'mixed' land use. In our assessment 11 of these appeared to have been partially affected by a programme of removal. But no less than 41 sites still remained as low-income housing. At the very outside less than one-half of all the settlements studied had been significantly affected by the rehousing programme. Moreover, the evidence suggested that where redevelopment had occurred it had not been informed by pressures from commercial capital. Rather the changes came about through public sector initiatives: mainly the construction of schools and roads, or road-widening schemes. There was no clear evidence of changes to commercial useage as a widespread or generalised speculatory process (Ward and Melligan 1985).

Thus if 'switching' of capital investment is occurring in Mexico City then it is not taking place systematically and certainly not in a way that is leading to significant changes to **existing** residential and commercial areas. It is clearly visible in land development processes at the periphery whereby land is converted from agricultural to commercial use. But it appears to have exercised far less importance in 'gentrifying' downtown areas than I, for one, had initially anticipated. In part this is due to the social 'construction' of consumer demand through the built environment and which I consider in Chapter 7. In part, also, it is an outcome of access and the evolution of the transportation system which I consider below.

Mexico City's transportation system

Favouring the better off: private companies and private cars

The physical expansion of the city and, in particular, the establishment of major industrial centres in a northern arc of the Metropolitan Area, required the emergence of a transportation system that would get workers from the peripheral *colonias populares* to the factories. Yet it was not until the creation of the Metro in 1968 and, more importantly, its expansion from 1977 onwards that direct state intervention in favour of collective systems of mass public transport really emerged. Even now the philosophy remains firmly one of a mixed public/private system, although there are signs that the government may, at last, be contemplating some moves against the use of private cars. However, even though there have been positive developments in transportation planning in recent years, the state has treated the private sector extremely favourably. Below I look, first, at the responsibilities and role of the private sector.

Forty-five per cent of the nation's vehicles are registered in the Metropolitan Area (Lizt Mendoza 1988). As Table 4.3 indicates, 'low-capacity' vehicles – defined as private cars, taxis and collective taxis (increasingly

Table 4.3 Evolution of means of transportation for low versus high-carrying capacity vehicles

| | Percentage of total journeys undertaken | | | | |
	1966	1972	1979	1983	1985
Low-capacity vehicles (taxis, *colectivos* and private cars)[1]	10.7	31.5	32.2	32.1	29.0
High-capacity transport (Metro, buses, trolley-buses and trams)[2]	89.3	66.6	65.5	67.2	54.0
Others[3]		1.9	2.3	0.7	17.0

Source: Adapted from Navarro Benítez (1989: 33).
(1) Includes collective taxis on fixed routes.
(2) Only Ruta 100 buses and other state-run enterprises.
(3) Includes casual pick-up taxis without fixed itinerary and suburban buses operated by the private sector.

10 seater *combis* and larger-capacity microbuses) – carry just under one-third of total daily journeys. A not unreasonable proportion one might imagine. But it must be remembered that we are dealing here with a poor population in which the large majority cannot afford these means of transport – in effect they are largely excluded. Moreover, the significance of these 'low-capacity' means of transport is far greater than the one-third of the population carried. Eighty-five per cent of pollution comes from vehicles – practically all of it from the disproportionate number of private cars (Legoretta 1988: 286; Castillejos 1988: 302). Thus, 34 per cent of daily journeys (6.7 million) are provided by some of the 2.5 million private cars, and 125000 taxis and *colectivos* (Domínguez 1987). Compare this with the remaining journeys which are provided by only 16000 units of 'high-capacity' means of transport, most of which are buses (ibid.). Now that the DDF is improving its anti-contamination controls on the *Ruta 100* bus system (6631 vehicles) which were notoriously bad sources of pollution, the blame for the majority of this contamination lies firmly with the low-capacity vehicles and users. Moreover, other social costs need to be accounted. The congestion caused by private vehicles slows down the movement on roads to 16 km/hour at peak times and this also affects high-capacity transport systems (Lizt Mendoza 1988). Capital investment in road construction and improvements, relatively low fuel costs, low repair and service costs, non-punitive costs on car tax and circulation licences, all encourage private car ownership and usage. In Mexico City the only relatively high-cost item is insurance. These low costs represent hidden subsidies to private car users in particular. The increase in private car usage as a proportion of total daily journeys from around one-fifth to one-quarter in the decade through to 1985 is apparent in Table 4.4. The General

Table 4.4 Journeys per day for different types of transportation

	Number (thousands), and percentage of total journeys undertaken				
	1971	1975	1980	1986	2000 (estimates)
	%	%	%	%	%
Buses[1]	6209 53.6	7414 50.5	8749 49.2	9300 42.3	16800 47.3
Metro (length km)	901 7.7 (39.9)	1510 10.3 (41.4)	2098 11.8 (46.2)	6515 29.0 (114.9)	7120 20.0 (240)
Electric service (trolley & trams)	547 4.7	665 4.5	607 3.4	700 3.1	2700 7.6
Collective taxis	371 3.0	438 3,0 ⎫	2392 12.6	2300 10.5	2500 7.1
Private taxis	1061 9.0	1261 9.0 ⎭			
Private cars	2206 19.0	2880 19.6	3532 19.8	5500 25.0[2]	6400 18.0[2]
Other means	300 2.6	360 2.5	423 2.4	– –	– –

Source: Adapted from Navarro Benítez (1988b: 46; 1989: 34).
(1) Buses includes urban and 'suburban'.
(2) Includes taxis and colectivos in the State of Mexico municipalities; also 'others' from 1986 onwards.

Transport Coordination aims to reduce this to 18 per cent by the turn of the century but this is unlikely to occur without the withdrawal of some of the implicit subsidies identified above.

The proposed car use controls that the Federal District Department is now contemplating will be the first attempt ever to move against private car usage in the city. The DDF is proposing to introduce mandatory anti-contamination controls on all cars from 1992 onwards. Only 5 per cent of vehicles in operation in 1988 were estimated to be operating at optimum levels in terms of air/gasoline mixture (Legoretta 1988). Also, in order to reduce the intense level of contamination suffered during the period January–February when the Central Valley is especially susceptible to temperature inversions, the DDF proposes to issue a car ban one (working) day a week in 1990 according to the displayed colour of each car's licence. If implemented and adhered to, this might be expected to reduce significantly car circulation on any single day.

A paradox revealed by Table 4.3 is that, although the state took concerted action to intervene in stimulating high-capacity transportation systems from the 1970s onwards, its failure to control rising car ownership and usage together with the dramatic expansion of collective taxis, has meant that the relative importance of **low-capacity** vehicles rose from 11 per cent to 32 per cent (Table 4.3). In part this is due to the reorganisation of collective taxis. Not only has the number increased, but the traditional pattern of large saloon cars carrying a maximum of six passengers along a few set routes has been overtaken by a widespread use of green and white *combis* carrying ten or eleven people. More recently still, larger microbuses have begun to appear on certain routes. The routes themselves are tightly organised, criss-cross the city, and are much more tightly integrated with other transport systems than they were a decade ago (Sutherland 1985). Although there seems little doubt the service they provide is much improved, they are also subject to many of the previous criticisms of private cars (Navarro Benítez 1988a). It is my view, however, that provided they are well maintained they are far less villains of the piece than are private cars – given their much higher occupancy ratio.

The criticisms of high social costs apply particularly to low-capacity vehicles, but until the state seriously undertook to intervene in mass collective transport the effect of government policy was to systematically favour the private sector. Before the late 1960s Mexico City's transportation system evolved in a rather *ad hoc* fashion in response to private vested interests at different points in time. It was basically a privately operated system which began with a (foreign-owned) tram-based service before the Revolution, and developed subsequently (1917–46) into a myriad collection of privately operated bus routes (Navarro Benítez 1988b). State intervention did not seek to cut across these interests in any way. Quite the opposite: bus operators were rewarded for their participation in and support for the post-revolutionary state apparatus and were encouraged to expand and to displace the foreign-owned trams (ibid.). It was not until 1946 that the state intervened formally in transportation matters, first to expropriate the trams, and secondly to create a trolley-bus network to complement that provided by the buses. However, its role in stimulating collective systms of mass transportation remained extremely limited until it began to develop the Metro in 1968.

Until that time state intervention was focused upon the development of the road network and particularly that which most favoured the private car: rapid no-stop highways such as the *Viaducto*, the *Circuito Interior* and, the suburban *anillo periférico* (Plate 4.1). Other major roads were also widened and lengthened throughout the 1950s and 1960s serving both private cars and bus routes (e.g. Insurgentes North and South, Calzada Tlalpan).

Many of these developments quite deliberately favoured not only private transport but opened up new areas of urban land development and speculation especially in the south of the city. For example, an important motive for the creation of the 'Camino al Ajusco' in the mid-1970s was to facilitate the proliferation of real estate development on the *pedregal* south of the *periférico*. It also provided more direct access to a State Secretary's *rancho*. Those with prior knowledge were able to acquire large land holdings and to make killings from the subsequent land valorisation windfalls that the new road generated. Of course, not all new road routes were motivated by private gain. Occasionally they avoided lands of powerful politicians or private interest groups where state expropriation would have been an embarrassment. This accounts for some of the twists and turns in the *periférico* route in the west. Large-scale construction firms such as ICA had also been pressing the government to raise investment in transportation systems, most notably the Metro; but Mayor Uruchurtu held

Plate 4.1 The orbital motorway or *anillo periférico* looking north across Chapultepec Park

Plate 4.2 *Eje vial* and a part of the most recently developed (overhead) Metro line

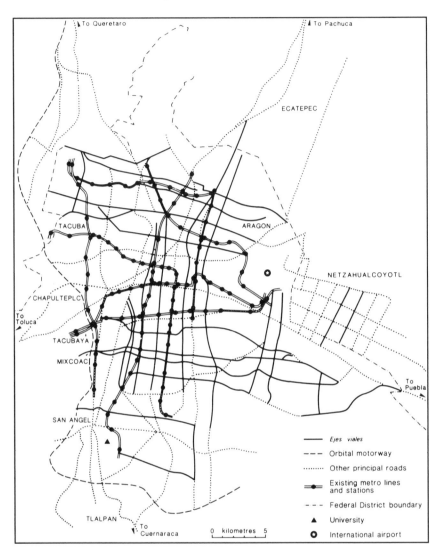

Figures within map: To Queretaro, To Pachuca, ECATEPEC, TACUBA, ARAGON, NETZAHUALCOYOTL, CHAPULTEPLC, To Toluca, TACUBAYA, MIXCOAC, To Puebla, SAN ANGEL, TLALPAN, To Cuernaraca

Legend:
——— Ejes viales
– – – Orbital motorway
········· Other principal roads
Existing metro lines and stations
– – – Federal District boundary
▲ University
◉ International airport

0 kilometres 5

Figure 4.2 Principal transport networks in Mexico City, 1989

out against them for as long as he could. His political demise occurred in part as opposition rose among powerful business interests whose real estate and construction proposals were being blocked.

Nor did investment in road construction on behalf of the private sector decline once greater public commitment had emerged to collective transportation systems. Sixteen *ejes viales* were constructed in 1978–9 comprising three-to-five lane one-way highways equipped with integrated traffic signalling. Although built at enormous expense and not without considerable public outcry over the way in which they were constructed, the *ejes* have done much to facilitate rapid traffic flow around the city (Figure 4.2 and Plate 4.2). Although many of the *ejes* have an exclusive contra-flow trolley lane (to avoid it being used by other vehicles), these *ejes* by and large are not heavily used by public transportation systems. Once again private cars and taxis were the principal beneficiaries.

Public transport policy

At the outset the Metro was designed to confront two problems: first to ease the congestion in the inner-city area; second, to help 'dignify' and rehabili-tate the Historic Centre (Navarro Benítez 1988a). Despite its inauguration in the late 1960s the Metro did not really begin to develop its true role until the early 1980s. The original network comprised only three lines which, although modern and fast, covered inadequately the central city and intermediate ring areas along a total network length which was only 40 km. The system did not extend to the heart of the industrial area in the north, nor to any of the main *colonia popular* areas. Thus at best it served as a complementary system to those users coming to the DF by suburban bus and wishing to go downtown and then perhaps to get another bus northbound to the factory areas. During rush hours congestion on the system was intense particularly at nodal points like Pino Suárez Station. Conditions were so bad that police segregated men into separate areas of the platform from women and children and into specified carriages. On the positive side, the system was clean, quiet, fast, extremely cheap and heavily subsidised. In 1978 the one-peso flat rate fare cost the equivalent of US 5 cents; and although it was increased to 20 pesos in the early 1980s, and to 100 pesos since 1986 and the level of subsidy has been reduced, the Metro remains the cheapest form of transportation that is genuinely available to everyone. In real terms it continues to cost around US 5 cents, and still carries a heavy subsidy. A multiple ticket usable on other integrated transport networks is now also available.

Expansion of the system began in earnest in 1979–80 with extensions and new lines over the next ten years which, for the first time, reached towards the working-class heartlands and into the industrial areas of Azcapotzalco and Vallejo in the north west (Figure 4.2). Particularly important was the new line which runs east to north and avoids the city centre. The total network length has almost tripled in ten years and a further doubling is proposed through to the year 2000. New lines were extended south to the University City and down the city's west side – both poten-tially middle-income user oriented. Moreover, around 70 per cent of the equipment is now produced nationally (rather than in France which developed the prototypes and most of the earlier rolling stock), so that increased investment no longer accentuates the loss of valuable foreign exchange (Domínguez 1987). However, the Metro remains a Federal

109

District Department enterprise and with a single exception at 'Cuatro Caminos' Station, has not developed beyond the DF boundary, nor does an integrated and complementary network exist in the State of Mexico. COVITUR was created as a DF enterprise in 1978 to coordinate and to develop the Metro operations. However, in the State of Mexico no counterpart exists, although COTREM was created in 1982 in order to tackle transportation problems and to liaise with COVITUR and the DDF (Lizt Mendoza 1988; Flores Moreno 1988).

For those living outside the Federal District, and also for many city residents, buses provide the main form of transport – often in conjunction with the Metro. Outside the DF these are run by private companies in contrast with the *Ruta 100* system operated exclusively in the DF since the private concessions were expropriated by Hank González in 1981. Buses form the primary means of high-capacity transport (Table 4.3) and their relative importance has not changed greatly since the late 1960s, accounting for around one-half of all daily journeys. There are indications of a sharp drop in the bus service in the 1980s and severe criticisms were voiced by President Salinas during his campaign that the *Ruta 100* was not fulfiling its obligations adequately. Although part of the criticism was politically motivated and directed at the intransigent union leadership, the problem was compounded by insufficient buses in operation, and by the fact that the service was too irregular and inefficient (Navarro Benítez 1989). Although they are better equipped than their counterparts of ten years ago and produce far less contamination, one gets the impression today of a far lower intensity of bus traffic on the streets in the Federal District. Moreover, the price differential between bus and *colectivo* fares has narrowed in recent years as the latter have increased their scale of operations and the regularity of their routes (Navarro Benítez 1988b; cf. Sutherland 1985).

In order to reinforce state intervention in mass transportation systems there are attempts to develop electric trams and trolley-buses. The 'light train' system links up with the Metro at Tasqueña and extends the service to Huipulco, 5 km further south. An important element in future policy proposals is to expand the role of trolley-buses (Table 4.4).

The important point to appreciate here is that the DDF now, at least, has an integrated transportation policy, and the *ad hockery* of yesteryear has declined. The service provided remains one of the best and cheapest (to users) in Latin America. Compared with earlier generations of workers of the 1950s and 1960s, today's journey to work is less onerous and less time consuming. This is due in part to improvements in the transportation system; in part it reflects the improved and changing organisation of space and land-use functions in the Metropolitan Area. But the DDF's transportation policy is also shot through with inconsistencies. For example both the public-sector elements of the system and the massive road investments are heavily subsidised by the rest of the country through fiscal resources and privileged appropriations to the DF. During the early 1980s between one-fifth and one-third of the (then especially high) DDF expenditure went on

Metro investment and subsidised travel through COVITUR (see Table 3.1), while the usual proportion had fluctuated around 13 per cent. Construction of the *ejes viales* in 1978–9 also consumed something like 18 per cent of the DDF budget compared with the usual 5 per cent on public works. And although the government has begun to develop a coherent commitment to mass transportation, this has not led to a fundamental policy change nor political willingness to reduce indirect subsidy and supports for the private sector, nor to penalise low-capacity vehicles. Perhaps growing awareness and public preoccupation about contamination will strengthen local government resolve to adopt a more aggressive stance towards private car owners in particular, and to encourage a switch to greater middle-class usage of the Metro or other forms of public transport. Whether or not the Metro could tolerate the increased use – particularly on certain routes and at peak times – is an open question. For many, myself included, the principal disincentive not to use the Metro remains the high level of discomfort associated with the overcrowding at peak times. But so long as the current policies continue they will crystallise the inequalities that already exist within the system rather than leading to progressive changes. Despite important overall improvements, the transportation structure continues to reproduce social inequality in the city.

The politics of transport policy

The creation of a transport system does not occur in a vacuum. It responds to the economic, investment and political imperatives of the day. Public protest and class struggle generated around means of transportation are also likely to influence state responses. Yet by and large Mexico City has avoided large-scale protest movements developed around such issues – certainly compared with other Latin American cities such as Bogotá, and São Paulo. The high levels of public subsidy and the relatively low fares derived from low fuel prices are probably the key reasons. Considerations of low comfort levels and high social costs associated with travel on public systems have not led to protest.

Yet investment in transportation has not been immune from political considerations. The 'Bus Owners Alliance' (*Alianza de Camioneros*) was closely associated with the government during the 1920s–40s, and offered government a wedge to drive between foreign investment in the tram system before it expropriated the service in 1946. The close government–*Alianza* cooperation continued subsequently during the 1960s and early 1970s despite a deterioration in the quality of bus transport during the period. Keeping the bus companies sweet was important for government in order to get workers to their places of work at low cost, and also to ensure that buses were available to the CNOP in order to transport *colonos* and popular groups to public meetings in support of the PRI and government functionaries. Echeverría, in particular, could ill afford for these reasons to alienate the bus-owning and bus-operating sector. There were other reasons too: his wife's family had strong business interests in private urban bus companies. This helps explain the total freeze on further Metro development during his *sexenio*, combined with the fact that the initial Metro development was closely associated with his predecessor (Díaz Ordaz) and there was little public kudos to be had by Echeverría for further extensions.

Politics and vested interest also help explain Mayor Hank González' transportation policy. He identified the traffic chaos as the 'capital sin' of the DF (Navarro Benítez 1988a: 154). In the late 1970s the Vallejo Industrialists' Association were complaining that they were losing 224 000 worker hours a day due to long distances and journeys to work of the 120 000 workers engaged in their 900 firms (Rodríguez 1985 cited in Navarro Benítez 1988b: 42). More important was Hank González' intention to undertake major public building and construction programmes in order to distribute patronage and largesse among his own political supporters. It was no accident that he alighted upon the *ejes viales* and the Metro expansion, both of which suited his spending programmes, particularly once oil revenues came on line (Teichman 1988: Navarro Benítez 1988a). In the following chapter I will explain how the adoption of a formal planning system suited Hank González' political project. Suffice to mention here that the *ejes* programme generated a sharp threat to the Mayor when public protest developed around the disruption caused by construction works, and from residents whose tree-lined streets were being bulldozed and their properties compulsorily purchased. Although many injunctions were sought, only one *eje* was incomplete when the system was inaugurated in 1979.

Unlike the protection offered to the *Camioneros* by Echeverría, there was little love lost between Hank González and the *Alianza* whom he criticised for the inefficiency of their operation and whose share of the market he proposed to reduce from 42 per cent to 19 per cent between 1978 and 1982 (Navarro Benítez 1988b). Eventually, in 1981, under his instructions the privately-run bus service in the DF (described as an 'octopus') was expropriated to form the basis of the state run *Ruta 100* in conjunction with the 118 new trolley-buses inaugurated in 1977 (ibid. 157). In 1988–9 the *Ruta 100* was itself the focus of·politically motivated attack by President Salinas' determination to purge unions of their corrupt and intransigent leadership (Cornelius 1989).

Thus political regimes have in the past had an important impact upon transportation policy in Mexico City although there are indications that today there is far greater continuity of policy between *sexenios*. The lack of continuity across the DF–State of Mexico border remains a major problem, however, and one that will steadily increase as a growing proportion of the Metropolitan Area population live in the surrounding municipalities. Questions about a coordinated transportation policy between the two entities; about who should pay the costs of providing public and private services (particularly where passengers pay taxes in the State of Mexico but commute into the DF for work) and so on, demand first a coherent political philosophy of urban development and, second, a unified metropolitan planning system. We saw in Chapter 3 why the former is unlikely. In the following chapter I propose to examine the potential for the creation of a unified planning system. But don't hold your breath.

5
Planning in Mexico City: decorative or indicative?

Previous chapters have demonstrated a clear need for some sort of planning authority to monitor, regulate and control land-use development citywide. In this book I have sought to identify many of the problems associated with rapid urban growth, namely: increased private car ownerhip, long journeys to work on inefficient transport systems, heavy pollution levels, irreversible damage ,to the city's ecological system, inadequate levels of servicing and public utility provision to the majority of residential districts, and so on. In Chapter 3, I concluded that these problems can only begin to be resolved by a political commitment to improved life chances and living conditions for the majority. Urban planning by itself will not overcome problems that are structurally derived. No matter how efficient, imaginative or politically supported planners are, their efforts will comprise 'technical tinkering'. But whether planners and planning groups are the instruments of reactionary politicians, overworked 'mollifiers' doing the best they can in a liberal tradition, or the advocates of the people acting as evangelistic bureaucrats will depend fundamentally upon the political conjuncture in which they operate and the **political space** offered them by their masters.

In Mexico the key problem was that until the late 1970s urban planners occupied no political space whatsoever. Unlike the United Kingdom where the 'crisis in planning' arose because planners had got it wrong; in Mexico, the crisis was because planners didn't exist as such. Until that time there had never been any systematic implementation of urban development plans anywhere. Within the Metropolitan Area any restrictions placed upon urban growth or proposed land uses were the result of particularistic decision making by politicians or officials; they were not based upon legislated norms and regulations. This situation has not been resolved, as I will show in this chapter. Plans are still not being implemented systematically. Within the planning process there is no public participation

114

to speak of. There remains too low a level of coordination between planning agencies in the Federal District and those of the surrounding State of Mexico. But, despite these caveats I will argue that there is some cause for optimism that a genuine urban planning process is emerging, and that, taken overall, this will lead to progressive rather than regressive outcomes for the majority of the city's population.

Traditionally 'planning' in Mexico has usually meant economic planning and until the last decade or so relatively little concern was expressed about physical or urban planning. The emphasis lay upon the allocation of financial resources, fiscal controls, industrial development incentives, monetary and exchange policy and so on, usually through the Treasury Ministry (HCP) and the Programming and Budgeting Secretariat (SPP). Subject to the overall guidance of the Presidency they, in effect, controlled planning. Other lesser departments acted in a rather 'maverick' fashion aiming always to win Presidential approval for their actions and not to be seen to lose advantage to other sectors of the public bureaucracy – in the manner outlined in Chapter 3. Generally each of these departments would have its own so-called planning office. Within this highly competitive mould, the desire for individual sectors to coordinate their actions within a single overall physical plan was unknown.

Since the 1970s, however, the position has begun to change for several important reasons. First, there is a growing consensus that planning is desirable. Urban development in a country the size of Mexico, or in any large city, is a complex business. One cannot expect individual sectors to take into account all needs, nor to take responsibility for evaluating and coordinating all of them equally. Whether this coordination role is a function for planning departments to fulfil is an open question. In Mexico it has usually remained the preserve of the Executive, the State Governor, the Mayor or Municipal President.

Second, physical planning is likely to become increasingly significant if only as an ideological tool to enhance state control rather than as a regulatory framework for urban development. Formally 'approved' plans can serve to justify political actions. Sometimes, too, they are a prerequisite for acquiring credit from international lending agencies (Gilbert 1976a). Although political considerations remain paramount, the influence of technocrats has risen in recent years. This does not mean that the influence of urban planners will expand incrementally. Indeed, their role and influence will continue to wax and wane with different administrations. Over the past four governments the planning 'star' rose with President Echeverría (1970–6), reached its height under López Portillo, but then slipped back when a confirmed economic planner (De la Madrid) took office (1982–8). Although President Salinas' position vis-à-vis urban planners is much the same as his predecessor's, he seems a little more likely to foster urban planning, particularly in Mexico City. In part this is because Mayor Camacho was previously the Urban Planning Minister and is now head of the Federal District Department; but it was also reflected in the interest expressed by the then Governor of the State of Mexico (Ramon Beteta) in physical planning and improved coordination between the two entities. Beteta was a political heavyweight and a political ally of Salinas. However, it remains to be seen whether Beteta's sudden resignation in 1989 will weaken significantly the drive towards a more integrated planning system betwen the DF and the State of Mexico.

In this chapter I want to ask how and why urban planning has evolved in Mexico. Is it related to the growing complexity of the urban environment, to changing external economic and political pressures, to internal pressure from social groups, to the whims of leading government personalities, or what? Second, what is the nature of planning activity in Mexico City? What are the main constraints acting upon planning and how effective were recent initiatives? Here I propose to examine in particular detail the period 1978–82 during which planning gained considerably in importance. Specifically I propose to examine the fate of the 1980 Federal District Urban Development Plan. Third, I ask what all this means for the general public. How far do they participate, and what is the likelihood of their ever becoming truly involved in planning decisions? Finally, in the conclusion, I ask whose interests are served by planning. Has it led to an improvement for the poor, or does it provide yet a further means for suppressing their actions? I hope an answer to some of these questions will allow us to make an informed assessment about the rationale for planning in Mexico.[1]

The structural impediments to physical planning

In Mexico as elsewhere in Latin America, urban planning is a relatively recent phenomenon. Although national planning systems existed during the 1950s in a few countries such as Colombia (1953), Nicaragua (1952) and Ecuador (1954), and while some regional or special projects also had significant planning structures, urban planning, if it was considered at all, was relegated to become a **sub-set** of these broader projects – **such as that** responsible for planning the new city of Ciudad Guayana (Rodwin *et al.* 1969). Investment programmes in social welfare, agrarian reform initiatives and so on evolved during the 1960s in part because of the support received through the 'Alliance for Progress' and were important because they to 'some degree legitimized the use of planning as a means of promoting development' (de Mattos 1979: 78). But the emergence of planning structures at this time was tightly constrained to aspects which dovetailed with the interests of national economic elites (Wynia 1972).

Planning has also suffered from several structural weaknesses. In part planners were to blame for they saw themselves, somehow, as 'above' the institutional political system (Cibotti *et al.* 1974: 40). They were overly concerned with technical criteria and regulations and often ignored the reality of the ways in which decision making occurs throughout Latin America. In their excessive dependence upon foreign techniques such as linear planning models, input–output analysis, growth poles, and urban structure plans they failed to identify the role of dominant groups in determining development processes (Kaplan 1972: 28; Moore 1978; Gilbert 1984b). For example, planning invariably threatens important interest groups. Proposals such as redistributive tax reforms, controls on land speculation, compulsory purchase, and development restrictions in certain areas are likely to engender conflict with those interests.

Planning also posed a threat to the traditional forms of political mediation exercised through patronage. As Wynia states (1972: 84), 'planning is an orderly process, trditional mediation of political conflict is not'. For politicians the priority is political control, not the efficiency of development (Gilbert 1981). Politicians need to be able to exercise discretionary control over the allocation of resources and to be able to act in a personalistic way. In Mexico, the precarious 'balancing act' referred to in chapter 3 whereby competing economic and political alliances must be accommodated between successive administrations, evokes little sympathy from politicians for a decision-making framework influenced by planners.

A further constraint has been the fear by many politicans that they would become overdependent upon *técnicos*. Invariably in the past the latter have not formed part of a President's personal trusted team and an Executive is unlikely to view favourably a growing dependence upon a body of technicians whose data processing and information handling becomes indispensable. Put simply, the Presidential calculus may be firmly invested against formal incorporation of the planning process (Wynia 1972; Gilbert and Ward 1985).

Finally, there was the fear tht plans inevitably lead to a greater dissemination of information to the public. In societies such as Mexico where decisions are often made behind closed doors according to highly particularistic criteria, the last thing that decision-makers want is informed criticism. Theoretically, too, planning requires active participation of the population at large. It should be open, democratic and participative. It would be naive to suggest that these epithets apply fully to planning processes in the UK or in the United States, but they are certainly an anathema in most Latin American countries today. Perhaps we should not expect too much, too quickly, from societies such as Mexico which have fundamentally different traditions of decision making and planning.

The emergence of planning in Mexico

Before 1970 national planning in Mexico referred to economic planning and comprised a process of 'mutual adjustment' led by a 'central guidance cluster' of four major institutions: the Presidency, the Ministry of Finance, the Central Bank, and *Nacional Financiera* (Schafer 1966). A single, centralised planning agency to fulfil this purpose had been shunned earlier by President Cárdenas (1934–40) and was never again taken up. Nor had any integrated regional planning framework ever been established. Rather, initiatives were partial and in addition to the three Metropolitan Areas three other broad investment and development areas had emerged: the Gulf Coast, the *Bajío* (central-north west) and the northern Frontier Zone.

State promotion of regional development was weak and unintegrated and comprised mostly one-off programmes such as the riverbasin projects of 1947 and 1961; the elimination of fiscal advantages for industries locating in the Federal District in 1954; the creation of small industrial parks in a handful of cities; and regional development plans for the states of Yucatán and Oaxaca, both of which were prepared by the Ministry of the Presidency after its creation in 1959. These actions had limited impact, not because they lacked technical expertise but largely due to the absence of any group within the urban-industrialist or rural sectors that would commit itself to a modern agrarian industry or would take up the question of regional inequalities (Unikel and Lavell 1979).

As part of his strategy of 'shared development' President Echeverría (1970–6) developed planning activities through the creation of various rural development agencies (Goulet 1983). More specifically as far as Mexico City was concerned, he adopted measures designed to promote the decentralisation of industry and the stimulation of development 'poles' outside the city. Incentives were provided for industry which discriminated against locations in the large metropolitan zones. Funds were established to promote industrial development, and commissions (the COPRODES) were created in each state to encourage collaboration between private and public sectors to stimulate socio-economic development. From 1973 onwards the Executive gave increasing weight to urban-industrial policies culminating in a Human Settlements' Law passed in 1976: probably the most important single piece of legislation in the field of urban planning in Mexico.[2] This Law created the basis for the state to intervene in a consistent and integrated way in the planning of human settlements, and it identified the levels of responsibility for policy making: national (i.e. federal), state, conurbation and municipality.

López Portillo consolidated planning activity within a Ministry of Human Settlements and Public Works (SAHOP). Within a year a National Urban Development Plan was published which aimed to confront the huge disparities in the distribution of national population. The Plan established policies for territorial organisation of population taking the Population Commission's (CONAPO) projections of a reduction of population increase from 3.6 per cent in 1977 to 2.5 per cent in 1982 and to 1 per cent by the year 2000. The aim was to restrict the growth of the three largest metropolitan areas (Mexico City, Guadalajara and Monterrey) and to generate an urban hierarchy with 11 centres of a million people, 17 centres with 500 000 to 1 million, and 74 centres of over 100 000 was to be created (Mexico SAHOP 1978: 42–4).

A national framework of eleven integrated urban zones was established with programmes designed to shape efficient urban systems within each.

Population centres were subject to policies of either (a) stimulus; (b) consolidation; or (c) ordering and regulation. Mexico City, needless to say, fell within the latter category. The functions of the Human Settlements Ministry was to coordinate execution of the plan at the national, state, conurbation and municipal levels, but it fell to another ministry (Programming and Budgeting SPP) to **promote** it. This dependence upon the goodwill and support of another sector was a major stumbling block. Moreover, the National Urban Development Plan was further dependent upon the goodwill of other sectors if it was to be operative. Particularly important was the attitude adopted by the then Ministry for the Promotion of Industry (SEPAFIN) whose National Industrial Development Plan, although ostensibly congruent with the National Urban Development Plan, in fact added a further sixteen priority areas to the eleven zones already established, and in effect rendered SAHOP's initiative virtually inoperable. Despite its apparent 'activity', planning remained passive in so far as it followed the pattern established by the so-called 'efficient' sectors of economic growth. It therefore validated the economic imperatives of the day (Unikel and Lavell 1979).

At a regional level a potentially important planning initiative was developed in 1978 with the creation of the Conurbation Commission for the Centre of the Country. This covered the Metropolitan Area and large areas of the surrounding states of Mexico, Hidalgo, Puebla, Tlaxcala and Morelos, and included each of the state capitals. The Commission's Plan focused primarily upon population and economic growth of urban centres lying some way beyond the existing built-up area. These centres such as Huehuetoca, Teotihuacán, Chalco and Amecameca (see Figure 1.1) were to be linked by a major orbital highway (the *'libramiento'*) and in some segments by a railway as well. The plan offered a strategy and an overall view of regional development, but lacked any specific mechanisms to ensure its implementation (Campbell and Wilk 1986). As such it fell pretty much at the first hurdle. Between 1978 and 1988 the Commission hardly met and was wound up in 1989 to make way for a Standing Council for the Metropolitan Area.

Since 1983 the traditional dominance of economic planning has been reasserted by President De la Madrid whose background was in economics, and during his period as Minister of Programming and Budgeting (SPP) he had engaged in intense bureaucratic infighting with the physical planning axis of SAHOP and with those (such as Hank González) in the Department of the Federal District (DDF). The latter, in particular, was more closely associated with expansionist philosophy supporting increased oil production levels, led by Petroleos Mexicanos (PEMEX) and its boss Díaz Serrano (Teichman 1988). The result was a sharp downgrading of physical planning between 1983 and 1988. SAHOP was emasculated: the large slice of its resources represented by public works was removed, and it was renamed as the Ministry of Urban Development and Ecology (SEDUE). From 1983 there was only one 'Plan' (the President's National Development Plan,

1983–8). All others were 'programmes', and in 1984 SEDUE published a National Urban and Housing Programme which was little more than a watered-down and less ambitious version of the previous Urban Development Plan. This 'new' programme identified 168 urban centres, the three largest of which were subject to policies of control and consolidation. A further 59 centres were deemed 'middle-sized' to be the focus of development according to local conditions. Some were scheduled for industrial growth, while others were designated to offer support to agriculture and tourism. Their selection appeared to be rather unsystematic, based in part upon existing economic processes and partly upon a political need to ensure that all states were included (Campbell and Wilk 1986). If Unikell and Levell's (1979) criticisms (mentioned above) of the shortcomings of the previous period of planning were a little harsh, they would certainly apply to initiatives in 1983–5.

When Camacho took over at SEDUE in 1986 there was too litle time remaining in the *sexenio* to turn things around. However, responsibility for earthquake reconstruction largely fell to him, and his competent and efficient disbursement of these large-scale resources, and his politically sensitive handling of what had threatened to become a major political problem in the downtown area, won him much respect. While not a committed planner himself, the survival of a planning ministry into the Salinas administration probably owes much to his performance as its chief in 1986–8. Almost certainly in the knowledge that he would be the next *Regente*, from mid-1988 he and (the then presidential candidate) Salinas began to develop studies and discussions with the State of Mexico authorities about planning structures and appropriate policies for the Metropolitan Area. However, at the time of writing (March 1989) little advance had been made or seemed likely until debt renegotiations were settled (achieved in July 1989).

While the last two decades have seen an important growth in Mexico's commitment to planning, its fortunes have fluctuated. It seems likely that some secretariat responsible for coordinating urban development will remain, but it will invariably be one of the most 'lightweight' public sectors. Even during its most active phase under López Portillo, the achievements were extremely limited. A lot of plans were prepared but relatively few passed state legislatures or were formally signed by the President. Even major initiatives such as the National Urban Development Plan foundered ultimately because the cooperation of other sectors was not forthcoming.

Planning initiatives in the Metropolitan Area

The effect of physical planning has always been more important in Mexico City than elsewhere in the country. The period of activity in national planning during the late 1970s described in the preceding section was also marked by the most dynamic phase of urban planning that the capital has

Table 5.1 The nature of different planning legislation passed for various periods since 1928

	Period					
	1928–52		1953–70	1971–84		
Category of planning legislation	(28–41)	(41–52)	(52–70)	(71–6)	(77–82)	(82–4)
A. Formulation of substantive planning and zoning legislation (includes 'Organic' laws)	7 (5)	(2)	1	(5)	13 (6)	(2)
B. Allocation of responsibilities and creation of bodies concerned with planning	4 (1)	(3)	0 (2)		6 (1)	(3)
C. Legislation concerning specific planning problems or land use (housing, roads, industrial sites)	5 (1)	(4)	6		1 (1)	
D. Changes, annulments, clarifications and administrative procedures	10 (0)	(10)	2 (5)		6 (0)	(1)
Total	26		9	26		

Source: Diario Oficial.
Data indicate individual pieces of planning legislation.

undertaken. Therefore, it is useful to analyse Mexico City's planning experience in detail in order to evaluate its rationale, its potential and the impact that it has had upon the lives of its inhabitants.

From 'decorative' to 'indicative' planning

Since 1928 when the city 'lost' its municipal status and became a special entity, legislation for city planning has fallen into three broad phases (Table 5.1). First, the period between 1928 and 1952 when several important pieces of legislation were enacted, the most significant of which was the 1936 Planning and Zoning Law and its precursors which, with minor modification, remained the basis for planning until 1970.[3] A Planning Commission was established, which in conjunction with the Directorate of Public Works was to create a regulatory plan which would be the key instrument in 'regulating the ordered development of the Federal District' (*Diario Oficial* 17 January 1933, Articles 2–4). In addition Federal District Consultative Councils and their local *delegación* equivalents were established as channels through which the public were invited to express opinions about servicing needs and public works. Throughout, the key

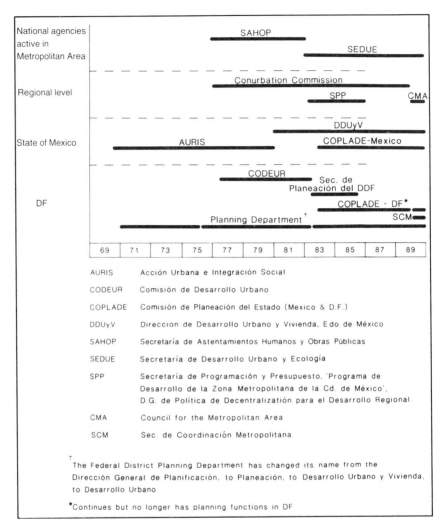

Figure 5.1 Departments and agencies with responsibilities for urban planning in Mexico City, 1970–89

organs of planning remained under the firm control of the Mayor. The 1940s saw the consolidation of these arrangements. Few new substantive pieces of legislation were passed, but the existing structure appears to have been strengthened and specific problems were dealt with through sectoral plans for industrial zoning, rent controls and so on.

In marked contrast the second period 1953–70 is marked by an almost total absence of any new planning legislation or initiative. This is explained by the influence exercised by Mayor Uruchurtu who held office throughout most of the period and for whom 'planning was alien to the spirit and

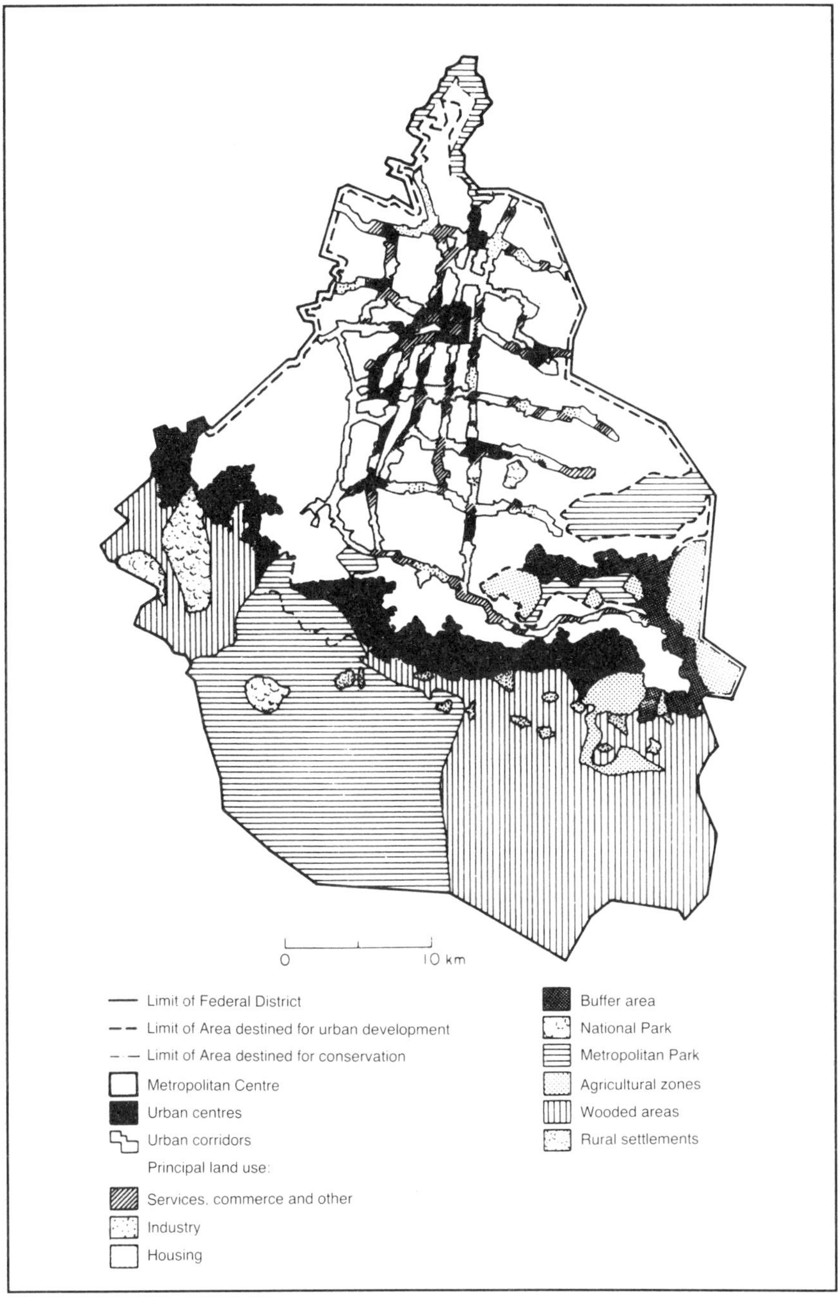

Key:

— Limit of Federal District
– – Limit of Area destined for urban development
– — Limit of Area destined for conservation
☐ Metropolitan Centre
■ Urban centres
⬠ Urban corridors
Principal land use:
▨ Services, commerce and other
▨ Industry
☐ Housing

■ Buffer area
▨ National Park
▤ Metropolitan Park
▨ Agricultural zones
▥ Wooded areas
▨ Rural settlements

0   10 km

Figure 5.2   Proposed land uses in the Federal District Urban
Development Plan

123

methods of . . . operation, which stressed secrecy, flexible interpretation of laws and regulations, rapidity, and spectacular short-term results' (Fried 1972: 680).

The third period (1970–88) covers the three administrations analysed in this chapter. Without doubt this is the most significant period in urban planning both nationally as well as in Mexico City (Table 5.1). The Echeverría *sexenio* provided the groundwork for the emergence of a fully fledged planning system that emerged between 1980 and 1988. The Federal District Organic Law was overhauled and initiated a slow process of decentralisation of many fuctions to the *delegaciones*. It renewed the existence of Consultative Councils, although as was argued in an earlier chapter these were not in fact activated fully until the following administration. For the first time an independent Planning Directorate was created, responsible to the DF Secretariat of Public Works (see Figure 5.1). It was charged with developing the Master Plan, and with planning and zoning. Before that date an office charged with responsibility for the Master Plan (*Oficina del Plano Regulador*) existed as a sub-department in the Department of Public Works.

In the State of Mexico planning functions were charged to AURIS (Urban Action and Social Integration) between 1969 and 1982, since when the State General Directorate of Urban Development and Housing has taken primary responsibility (Figure 5.1). In 1976 the Federal District Urban Development Law was passed which made mandatory the existence of a City Plan, and Sub-plans to cover each *delegación*. In addition the urban area was to have a proper zoning system. Despite these initiatives no planning system was made operational until the end of the decade when Mayor Hank González adopted a new Master Plan (1980), Sub-plans and a Zoning Law (both passed in 1982).

Planning in Mexico City

The new Master Plan applied only to the Federal District and referred to the Metropolitan Area in so far as it identified a total population target not in excess of 21.3 million by the year 2000, 14 million of whom were to be accommodated within the federal District (Mexico DDF 1980). The plan's principal objective was to improve access of the population to centres of economic activity and to the 'benefits of urban development' such as land, housing, infrastructure, services and utilities. The strategy proposed four major actions in urban areas and two in the non-urban districts to the south (Figure 5.2). In the urban area it aimed to create or consolidate nine centres to provide the locus of commercial and industrial activity and, to a lesser extent, housing. Each centre was to be complemented by sub-centres and by *barrio* centres. Collective transport systems were to continue being developed, as were the ring motorway and the urban highways (*ejes viales*). The important routeways were to be consolidated as 'urban corridors', and finally, a land-use zoning system was to be implemented. In many respects these measures validated existing processes and land uses. However, their identification and scheduling for reinforcement was positive in that it concentrated resources in selective locations that were already important in people's daily lives. As has been shown in preceding chapters, increasingly these sub-centres are the loci of 'satisfiers' in spheres such as housing, markets, and work.

In the non-urban areas the plan hinged around strict controls to prohibit development in the conservation area and temporary land-use developments such as sports fields, and picnic sites in a so-called 'buffer' zone. The aim was also to reduce the amount of newly incorporated land from 12 km^2 per year between 1978 and 1982; to 8 km^2 between 1982 and 1988; and to 4 km^2 during the period 1988–2000. Densities throughout the DF were to be increased, especially through measures that were designed to oblige owners of vacant plots to utilise their land productively. Some 18 per cent of plots were estimated to be unused (*baldío*).

The plan was passed in 1980 and a year later a whole series of sub-plans (the *planes parciales*) were approved, one for each *delegación*, and another for the Conservation Buffer Area (Mexico DDF 1980). In turn each partial plan incorporated *barrio* (neighbourhood) plans which identified permitted land uses in each area (Mexico DDF 1982). Formal zoning regulations were introduced in mid-1982. But these measures are meaningless without effective implementation. The planning office simplified the process where-by planning permissions could be obtained obliging applicants to go to a single 'window' at their local *delegación* office. Thereafter the application was despatched to appropriate offices for consideration, but this obviated the need for the individual applicant to go from office to office. The chief planner also, to a certain extent, forced the hand of *delegados* by closing selected unauthorised enterprises or building works. Inevitably this invited conflict between the importance of technical or political criteria in decision-taking and was only sustainable so long as it was supported by the Mayor (which was usually the case). (Both the planning chief and the Mayor came in for intense and embarrassing public criticism over allegedly underhand (i.e. discretionary) residential building development allowed in Bosques de Chapultepec: an elite residential district in parkland to the west of the downtown area.)

The 1980 plan contained several intrinsic problems, including its failure to address economic or social development issues so that economic, marketing and employment structures were excluded. Nor did the plan address the problem of complementarity with planning initiatives for the built-up area beyond the Federal District boundary. Nevertheless it was realistic in so far as it attempted to harness existing processes. Most of the new centres already existed informally and the proposal was to consolidate and integrate them. Also the 'buffer' zone aimed to restrict growth to that area in which expansion seemed inevitable, and thereby increased the possibility of preserving the conservation area beyond, which, otherwise, would have been quickly eroded. However, relatively few people engaged in capturing land or undertaking construction in this buffer zone appear to have heard of the Plan – not an unimportant consideration when evaluating its success (Aguilar Martínez 1988, 1987). In Tlalpan – a southern *delegación* spanning a crucial part of the 'buffer zone' – some 313 hectares of land was developed between 1980 and 1984, and more than three-quarters of the individual developments were by lower-income or middle-income groups on plots much smaller than the regulations permitted. Thus they were illegal. Nor did many people living in the buffer zone know about the DF Urban Development Plan and its regulations. Most of the 10 per cent who did were from higher-income groups (Aguilar Martínez 1987).

Although they patently were not working terribly well many of these initiatives lost impetus or were quashed between 1983 and 1988, even though for the first two years the previous planning chief was kept on. Paralleling the shift away from physical back to economic planning at the national level, Mexico City's incipient urban planning process has been placed on the back burner. Although a new DF Secretariat for Planning was created with strong political backing from Mayor Aguirre, this had little to do with physical planning. Rather its focus was upon the Federal District's contribution to the National (economic) Development Plan. Physical planning remained the responsibility of a politically weak DF General Directorate of Urban Development and Ecology. While the personnel in this department remained broadly stable it suffered from a lack of funds (see Table 3.1) and from a lack of credibility. Between 1983 and 1989 its name changed several times: a sure sign of political weakness, insecurity, and lack of clarity of function.

Nowhere is this lack of clarity more evident than in the fate of the Programme for Urban Reorganisation and Ecological Protection (PRUPE) which appeared from the planning office in late 1984. In its original form the proposal was to expropriate 77 000 hectares in the south of the city as a conservation zone, with the implication that many settlements already established in the region would be subject to removal (Schteingart 1987). Predictably this created a huge row from virtually all sides of the population and through a series of 'consultations' in the following ten months the PRUPE was gradually watered down. By August 1985 it comprised a declared area in which further urbanisation would be prohibited; the ecological zone defined; and the 37 villages and settlements in the south clearly demarcated (*La Journada* and other newspapers 24 August 1985). Effective controls or legislation which threatened local interests had been dropped as the measure was totally emasculated.

This rather absurd initiative ran alongside the regular revisions to the DF Urban Development Plan undertaken in 1984 and 1987–8 (*Diario Oficial* 16 July 1987). The principal difference between these revisions and the earlier 1980 plan related to what was proposed in the conservation zone in the south of the city. The pragmatic concept of a buffer zone beyond which conservation would be enforced was abandoned in favour of the PRUPE. Thus, to the extent that the concept of PRUPE was eroded, so too was the credibility of the plan (now called the Director Programme for the Urban Development of the Federal District). The operation and enforcement of planning permissions initiated 1980–3 appears to have been more lax thereafter. But greater attention was directed to the partial plans which were elaborated in great detail. These were produced as pamphlets in which the *delegación*'s proposed zoning was mapped out and a detailed table of codes relating permitted and non-permitted uses was displayed. Provided that one could read a map and make sense of clear, but rather complex, tables, the material was excellent. However, as a basis for popular consultation about the proposed planning law, applied to an adult population many of whom have not completed primary education, it was not terribly realistic.

As I will argue later, the authority for urban planning has been dissipated by the existence of a multiplicity of agencies with overlapping and/or competing responsibilities within the Metropolitan Area. In the surrounding State of Mexico there have been some recent attempts to develop corresponding plans at the municipal level. These have been prepared through the State Urban Development and Housing Department in conjunction with the respective municipal authorities and to some extent with the DF planning teams. However, in terms of a planning process which embodies legislated plans, zoning and regulations for the implementation of a plan, the process is nowhere as advanced in the State of Mexico. Detailed land-use maps have been prepared for surrounding municipalities (Garza, *El Atlas* 1987), and some attempt has been made to ensure broad consistency of land uses in adjacent neighbourhoods on either side of the DF/State boundary. But categories of land use are not the same, and the lack of regulations means that they portray the outcome of unregulated processes, rather than serving as prescriptive guides to control future development. They are what they say they are: land-use maps. But, to the extent that the DF Director Programme and partial plans lack 'teeth' and also fail to guide processes, one might argue, not unreasonably, that the distinction between plans and land-use maps matters little.

Nevertheless for a brief period during the late 1970s and early 1980s the planning department functioned much more systematically and effectively than ever before. Since then planning has continued albeit in a diluted form. But, as I argue below, there are sound reasons to account for the emergence of planning at that time which relate largely to its functionality to the maintenance of the Mexican political system. In addition President Salinas, Mayor Camacho and then State Governor Beteta were acutely aware (and apparently resolved) of the need to achieve tighter coordination of urban management and planning at the level of the Metropolitan Area. During 1988 an *ad hoc* Metropolitan Coordination was created comprising close advisers to each of these three men, and Salinas stated his intention that a Standing Council for the Metropolitan Area be created (*La Journada* 1 June 1988). Moreover, the new DF planning chief is a former sub-director of the 1979–83 planning 'team', and was Camacho's adviser and representative on the *ad hoc* committee. One should not expect too much of planning *per se*, but I expected it to find greater favour in the current administrations than it enjoyed between 1983–8. However, up until mid-1989 there had been little to substantiate my expectations. To my surprise it became quickly apparent during my most recent round of interviews to find that neither the current planning chief nor Camacho himself appear greatly interested in developing the role of physical planning. One-off troubleshooting is more the order of the day, combined with lightweight, relatively inexpensive but highly visible mini-projects (*mini-urbanismo*). In my view this approach is little more than a 'bread and festivals' strategy of social appeasement. Physical planning seemed as far from the minds of the current team as was the case under Mayor Sentiés during Echeverría's administration.

The status and authority of Mexico City's planning department, 1970–89

It is one thing to identify the 1970s and 1980s as an important period in the history of planning but, as I have already suggested, it is quite another to argue that a process of city planning has been implemented. In this section I argue that the authority enjoyed by planning is constrained in two ways: first by its institutional structure; and second by its low budget.

In Figure 5.1, I have identified those offices or agencies with a significant interest and role in planning within the city. It is not exhaustive and excludes several of the big-spending departments such as the transport commission and the water agency which also have their own 'planning' offices. It demonstrates the difficulty that any single agency has in exercising **authority** over the planning process. There is a clear **multiplicity** of offices with responsibility for planning. In part this may be explained by the existence of two federal entities across which the city sprawls. But it also reflects the political tradition for incoming administrations to create new departments to compete with, or to take over, some of the duties of those already in existence. This enhances the opportunities for patronage by providing jobs within the bureaucracy. It also allows the Executive and Mayor to manipulate and play-off one political faction against another: part of the 'balancing act' to which I referred earlier. Despite the fact that more recent administrations have set great store by administrative efficiency, it is apparent that there has been a proliferation of the bureaucracy with responsibilities for planning in Mexico City.

The government has never seriously sought to create a **citywide** planning authority. The Conurbation Commission did not fulfil this role but was an advisory body at a much larger scale which covered five central states and the Federal District. Nor did the 'Programme for the Metropolitan Region' established in 1984 with a technical committee in Programming and Budgeting (SPP) which was pitched at a regional scale and comprised a broad normative document with no executive status. Its thrust was less physical planning and more the coordination of resource allocation to municipalities.[4] The COPLADES, too, are committees with a broad representative base designed to stimulate local participation of the public and private sectors in economic development, rather than being an executive body for physical planning. Although it is not a citywide planning body, the Metropolitan Area Council may lead to greater effective liaison between respective planning bodies.

Thus for city planning to be effective under existing conditions requires close collaboration between the principal planning agencies on either side of the Federal District boundary. Cooperation of this nature was always unlikely given that personnel invariably form part of different groups built around major political figures (*camarillas*) and that competition between these bureaucratic factions is the hallmark of the Mexican governmental system. A classic example was the elaboration of SPP's 'Metropolitan Programme' which was elaborated **without** serious consultation and input from SEDUE, the Conurbation Commission, or the Urban Development Departments in the State of Mexico and the Federal District.[5]

A second constraint on planning is that it is poorly funded. Since its elevation to become a separate directorate in 1971, the planning department has had one of the smallest budgets of the Federal District Department. Although in real terms expenditure on planning doubled between 1971 and the end of the decade, relative to other departments it declined from between 2 and 4 per cent of the total to around 1 per cent. However, relative cheapness does not guarantee continued existence nor immunity from savage expenditure cuts. During the 1982 crisis when the Directorate had recently and successfully implemented its Master Plan it suffered higher proportional cuts than many other departments. Its authorised budget was cut from an initial 1300 million pesos to 700 million pesos early in the year, and then further to around $280 million in August. Planning, for all that it is a relatively cheap exercise, is no less liable to cuts than any other department.

The politics of plan implementation

An important feature of plan implementation is the way in which it may serve a useful political purpose for the City's Mayor. Hank González, for example, had little sympathy or interest in planning when he took office. Rather, as demonstrated in Chapter 4, his primary concern was to engage in major construction works that offered opportunities for disbursing patronage and for self-enrichment. Yet he realised that a Master Plan offered several advantages. First it complied with the Law which demanded the existence and regular review of a Master Plan. By itself this is an inadequate explanation: it would have been quite easy to produce a flimsy plan or a suitable revision of a version of the Master Plan presented but not implemented in 1976. Indeed for the first eighteen months the

Mayor kept the earlier plan 'on ice' and showed little inclination to revise or to implement it.

A second reason, was that it provided justification and backing to the Mayor's fight for extra resources to carry out the building programme already underway. Considerations of this nature certainly prompted his desire to update the Master Plan. During 1978–9 there was an enormous increase in expenditure undertaken on the building of new rapid highways with integrated computerised traffic signals (the *ejes viales*). Opposition to these building programmes was encountered within cabinet and also on the streets, where protest had erupted against the destruction of tree-lined avenues and the eviction of residents due to street widening associated with the construction of the highways. The Mayor needed to be able to demonstrate that this programme (and others that were in the pipeline) were properly thought-through and integrated within a Master Plan. Thus the plan required speedy elaboration but, for political reasons, it was entrusted to SAHOP rather than being drawn-up in house within the DDF.[6]

Third, planning was implemented around this time because the traditional forms of mediation were no longer adequate. Patron–client links which had predominated between high-ranking government officials and local communities were replaced from 1977 onwards by a more formal arrangement of state–community relations embodied within the neighbourhood councils' structure (*juntas de vecinos* structure [see Ward 1981a]), and as greater decentralisation of responsibilities to *delegados* was achieved. As part of this change the planning system began to be used to provide ongoing political legitimacy. This became imperative once the level of debate over urban issues had begun to be more informed. Increasingly through the 1970s interest in urbanism was no longer a preserve of elitist and relatively conservative groups such as the Architects' and Engineers' Professional Societies, nor was it an academic backwater: it had entered the mainstream of politics. For several years a radical school of architecture (*Autogobierno*) at the National University had trained graduates with a very different perspective about urban development, which challenged conventional approaches. Moreover, several other professional courses had emerged such as the Human Settlements Degree at the Metropolitan University. More significantly, perhaps, was the concerted and informed criticism that had begun to appear regularly in the press, many columnists of which were lecturing staff on those courses. Others were advisers to left-wing political parties which were beginning to flex their muscles after the political reforms of 1973 and 1977. Information and critical argument entered party manifestos and even into Congress through minority party representatives. The Coordinated Popular Urban Movements' Organisation (CONAMUP) had successfully united a large number of low-income settlements into a single force, and by 1980 was beginning to assert itself both nationally and locally. It was particularly active within the capital (Ramírez Sáiz 1983). There was, therefore, a growing sophistication of argument about urban development which demanded sound technical answers that could only be provided by a competent planning team. An ongoing planning system now became an important tool for political mediation.

However, the adoption of a formal planning system in the late 1970s also required certain compromises and trade-offs that some sectors of government and the PRI would be reluctant to make. Inevitably the publication of plans would add further to the dissemination of information about Mexico City's urban development. It would also require some curtailment of particularistic decisions by *delegados* such as issuing their friends with planning permissions for developments that were not authorised by the Plan, or the condoning of actions of certain groups in exchange for political support. These were threatened once run-of-the-mill decisions were much more likely to be decided upon technical criteria rather than political ones. But, for the government, these were relatively small concessions to make, and in any case they were probably inevitable once the level of public debate had risen.

Clearly the apparent reduction in the importance accorded physical planning since 1983 might appear to contradict my argument about the inevitability that Planning Departments play an increasing role in political management. In some of my most recent interviews with high-ranking functionaries I attempted to explore this point. Some officials expressed surprise that an urban planning department had survived at all. Given the backgrounds of the President De la Madrid and Mayor Aguirre, whose emphasis was upon economic planning, administrative efficiency; together with the president's antipathy towards many of the leading figures associated with physical planning under the previous administration, it was suggested that the continued existence of an 'urban development' department was unexpected. Yet it survived in a very weakened state, and its previous chief was confirmed in his post. The only explanations are either administrative ineptitude or, more likely, that some form of physical planning structure remained politically useful. It saved formally changing the Law to revoke the Master Plan with all the political embarrassment that would cause. It provided an important cushion for politicians to meet public criticism when urban infrastructure fails – as, for example, when there was intense flooding during the 1984 rainy season. A planning programme also gave the illusion of activity. Even the PRUPE, for example, while it backfired and did not win the support and approbation that the Mayor had expected, nevertheless engendered a long and wide-ranging debate which could be turned to good effect by the DDF authorities. It demonstrated that they were concerned and serious about the rising current of public debate on ecological issues. And it cost virtually nothing! Also planning may be used to head-off social unrest. In Mayor Aquirre's own words when presenting the revised plan in 1984: 'the Government of the Federal District cannot allow things to continue their present course, and cannot allow such an important problem for the maintenance of social stability to get out of hand . . . (*Ovaciones* 24 August 1984). Although physical planning remained very low priority, its survival in vestige form was politically useful.

To a certain extent this rise and fall in fortunes may be attributed to sexennial cycles. The current administration has indicated its intention to consolidate the role of integrated planning at a metropolitan level; and has brought ecological management to the forefront of the current political agenda. Land-use planning and the adoption of stricter controls over permitted land uses is likely to rise again in importance. It is anticipated that these responsibilities will be delegated to an expanded number of *delegaciones* but that local *delegados* will be kept on a tighter rein than was even the case under Mayor Hank González.

Public participation in planning

In many respects public participation is the acid test of whether or not a true process of planning exists. In the early 1980s several high-level planning officials in Mexico singled it out as the most important criterion in any definition of planning. They saw it as a means of ensuring that planning policy was carried out. By incorporating the public into the process and making them aware of the issues at stake, and of public authorities' obligation to install and maintain essential services, planners sought to establish a dynamic whereby proposals contained within the Master Plan would be implemented. Similarly a raised level of public consciousness might help sustain policies across *sexenios* and provide a degree of continuity previously lacking in the Mexican political system. However, these statements suggest a greater concern for information dissemination than public **participation** in decision making or in the effective ordering of local priorities. In my conversations with those planning officials most sympathetic to the idea of public participation even they demonstrated little understanding about how the public might actively be involved.

Public participation was built into the preparation of the Master Plan primarily at the level of the *delegación* sub-plans and the neighbourhood *barrio* plans. The latter were the brainchild of Mayor Hank González himself, and the Planning Department incorporated them without enthusiasm. They felt that *barrio* plans made sense in small towns and villages but were unworkable in large cities. It was simply not feasible to build a pyramidal structure in which a plan was compiled from the bottom-up. Mistakenly perhaps the vehicle selected for the process of consultation and participation were the then recently elected neighbourhood councils. Over 30 000 questionnaire schedules were distributed through the *delegaciones*. Some 200 were returned. The circulation was ignored by almost all of the local mayors (*delegados*) and in retrospect the planning office realised that they should have made direct contact with the neighbourhood councils. One *delegación* insisted that they draw-up their own sub-plan which they did with considerable success. However, most of their proposals were ignored, largely because they were submitted too late, but also because they did not dovetail adequately with the Master Plan (*Unomásuno* 3 July 1982).

132

Because of external political pressure the plans had to be completed within three-and-a-half months so it was impossible for the central planning office to delegate responsibility. Neighbourhood plans and sub-plans were prepared by consultants closely supervised by the Planning Directorate. Public participation was purely nominal and while the planning chiefs argued that they would seek to ensure greater involvement in subsequent revisions they appeared to be unclear about how it could be achieved. Moreover, as I pointed out earlier in this chapter, the majority of the population did not know about the existence of an Urban Development Plan (Aguilar Martínez 1987).

Other opportunities for participation in urban development were through the 'popular initiative' and through the holding of a Referendum (Aguilar Martínez 1986; Ramírez Sáiz 1983; *Unomásuno* 21 January 1985). But from the point of view of the government both presented a major threat and constraint to executive action. The regulations for the calling of a referendum have never been elaborated satisfactorily and this was a frequent demand made by political parties during the DF Popular Consultation of 1984. As it stands the initiation of a referendum lies with the Executive or with Congress. It must also affect all DF citizens in areas related to social needs, and does apply in matters of public finance and fiscal affairs. Little wonder that no referendum has ever been held. However, the changed composition of Congress since the 1988 elections and the opposition parties relative strength in the DF, may make this a possible route for urban protest in the future.

The important point is that public opinion and involvement was not sought in any of the major urban projects that were undertaken between 1978 and 1982. In neither the *ejes viales* highway system nor in the New Wholesale Market project was there any public participation or consultation. However, both generated fierce debate. In the case of the *ejes viales* public protest was the most intense ever experienced on an urban development project. Largely middle-class in origin, local resident groups and defence committees arose in an attempt to prevent the land clearance necessary to create the grid of the proposed sixteen multi-lane highways. The groups that were formed enjoyed only minor success. One of the sixteen roads was shelved when injunctions served against the Federal District were upheld. Mostly, however, these failed or were sought too late when the bulldozers were tearing down houses. A second success was the announcement that 'betterment' taxes to recoup some of the enhanced land values from property owners who benefited from the project were to be waived by the authorities (*El Día* 1 June 1979). Those who protested against the environmental loss due to the removal of trees were expected to be appeased by promises to transplant them elsewhere. Apart from these rather trivial concessions little was achieved. The protest groups remained isolated and failed to organise a united front against the authorities. Once defeated they rapidly disbanded. The only urban development projects where 'popular' participation has been actively encouraged are minor public works associated with *barrio* servicing. But in these cases the primary aim has been one of reducing overall costs through the use of community labour.

It might be argued that participation in planning has been achieved through the neighbourhood associations and through the Consultative Council of the Federal District. Monthly meetings between top Federal District officials and the *juntas de vecinos* served to reinforce this structure of neighbourhood participation and occasionally groups had their demands met after participating in *junta* meetings (Ward 1981a). During 1982 protests from well-organised middle-income residents' associations used the platform provided by the monthly *juntas* to denounce certain local mayors and developers for contravening zoning regulations established in the Master Plan. But senior DF officials (other than the local *delegado*) have not regularly attended such meetings since 1983. Nor do the *juntas* appear to lead anymore to direct positive outcomes for local neighbourhoods (Jiménez 1988).

After 1983 the term 'participation' was widely emphasised by President De la Madrid. First a series of 'popular consultations' were established to feed-in ideas and opinions to inform government policy. Although these meetings have generated substantial involvement from a wide range of interest groups, there is little evidence that proposals have been taken on board. Secondly, in May 1983 a 'National Democratic Planning System' was established under the aegis of SPP. Its functions covered the organisation of 'popular consultations' and specific forums such as municipal reform; to make proposals for the implementation of state-wide planning systems; to create regional plans; to assist the implementation of the National Development Plan; to coordinate the President's State of the Nation Report, and so on (Mexico 1983: xviv). There was little in either of the two structures to suggest genuine participation: at best they were consultative, and at worst became channels for the dissemination of information on behalf of government.

Therefore public participation in the planning process in Mexico is more nominal than real. In many ways the failure to incorporate a far higher level of active and real public involvement constitutes the most important single caveat to the argument that a planning system has been introduced in Mexico City. Moreover, as I argued in Chapter 3 it is difficult to envisage greater devolution of decision-making powers to local groups occurring in the immediate or medium-term future. Planning may persist, and structures designed to facilitate community–state interaction and popular participation may continue to evolve, but their *raison d'être* will be one of maintaining the status quo. Genuine innovations to empower local organisations and opposition parties will require fundamental societal and political changes.

Conclusion: planning for whose interest?

In 1979 a principal planner at the Human Settlements Ministry said during interview that, in his opinion, planning in Mexico was 'still in the dark ages'. This was at a time when urban planning was at its most active, but only a few of the plans prepared by SAHOP were actually implemented. Even in the Federal district where the experience had been much more positive, planning was implemented primarily for political reasons. Moreover, neither fundamental changes in the rationale governing urban decision making nor genuine public participation within the planning process had been broached. Nevertheless it is worth while asking, by way of a conclusion, in whose interest planning has operated in contemporary Mexico. Has the position of the urban poor in Mexico City been helped or hindered by the existence of the 1980 Master Plan and associated zoning regulations?

The Plan would appear to have had little impact in preventing illegal physical expansion in the south of the city and encroachment upon the 'conservation area' (Aguilar Martínez 1986). The cushion that the 'buffer zone' represented was removed from subsequent versions of the Plan. One of the original functions of the PRUPE was to justify and legitimise evictions of settlement in the area. However, the furore surrounding the publication of the PRUPE, and its substantial revisions as a consequence, meant that the programme that was implemented lacked teeth. In the absence of effective land-use planning controls, *delegados* have taken a hard line against encroachment by settlers. This involves boundary fences, guard posts, mounted police patrols and summary evictions of any new irregular settlements (Pezzoli 1989). If planning *per se* has proven ineffective within the DF then the situation is even more acute at the rapidly expanding urban periphery in the State of Mexico.

Planning initiatives will lead to different advantages for various social groups. As we have observed, government planning has been used primarily to legitimate decisions. The principal motive for revising the Master Plan was to incorporate the new urban highway system and the extensions to the Metro, both of which had been decided upon behind closed doors by the Mayor and his advisors without consultation with the planning department or the public. Today the Plan provides further legitimacy to justify decisions to evict squatters and other groups from newly formed irregular settlements. Elsewhere it may justify decisions not to extend services. Ideologically, too, the planning department strengthens the ability of the government to meet criticisms about its handling of urban development problems. On the other hand, the adoption of planning implies certain disadvantages for government. It reduces flexibility of decision making. This does not mean that particularlistic decisions and authorisations are no longer made: I have evidence that they are, but they are probably less widespread than in the past. Another disadvantage for government is the increased dissemination of information which makes informed criticism from opposition groups and from middle-income residents' associations much more of a problem than in the past.

Land developers and speculators may be affected negatively in so far as they no longer have quite such a free hand to develop what they want where they want. They will be obliged to comply with the more rigorous regulations that now exist. If they do not, then their developments may be closed down. However, they also benefit in so far as the Plan offers an amnesty and effectively condones previous illegal transactions that they may have made. Moreover, the incorporation into the Plan of land and land uses that were previously excluded, and which they own, is likely to raise land values to their advantage.

For the general public, outcomes are mixed. Middle-income groups are more likely to adhere to zoning regulations and to seek formal planning permissions as they have neither the resources nor the political weight to overcome planning regulations. However, they may be expected to gain in so far as they are able to press more strongly for the exclusion of any undesirable land use from their neighbourhood. Low-income housebuilders are unlikely to seek full planning permissions, but they may benefit where their previously unrecognised settlement is included on the Plan and in the zoning. This enhances their security of tenure and may strengthen their claim for service provision. It may also work the opposite way and isolate settlements beyond the servicing grid. One group of *colonos* who approached the planning chief about the possibility of services being installed to their settlement were informed that according to the Plan they were beyond the servicing network. Their only recourse, he said, was to participate in the next revision of the sub-plans to ensure that the servicing net was extended to cover their area (*Unomásuno* 8 April 1983). For those seeking to enter the irregular land market for the first time the existence of the Plan may justify their eviction. However, the existence of the 1980 Plan cannot be blamed for settlement eradications which also occurred widely before it was implemented. In the past planning *per se* has not usually been a cause of evictions, though it may be used to justify them.

To the extent that implementation of the Master Plan will lead to a more rational land use; improved access to place of employment, markets, public services, recreational areas; and to the conservation and preservation of the natural environment, then everyone will benefit. Yet, as I have argued, progress towards a fully fledged planning system in Mexico is both slow and ephemeral. The changes that have occurred over the three *sexenios* are significant, but superficial. The emergence of planning forms part of an accretional response of the state in Mexico to maintain the underlying structure. Certain concessions have been made but they are modest and, overall, the benefits that planning generates for the state in terms of enhanced legitimacy, greater social control, and access to financial resources suggests that the continued existence of some form of physical planning structure is assured. For these reasons alone its relevance for the state is likely to grow. For those officials who believe that planning may assist in the improvement of conditions for the poorest sectors of society my conclusion is not totally negative. Although the scope for improving conditions for the least advantaged groups is constrained, it is there. Sometimes societal inequalities may be reduced slightly by curbing the excesses of the more powerful. Sometimes, too, the demands of the poor can be strengthened by identifying the obligations of public authorities to comply with the Plan. There are indications that a little headway in this direction has been made within the Federal District especially between 1980 and 1983.

If planning as an open, democratic and largely technical process is ever to exist in Mexico then the key is almost certainly one of public participation. Only by actively involving the public in decision making is continuity across *sexenios* a possibility. This does not mean that aspects of the plan would not be expected to change as governments change. It is perfectly reasonable to expect that different administrations should have different development priorities. It is also reasonable for politicians to continue to expect to be able to appoint top personnel of their own persuasion to head the planning department or ministry. But the institutional apparatus for planning should be clearly defined and remain fundamentally unchanged, as should the bulk of the staff and channels of public participation. Once established, plans should be implemented according to technical criteria and be open to public scrutiny. Any major shifts in content would have to be approved by the public. But, so long as the current practice remains, where a six-yearly change of administration brings major changes of institutional structure for planning, changes in planning policy, content and process of evaluation and implementation, then the planning process in Mexico will remain fundamentally an instrument of political control.

6
The reproduction of social inequality: access to land, services and health care in Mexico City

Compared with elsewhere in the country, residents of Mexico City enjoy privileged access to social expenditure. Indicators for various dimensions of social welfare reflect this spatial inequality (Mexico COPLAMAR 1982). This does not mean, however, that within the city access to those resources is not spatially nor socially differentiated. Moreover, the means whereby these resources are provided, 'filtered' or fought over are also the principal mechanisms through which social differentiation is replicated and, in some cases, intensified. This constitutes the main argument of this chapter. I want to examine four key issues. First, how does the changing environment of social welfare provision in Mexico City offer opportunities for *political mediation* by the state? By 'social welfare' I mean a wide range of areas of provision including social security, social services, health care, education, urban planning and community development, and infrastructural services such as water and electricity (Ward 1986). This can be analysed by examining both the content of programmes as well as the way in which these are managed by the bureaucracy. Second, what is the effect of the *stratification* of delivery systems upon patterns of social inequality? Here it is necessary to examine the multiplex nature of provision and its impact upon the take-up of benefits and the disposition of different social groups to press for improvements. Third, how far does *negotiation and demand making* between the state and the community replicate or dissipate existing social divisions? Fourth, how far has the improved technical 'content' of social welfare policy (greater efficiency, more appropriate and low-'tech' solutions, expanding distribution and so on) led to a reduction in levels of inequality in Mexico City?

Space does not allow me to address these questions systematically in the context of each and every dimension of social welfare provision. Therefore,

138

in each case, I propose to bring to the foreground a different aspect of provision as an example for analysis. I acknowledge that not all dimensions of social welfare provision considered highlight to the same extent answers to these questions. Thus I have been selective. But I would argue that the general principles identified for one particular area also may apply to a greater or lesser extent elsewhere, and that in all cases the outcomes lead in a similar direction. My purpose is to shed light on the nature, rationale and effects of social welfare provision in the city.

The housing and service provision bureaucracy in Mexico City

The growth of state intervention

An important question about public intervention to emerge in recent years is why the state takes responsibility for providing certain services and not others. Numerous writers have attempted to explain the growth of state intervention (O'Connor 1973; O'Donnell 1974; Collier 1979; Harvey 1985). In particular, Castells' work (1977, 1979) has attracted attention. In the case of advanced capitalist societies he argues that growing state intervention is an inevitable outcome of the falling rate of profit in the capitalist economy. In order to maintain the rate of capital accumulation the state undertakes responsibility for providing services that are 'collectively consumed'. Generally speaking these services are those which offer low profit to the private sector but for which there is rising demand from organised working classes:

> . . . the intervention of the state becomes necessary in order to take charge of the sectors and services which are less profitable (from the point of view of capital) but necessary for the functioning of economic activity and/or appeasement of social conflicts (Castells 1979: 18).

But as President Solinas emphasized in his first State of the Nation address, public intervention does not necessarily mean public ownership. The private sector may be heavily subsidised rather than being nationalised. In Mexico City until 1981, bus services were exclusively run by private companies with large state subsidies on fuel prices, a structure which continues to apply outside the Federal District. The state only tends to become the sole provider of a service when the size, complexity and inherently monopolistic nature of the product has created problems: as when the private electricity company was incorporated into the public sector during the 1960s as the demand for power increased. During the 1980s in Mexico there has been growing interest in the privitisation of services and utilities, taking a lead from the World Bank and experiences such as those of the United Kingdom (Roth 1987). Airlines, hotel chains and, most recently of all, telephones, have been transferred from public to private hands. In addition, in Mexico City the authorities have sought to reduce the levels of subsidy on a variety

139

of goods and services. Moreover, they propose to adopt more efficient systems of recovery of the real costs of service provision and consumption, together with more effective tax and rates collection. However, some level of subsidy is likely to remain and, even though the government might wish to devolve some responsibilities to private enterprise, it appears unwilling to contemplate the political costs of major price increases. But without the attraction of significant profits private enterprise is unlikely to elicit great interest in taking over many of these functions.

Whether or not one accepts Castells' argument, certain services and activities appear more likely to fall under the wing of the state, and some will be accorded higher priority than others. The ranking will relate to both growth and legitimacy reasons. Connolly (1981) argues that every activity falls along a continuum which runs from directly productive (and therefore beneficial to capital) to unproductive. A related continuum runs from activities with high social content (i.e. they both contain and integrate the population) to those with little social content. I would argue that in Mexico City concerted state intervention occurs primarily in those areas necessary to the acceleration of economic growth rather than in those vital to the welfare of the poor. When the poor benefit and receive water or electricity, it is after the needs of key productive enterprise and better-off social groups have been met. Social services such as education, housing, public health, refuse collection and market facilities which have little direct interest for the corporate sector, receive much lower priority and may even be neglected. The affluent can satisfy their needs through the private sector. Other groups are likely to benefit only in so far as they are able to exercise influence over the state. Inevitably, therefore, labour that is well organised or which occupies strategic industries such as power, railways, and petroleum are most likely to have their particular social needs met; the remainder will be less fortunate.

Responsibility for housing and servicing in Mexico City

A matrix was constructed to provide an overview of the differential involvement of public and private sectors in a range of activities in Mexico City (Figure 6.1).[1] This shows the main responsibilities of the private and public sectors with respect to low-income and higher-income populations at a variety of levels (local, regional and national). The influence exercised by international agencies is also indicated. The rows in the matrix show the major functions which affect low-income populations in their housing and settlement situations. Each row is subdivided to differentiate between those living in the 'conventional', legalised market ('U'); and those living in the 'irregular' low-income market ('B'). Clearly this is not intended as a watertight distinction but it is not misleading at the level of general-isation that I wish to portray. The aim is to depict the different roles of public and private sectors with respect to richer and poorer groups; and the

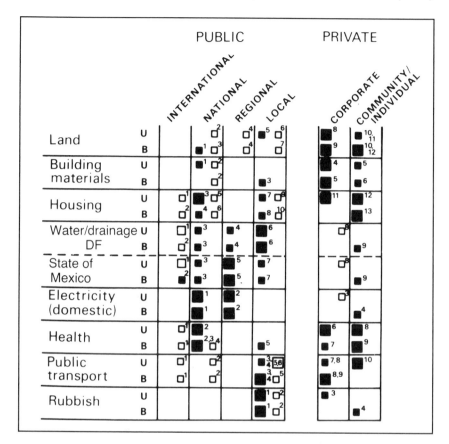

Figure 6.1 Matrix of responsibility for housing and servicing in Mexico City

NOTES TO FIGURE 6.1

Land

1. Lands provided by the state for *barrio* overspill developments, site and service schemes, etc. Agencies involved: BANOBRAS 1960–70; INDECO 1976–81; INFONAVIT 1977–83; FONHAPO 1981–pd.
2. National housing and economic policies, tax legislation on real estate, etc. all affect the supply of land.
3. National policy towards illegal land development affects willingness of developers to promote low-income settlement.
4. Conurbation Commission (1976–83) provides normative plans which affect future land uses and supply of land for residential purposes.
5. Agencies provide land for urbanisation (usually lower-middle-income housing) BANOBRAS 1960s–83; AURIS 1969–83; INDECO, 1973–6; CODEUR 1977–83.
6. Local zoning policies or tax laws affect supply of land.
7. Local policy towards invasion and illegal land occupancy and willingness to regularise and service affect propensity to supply land.
8. Real-estate companies' speculatory developments (usually legal).
9. Real-estate companies' speculative developments usually illegal, 1950s and 1960s.
10. *Ejidal* lands are alienated illegally by the *ejido*. Results mostly in low-income

Notes to Figure 6.1 – continued

settlements but some notable middle-income residential developments have occurred.
11. Small-scale landowners also provide land for subdivisions.
12. Invasions and small-scale purchases of land by groups of residents.

Building materials
1. National enterprises produce steel and other goods used in the building industry.
2. Price controls and restrictive practices affect total output.
3. Cheap supply centres provide materials for self-help. Sponsored by INDECO 1973–82; AURIS 1970–5.
4. 'Industrialised' large-company and monopolies sector.
5. Building materials produced by middle-sized enterprises.
6. Middle-sized enterprises, artisans, petty-commodity production, recycled throw-aways, etc.

Housing
1. International assistance for 'social-interest' housing and international conventional wisdom affect national housing policies. Specifically, the Alliance for Progress provided 'seed' capital for PFV 1963–4.
2. International agencies espousal of self-help affects national housing policy.
3. Social-interest housing projects provide housing. Specifically: BANOBRAS 1960s; INVI 1964–70; INDECO 1973–6; INFONAVIT 1973–83; FONHAPO 1981–PD.
4. Supply of site and service housing opportunities.
5. National housing policies, provision of credit, tax incentives, etc.
6. National housing policies towards self-help type solutions.
7. Housing projects produced by Habitación Popular, 1972–6; AURIS, 1970–5.
8. Development of self-help projects (Habitación Popular, 1972–6; AURIS 1970–5; INDECO 1977–82; FIDEURBE 1973–6; FONHAPO 1981–PD.)
9. Local policies towards social-interest housing and urbanisation.
10. Local policies toward self-help and towards illegal settlements.
11. Corporate provision of private housing.
12. Individual provision via private architects' offices, etc.
13. Individual self-help.

Water and drainage
1. International finance for water procurement and regional drainage schemes.
2. International finance and pressure to provide service to low-income communities; pressure from WHO, etc., to reduce mortality and morbidity levels.
3. National procurement and supply to regional authorities. Before 1977 SARH; 1977–83 SAHOP.
4. CAVM supplies 20 per cent of the DF's requirements. Sells to the DF in bulk.
5. CAVM sells water to CEAS which supplies households in the State of Mexico.
6. Procurement and supply within the DF. Water is obtained from wells and a proportion of the DF needs are brought from CAVM. Before 1977, responsibility of *Dirección General de Operación Hidráulica* and the *Dirección General de Agus y Saneamiento*. Since that date merged into single *Direccion General de Operación Hidráulica*. The DCGOH provides primary and secondary networks while domestic supply is the responsiblity of the *Delegación*.
7. Secondary supplies of water procured and supplied by municipal authorities in the State of Mexico.
8. Provision of network by urbaniser.
9. Self-help drainage, pit latrines, etc.

Electricity
1. CFE provides national grid.
2. *Companía de Luz y Fuerza del Valle de México* provides domestic supply.

Notes to Figure 6.1 – continued

3. Provision of domestic network by urbaniser.
4. Illegal wire taps supply households.

Health
1. Pressure from international health organisations to improve health standards and provision.
2. Social security affiliates. IMSS, ISSSTE, and those created for certain groups of workers in railways, military, petrochemicals.
3. State sector (SSA).
4. National policy regarding treatment of low-income groups.
5. DDF *Dirección General de Servicios Médicos* provides some medical services, blood for transfusions, etc.
6. Private clinics and hospitals.
7. Charities, Red Cross, etc.
8. Private doctors.
9. Private doctors, chemists, *curanderos*, etc.

Public transport
1. Tied aid from France for Metro.
2. National government policy towards fuel prices, subsidies and public transport.
3. Metro, trams and buses within the DF (since 1981).
4. Trolley-buses (*Servicio de Transporte Eléctrico*).
5. DF policy towards servicing needs of private transport: car parks, freeways, etc.
6. DF policy towards transport in general (COVITUR).
7. Taxis.
8. Collective taxis.
9. Buses in the State of Mexico. The privately owned bus service that operated in the DF was nationalised in 1981.
10. Private cars.

Rubbish
1. *Delegación* cleansing department and outside the Federal District in hands of the municipalities.
2. Incentives for interest groups to invest in recycling materials.
3. Private services, industrial-waste-disposal services, etc.
4. Self-help tips and dumping.

different ways in which poorer and richer groups in Mexico City are housed and serviced.

For every function, the matrix depicts which of six possible public and private 'agencies' is responsible for provision. The influence of international lending institutions, aid agencies, private lending and commercial organisations is depicted in the first column. There follows three public sector columns which demonstrate the responsibilities of national, regional and local government institutions. The final two columns deal with the private sector, one with the corporate and large-scale sector (i.e. manufacturing industry, commerce, large landowners, building companies), the other with the small-scale, individual and community sector (one-person businesses, individual home owners, community groups).

Where an institution, a group or set of individuals is deemed to exercise direct influence or responsibility over supply this is indicated by a shaded square; and the extent of influence is suggested by the size of square (small or large). Where influence or responsibility is indirect (by controlling prices, prohibiting land invasions, through planning, etc.) this is represented by an unshaded square. The numbers accompanying each symbol relate to the notes of explanation.

There are obvious limitations to the matrix. The portrayal is a static one compiled for 1979–80 and changes are only explained in the accompanying notes. I have not further subdivided each vector into the two administrative units of the DF and the State of Mexico, with the exception of the water/drainage row where important differences occur. It fails to identify the relationship between different actors, for example between the government and corporate sector. Nor does it offer any insight about the efficiency with which a responsibility is dispensed; while the public sector is depicted as being responsible for the poor, this does not signify that it performs this role well.

Looking across the matrix it is clear that the private sector dominates in the area of land provision: a point developed below. The corporate private sector exercises enormous importance in its role as owner and developer of land. Also important are the formerly agrarian *ejidal* communities which offer land primarily to poor groups. Building materials production and supply are also firmly the preserve of the private sector, and mostly corporate enterprise. The state's direct involvement is limited largely to steel production, though it does exercise indirect influence through pricing and through its role as regulator of the economy. Housing, too, is mostly an activity carried out privately, either through large and small-scale construction companies, or through self-building. Increased direct state action has led to greater availability of housing (see also Ward 1990). Overall, therefore, housing generated directly by government initiative is less important than that produced privately.

With respect to public utilities the state is the major supplier. With the exception of itinerant water sellers and the provision of bottled drinking water, it is the public sector which is wholly responsible for water and drainage, though different institutions are involved in procurement and supply. Electricity is much the same. Refuse collection is organised by local DF and municipal authorities, but there are also private corporate cleansing services which operate for some industrial and commercial enterprises. In the more recently established or more distant working-class *colonias* which do not enjoy a regular service, the poor, individually, have to burn, bury or dump their rubbish.

Health and public transport on the other hand are the responsibility of both sectors. As I will demonstrate below the state provides various tiers of health care to different social security affiliates and to the rest of the population through the government Health Ministry. But the private sector is also very important. While most affluent groups and many of the middle classes use private medicine, so too do the poor, usually by visiting their nearest local doctor. Similarly, transport services are shared between public and private enterprise. In Mexico City the Metro and trolley-bus services are run by the Federal District; so are most of the buses (since 1981). Taxis, *colectivos*, and of course private cars, all form part of the private sector.

We may now return to the questions posed at the beginning of the chapter and begin to examine the ways in which some of these dimensions of social welfare provision reproduce social inequality. First, access to land for housing development.

Reproducing social inequality through political mediation: access to land for illegal housing development in Mexico City

Methods of land acquisition in Mexico City

Although Mexico City has received the lion's share of resources allocated for government housing provision the supply has never come close to matching demand. Even during the 1980s under Da la Madrid when public-sponsored housing programmes reached their peak I estimate that nationally this only met approximately one-fifth of total annual demand (Ward 1990). Therefore the majority of the population have had to seek alternative 'informal' methods of shelter provision – most usually through illegal land acquisition and self-build.

In any society the process of land allocation is highly competitive between groups and in most capitalist societies it is the market which acts to allocate land. Those who can afford to pay more, or according to economic theory are less indifferent to location, acquire the more desirable areas (Gilbert and Ward 1985). In Mexico City the vast majority of the poor are at the bottom end of a single market, and the land that they bid for is cheap because full title is not provided, it is unserviced, poorly located, and undesired by economically better-off groups. To that extent they may be said to hold a monopoly over the land at the outset, but the process of commercial exchange penetrates this market very soon afterwards (see Chapter 7).

There are innumerable ways in which the poor acquire land, within the broad generalisation that they are usually illegal (see Gilbert and Ward 1985 for details). In Mexico City there are two basic alternatives: the first is to invade land and the second is to purchase land beyond the limits of the conventional, legalised housing areas. In Mexico City invasions occurred most frequently during the 1950s and 1960s when there was a formal ban on any new authorisations of low-income subdivisions within the Federal District. Large-scale invasions were more common after Mayor Uruchurtu lost office and during the earlier years of the Echeverría administration when the political climate encouraged popular mobilisation.

The purchase of land may also take many forms and is common throughout Latin America. In Mexico City it is by far the most important

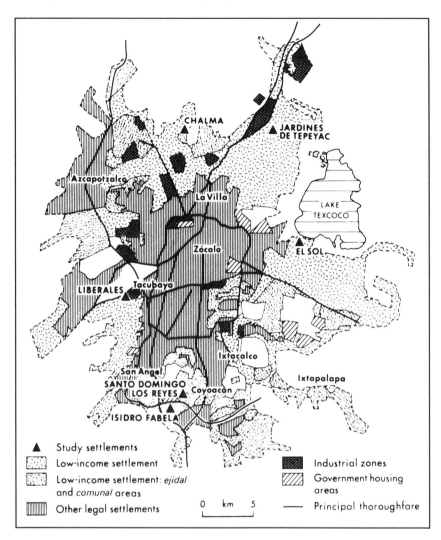

Figure 6.2 Distribution of *ejidal* land and irregular settlement in the Metropolitan Area

means of acquisition. Land is bought either through company-sponsored illegal subdivision (*fraccionamientos clandestinos*) in which some form of title is usually provided, but services are non existent or severely limited (see Plate 2.9). The enormous scale of some of these developments sets them apart from other Latin American, or indeed from most other Mexican, subdivisions. Settlements comprising several thousand families are common in Netzahualcóyotl and Ecatepec. Alternatively plots may be purchased on *ejidal* (community) lands and an estimated 16 per cent of the total city population in 1970 were living on land that was *ejidal* in origin: a proportion that has increased since that date (Varley 1985b; COPEVI 1979; see Figure 6.2). The sale of plots – again without services – takes place either directly by individual *ejidatarios*, or by their elected local representatives: the *comisariado ejidal* (Mexico SAHOP 1979; Varley 1985a). Whichever applies, the process is illegal because *ejidatarios* have use-rights only over the land which is, theoretically, inalienable. Nor is it only low-income groups that are involved: during the 1960s large tracts of *ejidal* were privatised for elite housing developments, while in the 1970s rich and poor alike bought plots illegally on *ejidal* lands in the south of the city (Varley 1985a, 1985b). Today the largest single area of active low-income settlement formation is on the far eastern frontier of Mexico City on the *ejido* of Ayotla in the Chalco Valley which extends over some 2500 hectares.

Below, I propose to examine how the process of illegal land development in Mexico City has facilitated political mediation and social control by the state and thereby perpetuated patterns of inequality. By 'political mediation' I mean the ways in which the state attempts to advance the interests of powerful and organised groups which it seeks to placate and, at the same time, manages to maintain social control and to legitimate itself through the securement of political support for the government – although, as I observed in Chapter 3, since the 1988 elections this process has also entered a period of crisis. Faced with austerity programmes during the 1980s the government intensified its efforts to maintain 'social peace' and continuing support from the labour sector (Carr 1986). Land for housing the poor has always been an important element in Mexican statecraft and my aim here is to analyse how successive Mexico City regimes have achieved similar ends of political control through handling land issues in two ways: first, through controlling the content of land development policy; second, through the ways in which the Mexican government has cultivated a bureaucracy to manage land issues.

Mediation through the content of land development policies

An analysis of government intervention in the land market must take account of both **action** and **inaction** on the part of the authorities. Failure to act may reflect policy choices and this has been (and continues to be) an important feature of Mexico's management of low-income land developments. Two types of response are identified. First, those actions that affected the **provision** of land for low-income settlement; and second, **remedial actions** such as regularisation, recognition and approval to extend services to unregularised areas.

Three broad periods of land development may be identified: a *laissez faire* phase before 1970 when many of the low-income *colonias* were formed against a backcloth of little government intervention. In Mexico

City during this time irregular settlements increased from 23 per cent of the built-up area and 14 per cent of the population in 1952 to 40–50 per cent of the built-up area and a slightly higher proportion of the total 8.5 million city population in 1970 (Mexico BNH 1952; Ward 1976a; COPEVI 1977a). The period between 1971 and 1977 saw a much more **interventionist** phase in which government created an extensive housing bureaucracy and in particular instigated large-scale remedial actions, although they were largely *ad hoc* in nature. Since 1977, handling of land development has been one of **technical management** in which interventions in **both** the sphere of land provision and remedial action have been more efficient and more systematic. In essence I argue that, since 1977, governments have sought to achieve social control less by manipulation and more by 'delivering the goods' (Ward 1986). Below I propose to analyse the primary mechanisms whereby land policies have sustained political mediation during these three periods.

Government policy towards the provision of land for low-income settlement between 1950 and 1970 differed on either side of the Federal District boundary. In the State of Mexico during the 1950s and 1960s the authorities acted consistently to further the interests of the land developers.[2] So-called 'Improvement Boards' established by the Governor from 1952 onwards, ostensibly to coordinate the installation of services in the region, achieved little beyond the promotion of lot sales on behalf of the companies. Moreover, the State authorities took no action against the common abuse whereby the same plot was sold several times over to different individuals. Despite comprehensive regulations governing the creation of low-income subdivisions (the *Ley de fraccionamientos* of 1958), neither the State nor the Federal Government pressed for sanctions against the developers. Indeed until 1969 authorisations for further developments continued to be given by the authorities even where the offending companies had been denounced by residents for their failure to satisfy the conditions laid down in earlier settlements (Guerrero *et al.* 1974; Connolly 1982).

In the Federal District, City Mayor Uruchurtu imposed a ban upon the authorisation of new subdivisions and this led to a proliferation of invasions and illegal subdivisions developed by owners whose land development plans were frustrated. Uruchurtu's sectoral jurisdiction did not extend to *ejidal* land and the informal supply of land on the *ejidos* was also assisted by government action and inaction throughout this period. Legally the use of *ejidal* land for urban expansion is prohibited under the Agrarian Law (Article 91). However, *ejidal* land may be disestablished 'in the public interest' in one of two ways; by *permuta* or exchange of one area of an *ejido* for equivalent lands elsewhere; and by expropriation. There was widespread abuse of *permutas* during the 1950s and 1960s to secure land for a variety of purposes not all of which can be justified as having been in the public interest. Large upper-income residential districts such as Jardines de Pedregal and part of Ciudad Satélite came into being in this manner. Low-income irregular settlement usually formed through the manipulation of a legal facility whereby part of an *ejido* may be set aside as an 'urban centre' to house the *ejidatarios* and other community workers. Application would be made to the Agrarian Reform Department for an urban *ejidal* zone, or for the extension of an existing one, but meanwhile lots were 'sold' by the *ejidal* community. The formal procedure to create an urban zone on an *ejido* is a long and complicated one, and often the later stages are never reached because after several years settlement has emerged as a *fait accompli*. It then becomes a matter to be resolved through legalising 'clouded' land titles – called 'regularisation' in Mexico (Varley 1985a).

Mediation through land development is also apparent by the removal of specific politicians whose policies were proving too inflexible. A good example is the concerted opposition that built-up against Mayor Uruchurtu's policies during the 1960s as a result of his consistent refusal to authorise or to approve servicing to low-income settlements within the Federal District and, perhaps more importantly, once his policies began to threaten the more powerful groups involved in speculative land development in the south of the city (López Diaz 1978). He had also consistently blocked initiatives for the development of a major collective transportation system which added further opposition – particularly from the large-scale construction sector. That his policies had become dysfunctional to the state by 1966 when he was forced from office is also confirmed by the more circumspect and conciliatory approach of his successors and by the rapid development of a Metro system (Cornelius 1975; Alonso *et al.* 1980).

Action to prevent the uncontrolled growth of irregular settlement was not undertaken until it was virtually too late and even then has only affected the sale of private land by the companies. Significantly, this occurred only when a mass-based organisation in the State of Mexico (*Movimiento Restaurador de Colonos*: the MRC) precipitated a political crisis in 1969 by calling a strike on further payments to the land developers. By this time, however, many company developers had begun to lose interest in the development of irregular settlement and transferred their attention (and gains) to the legal middle-income real estate market. Not until relatively late in the process did the state respond sharply to company-led low-income subdivisions. Several settlements have been 'embargoed' by the State of Mexico government: an option always open to previous administrations yet not exercised. It is usually achieved by requiring land developers to comply with servicing norms, and to make immediate payments of massive amounts of backdated taxes and fines relating to improper management of the subdivision. Failure to comply results in the development being sequestrated by the State authorities. However, as we have observed, this initiative has come too late to affect land provision significantly.

Although several land invasions occurred between 1970 and 1973 these are no longer tolerated. During 1977–9 firm action was undertaken by the Federal District authorities to remove squatters from newly established occupations. In one large-scale invasion attempt in the south of the city named after López Portillo's wife, *colonos* were evicted as many times as they reoccupied the land. Their temporary houses were destroyed despite injunctions taken out against the authorities to prevent this from happening. Eventually the squatters gave up, and the land remained vacant. Explicit instructions were given by Mayor Hank González to *delegados* to resist all new occupations and to raise the surveillance of vacant land.

As I described in Chapter 5, even a decade later the south of the Federal District remains a principal zone of conflict between government and would-be squatters. During 1988–9 there were frequent evictions of settlers in a well-established *colonia* of El Seminario in Tlalpan. It falls on the 'wrong' side of the road to Picacho in an area designated as an 'ecological reserve': a concept which counted for little until it was adopted by the Government as an integral item on its new and widely publicised 'ecological agenda'.

Given the breakdown in supply through company sales, the *ejidal* sector has become the most important means of land acquisition for the poor. Yet here, too, the government failed to take action. No direct attempt was made by either the Federal District or by the State government to use *ejidal* land for low-income housing purposes, despite the clear opportunity that it provided. One author, as early as 1965, noted: 'Land reserves of this kind, under public control, have long been advocated in many metropolitan areas, but few can match the good fortune of Mexico City in having such reserves readily at hand' (Frieden 1965: 86). Good fortune or not, the government failed to act. Although some effort to develop land reserves was made through newly established housing agencies such as INDECO and INFONAVIT these were very limited in size and potential (Makin 1984). CoRett, another new agency, offered greater potential scope in this respect. In addition to its main functions of regularisation of irregular settlement on *ejidal* land CoRett was also empowered to **develop** low-income subdivisions on suitably located *ejidos* (*Diario Oficial* 7 August 1973). The latter function, had it been seriously pursued, would have offered the state a major opportunity of developing land supply for the poor. However, strong opposition from the *ejidal* sector blocked this area of potential responsibility and it was subsequently excised from CoRett's charter (*Diario Oficial* 3 April 1979). Anything that interfered with the process which worked firmly to the advantage of some *ejidatarios* was to be resisted. Indeed, for the state, the process also had certain attractions: the *ejido* sector upon which it depended for considerable political support was mollified; at the same time the supply of low-cost land for the poor was sustained. Although the principal agents of land development might have changed, government passivity towards informal land provision has not.

The combined 'clamp-down' on subdivisions and invasions meant that the only source of land for the poor is provided by the *ejidal* sector. Yet little attempt has been made by successive governments to restrict illegal sales by *ejidatarios*. In 1979 an Inter-Sector Commission was established comprising the Ministries of Agrarian Reform and Human Settlements and CoRett in an attempt to expedite the identification and expropriation of *ejidos* whose land would be affected by future urban growth. Although this might offer a major step forward in the acquisition of rural land for long-term urban development, in the absence of additional preventive measures it is unlikely to succeed in controlling land alienation by *ejidatarios* in the short or medium term. Quite the opposite: faced with the danger of government intervention to deny them the possibility of illegally selling land, it is likely to stimulate them to sell or to find ways of slowing up the process of handover to government. Although firm action against particular *ejidatarios* might appear to represent a responsible undertaking in technical terms, politically it would be regarded as irresponsible leading to conflict with vested interests in the agrarian sector. By reducing the supply of land to low-income groups it would also engender potential conflict with the poor: from the government's point of view, better to leave well alone. This 'rationale' applies particularly in the State of Mexico where most of the *ejidal* land available for incorporation into the Metropolitan Area is distributed. Continuing expansion or irregular settlement in Ayotla and more recently in Chalco, together with the PRI's need to keep the *campesino* sector mollified between now and the 1993 (State) election, makes any strong intervention unlikely.

The content of 'Remedial' policies since the 1960s

Remedial actions on the part of the state were limited before 1970 on both sides of the DF boundary. Within the District, regularisation of selected settlements occurred either through persuading the landowner to install services and to give legal title or, more usually, by expropriation and resale to residents. In theory there was an agreement between the Electricity Company and the Federal District Department that power supply would not be connected until legal title had been obtained; in practice the supply was often provided.

The provision of standpipes, regularisation, and lightweight one-off campaigns such as the vaccination of children, the removal of rubbish from settlements, etc. were negotiated and provided primarily by the *Oficina de Colonias* in the Federal District and by the municipal authorities in the State of Mexico. But serious 'remedial' actions did not emerge until Echeverría took office. In the State of Mexico, as was noted above, the incoming administration faced an immediate political crisis brought about by the payments' strike by residents to companies. Government response is illuminating in that the crisis prompted a much more interventionist approach in the handling of the land issue especially in the area of **remedial action** which was tackled in several ways (Tello 1978; Ward 1981a). First, the immediate political problem was solved through a special deal whereby developers were reimbursed less 40 per cent to take account of the services they had failed to install; and residents received a 15 per cent discount on the overall purchase price and full legal title to their lots. Service installation was to begin immediately, also provided by the government, but the costs were to be recovered from residents over a ten-year period. The agreement was accepted by all parties although it has been strongly criticised for favouring the companies in so far as they were exonerated from responsibility for their illegal transactions, retained a large part of their profits, and escaped the burden of paying for services (Guerrero *et al.* 1974; Martín de la Rosa 1975; Ferras 1978).

Second, political mediation was achieved through remedial actions which identified land regularisation as an **issue in its own right**. Significantly, in no other country does regularisation feature with such prominence (Gilbert and Ward 1985), but in Mexico regularisation emerged as having critical importance from 1971 onwards and the creation of a battery of agencies to provide full legal title to *colonos* was an innovation. However, it can be argued that the nature of regularisation policies at this time reflected governmental needs more than those of residents whose main concern was for security of tenure (Ward 1982). The interpretation that this required full legal title was one provided by government rather than by the residents themselves. Full tenure was not required before *colonos* could sell their plots, nor was it necessary for services to be installed, for this requirement had usually been waived since the early 1960s. Security of tenure could easily have been provided by simple recognition of *de facto* occupance and did not require full legalisation through expropriation, indemnisation and the drawing-up of property deeds. The point is that there is a 'social construction' to illegality (Mele 1987; Varley 1989). Regularisation was seen as a medium of negotiation and social control in so far as it constitutes a cheap resource that can be granted or withheld by the authorities.

The regularisation of land in existing settlements has intensified since 1977. Agencies responsible for regularisation have become more efficient, and the number of titles issues each year has risen considerably in part as a response of efforts to simplify the process. But regularisation has also undergone an important qualitative change. Since 1977 it has become both a means to an end as well as an end in its own right. It is conceived as a mechanism to incorporate the populace into the tax base, and as a first step to recoup systematically government investment in services and utilities. Also, as I demonstrated in Chapter 5 it is a means whereby greater control over planning and building activities may be exercised. Once included in the property register the authorities attempt to 'clear' outstanding land tax debts that the *colono* is deemed to have. These may comprise backdated rates chargeable retrospectively for up to a maximum of five years. However, they often include a range of additional charges. In different settlements I found multiple examples of valorisation taxes relating to motorway construction undertaken several years earlier; charges for building permissions and many apparently arbitrary fines. Often failure to have paid these fees and fines previously led to surcharges being incurred. Where residents protested either through their leaders or *en masse*, the amounts charged became negotiable and, more often than not, a discount was arranged. This demonstrates how the authorities sought both to raise treasury resources as well as to use the procedure as a dimension of political mediation and control. During 1978 the existence of a deliberate policy link between regularisation and taxation was freely admitted by officials in the cadastral office of the Federal District.

Mediation through bureaucratic manipulation

In addition to constructing a changing land policy over time, administrations may achieve social control through the manipulation of the bureaucracy which has responsibility for irregular settlements. For instance, the **multiplicity** of agencies created by the Echeverría administration with regularisation duties within the Metropolitan Area led to numerous overlaps in functions. CoRett's charter gave it responsibility for *ejidal* and *comunal* lands yet, in the State of Mexico, AURIS was also involved in *ejidal* land. Similarly in the Federal District, FIDEURBE was created specifically with the task of regularising the most conflictive settlements (such as Padierna and Santo Domingo), and many of these were on *ejidal* or *comunal* lands. An added problem was that responsibility for several of these settlements had rested initially with a national agency, INDECO, so there was likely to be an overlap of functions and leader-agency networks brought about by the transfer of responsibility from the first agency to its successor. INDECO was an agency with a broad range of functions which meant that it operated nationally as a sort of roving 'troubleshooter' and was charged to resolve problems in specific settlements as and when they arose. The *Procuraduría de Colonias Populares* (PCP) had a similarly vague role to fulfil within the Federal District. It was the old CNOP-dominated *Oficina de Colonias* now reconstituted by Mayor Sentiés to act as a vehicle whereby he could intervene in low-income-settlement affairs. It had some regularisation duties but also distributed free milk, gave out presents to children at Christmas, organised clean-up campaigns, etc. The Director as *Procurador* saw himself, literally, as the 'advocate' or 'attorney' of the poor.

Inter-agency strife is a feature of this type of bureaucratic structure. The informal 'rules' governing inter-departmental behaviour at all hierarchical levels are, broadly, those of either outright conflict and competition; alliance; or tacit agreement not to meddle in each other's affairs. Of these three alternatives 'alliance' did not figure during this period in relations between the agencies identified above. However, between 1973 and 1976 there is ample evidence from my own fieldwork and that of others that both FIDEURBE and the PCP suffered from, and engendered conflict with each other (Alonso *et al.* 1980: 377–439). CoRett, too, occasionally meddled unnecessarily as when it declared that, were it to be in charge of regularisation in the settlement of Ajusco, the costs to residents would be much lower than those proposed by FIDEURBE (López Diaz 1978). Coming precisely at a time when the latter agency was trying to secure the cooperation of *colonos* it is difficult to interpret CoRett's action as anything but deliberate political sabotage.

Furthermore, conflict between agencies was facilitated between 1971 and 1976 by the structure of patron–client links that agency directors and personnel were expected to form with individual communities and by the proliferation of different leadership groups within each settlement, particularly the most conflictive. Each group of residents led, invariably, to a different agency so that it was common for one group to elicit support from the *Procurador*; another would seek out the head of FIBEURBE while others would go to the local *delegado* (Alonso *et al.* 1980). At the same time, when a group felt really threatened they approached President Echeverría himself who appeared well disposed to receive their delegations and to listen to their case. As a result rumour abounded, contradictory policies were espoused, and orders were countermanded. One agency head bemoaned the frequent practice of calling agency heads to open hearings with the President, which had the effect of undermining their authority without reducing their responsibility. Another described the experience as one of being on a 'constant war footing'.

Whether this bureaucratic structure and functioning were the result of accident or design is a matter for speculation. However, the important point to recognise is its **functionality** for the Echeverría administration. The existence of several agencies, all apparently active on behalf of the poor, gave the impression that much was being done. Important, also, was the personal contact that Echeverría maintained with grassroots organisations and which he demanded also from his agency directors. The President could appear as arbitrator on behalf of selected groups (Connolly 1982). Also, where one agency threatened to become too powerful, or another too weak, he could shift his support to re-establish the balance. Both land and the bureaucracy itself became the cannon fodder for political mediation by Echeverría.

The structure of the land and urban development bureaucracy and the way in which it behaved changed substantially from 1977 onwards. This was partly a result of the overall streamlining of the various sectors of government activity initiated by López Portillo as part of his Administrative Reform. It was also indicative of the growing technocràtisation of the bureaucracy in which politicians have been replaced by professionals (*técnicos*). In the Federal District it was part of a conscious effort to change the nature of state–community relations and to make land regularisation more efficient and less politicised.

The number of agencies with responsibilities for regularisation were reduced (Ward 1989b). More importantly not only were overlaps avoided, but authority was invested in a specific agency and not between them – as had happened before. Each got on with the job for which it was responsible and kept out of the others' way. The process of streamlining and tecnocratisation has continued since 1982.

Several important points emerge from this review of changing government response to irregular settlement. We have seen that land is an important mechanism for political mediation in Mexico City. So far as the provision of land is concerned the state's response has been passive.

In choosing not to act against the real estate companies or against those responsible for *ejidal* land sales it has favoured certain interests at the expense of the poor, and condoned illegal practices. At the same time the illegal supply of land for low-income groups has been maintained.

In establishing policy towards existing irregular settlement the covert aims of the state appear to have been paramount. The state has sought to use the land issue as a means of extending its influence over the poor and to maintain their quiescence. The way in which this has been achieved has altered significantly in recent years. Before 1977 control was sought primarily by political manipulation, cooption and patron–client links with the poor. Since that date, while social stability and social passivity remain fundamental goals, the state has developed a more structured framework in which to achieve them. Increasingly, it depends for its legitimacy and support on greater efficiency and delivery of resources desired by *colonos* and less upon traditional forms of mediation such as patron-clientelism and the PRI apparatus. In Mexico regularisation has become an important element in the political calculus. The nature of regularisation has evolved to reflect state priorities rather than those of low-income groups. It is not simply a means of extending full property titles to the poor, but increasingly a means of incorporating them into the tax base: a point to which I return in the next chapter.

Reproducing social inequality through stratified delivery systems: health care in Mexico City

In the Metropolitan Area of Mexico City high mortality and morbidity rates are associated with low-income areas and poor housing conditions. Those living in the eastern suburb 'irregular' settlements of Netzahualcóyotl were especially prone to intestinal infections brought about by the poor sanitary and water supply conditions that existed in those areas – at least up until the early 1970s. Those living in the working class neighbourhoods of Tepito and Guerrero in the heart of the city suffer from especially high rates of respiratory diseases due to cramped housing conditions and high levels of pollution (Fox 1972). Yet despite some shift of focus towards primary health care along lines outlined by the World Health Organisation (1978, 1981) the philosophy of health care in Mexico concentrates upon individualised health care and treatment rather than on collective programmes to improve general living conditions.

The stratification of health care in Mexico: who does what?

Public health care and social security provision in Mexico have evolved over more than four decades and, paralleling expansion in other areas of the

The reproduction of social inequality

Table 6.1 Population attended by social security organisations and by private and government sectors

	Metropolitan Area[1]		Nation[2]	
	Per cent	Thousands	Per cent	Thousands
Social security:				
IMSS	43.0	4935.8	29.9	20 000[3]
ISSSTE	15.5	1772.1	7.2	4800
Others	7.2	828.0	2.2	1500
Government: SSA and DDF	17.9	2045.9	15.6	10 500
Private sector	16.5	1884.0	14.9	10 000
Unattended	0	0	30.1	20 100
TOTAL	100.1	11 455.8	100.0	66 900

(1) *Source:* DDF, *Plan Director*, Chapter 7, based upon data provided by SSA. Data are for 1976.
(2) *Source:* López Acuña (1980: 108), based on data from José López Portillo, *II Informe*. Data are for 1978.
(3) Pre IMSS–COPLAMAR programme 15.

Mexican bureaucracy, present a pastiche of separate institutions, the individual fortunes of which have fluctuated with administrations.[3] But, as well as the widely documented tendency for organisations to evolve as a response to pressure from the most powerful social groups (Mesa Lago 1978), in Mexico coverage has also been extended to the not so powerful, and specifically to wider sections of the working population that include both blue-collar and white-collar workers. This has come about for various reasons. It is a result of political gestures initiated by the Executive to strengthen the popular ideology that the interests of the poor are being served. It has been used to win popular support for the government, while at other times it provides a means of compensating workers for declining opportunities and for the erosion of real wages.

In Mexico the principal social security institutions that have been established also organise their own medical service and here I propose to focus only upon this aspect of their functions. Access to health care for Mexicans falls into three main categories, each of which will be described briefly below.

Social security organisations

First there are the public social security organisations, the largest of which is the IMSS (*Instituto Mexicano de Seguro Social*) founded in 1944, originally for urban salaried workers. Since then it has been extended to include agricultural salaried workers (from 1954) and, since 1973, coverage has progressively been offered to all people in employment and even for the self-employed. However these groups accorded are an inferior membership status in which benefits are less comprehensive, are limited to non-specialist medical treatment and exclude maternity care. In view of these limitations it is perhaps hardly surprising that people have not rushed to join. Despite attempts to extend coverage to rural areas membership of IMSS remains overwhelmingly urban: 91 per cent in 1983 (De la Madrid 1984 *Segundo Informe, anexo Sector Salud*).

Next in size is the ISSSTE (*Instituto de Seguridad y Servicios Sociales de los Trabajadores al Servicio del Estado*), founded much later (1960) for state employees, it offers the most extensive and generous health and social security package. Affiliation increased fivefold between 1966 and 1976 mirroring the expansion of the state bureaucracy during that period. Expansion was particularly rapid during the early 1970s though resources per capita have declined steadily since then. Almost all of its affiliates are urban and, as we can observe from Table 6.1, a sizeable proportion live in the Metropolitan Area of Mexico City.

Government sector

The second major level of health provision comes from the public-governmental sector and most important here is the Ministry of Health (SS, formerly Health and Welfare SSA) which provides the main alternative source of health care for the bulk of the population not covered by any of the social security organisations or private medical insurance. In absolute terms the responsibilities of the Health Ministry have grown. In 1983 the Minister stated that between 15 and 20 million people in rural areas alone were without any access to health care (*Excelsior* 17 April 1983). Of the three institutions it is the worst endowed, yet for many of the poor it is likely to be a crucially important system. Estimates vary, but it seems likely that for between 18 and 20 per cent of the population of the Metropolitan Area the SS system represents the only alternative to private medicine (Table 6.1).

Private sector

The third level is the private sector. This includes both a private health care system as well as private charitable institutions such as the Red Cross and the Green Cross. Although limited in number and in the range of services offered, charities are often an important 'bottom line' of health care provision. Nor should the importance of a private health service in Mexico be underestimated. While the proportion of the total population covered by social security grew from 22 per cent in 1967 to almost 40 per cent in 1980, this leaves the majority dependent upon the public-government and the private sector. Moreover, as I will demonstrate below, private medicine is not a preserve of the rich: the poor also make extensive use of the private sector, especially for 'lightweight' consultations.

The rise in numbers covered by each of these institutions has had important implications for the manpower and health care resources that each is able to offer. There has been a sharp deterioration in the level of staffing and facilities offered by ISSSTE due in large part to a major increase of affiliates between 1973 and 1978. Per capita ratios of doctors, beds and nurses declined dramatically and its previous top position was lost to IMSS which managed to maintain its earlier levels despite an increased membership (Ward 1986). However, in neither case does the level of service drop to anything near the paucity of resources experienced by the Ministry of Health throughout the period. In the 1980s per capita facilities enjoyed by the social security sector have remained far better than those of the public-government sector. These different levels of benefits offered by the various 'tiers' are an important mechanism whereby inequalities are reproduced.

Policies are not formulated in a vacuum: they emerge within the political economy of a given time. During the early 1970s under President Echeverría the emphasis lay firmly on developing large-scale high-technology hospitals and medical centres which López Acuña (1980: 182) described as: 'white elephants which, voraciously, consume scarce resources allocated to health care in Mexico'. Partly as a sop to demands from the rural and urban poor Echeverría also espoused more 'populist' programmes which had potentially wide-reaching implications for improving community health care, but which ended up as little more than rhetorical gestures. They included the creation of child-care institutions and general purpose community development agencies which sponsored 'lightweight' programmes such as the distribution of free breakfasts, education about nutrition, rehabilitation and education of polio victims, health and immunisation campaigns. From the government's point of view these institutions were relatively cheap, offered flexibility to respond to specific crises, and reinforced an ideology that significant action was being undertaken on behalf of the underprivileged. In the previous section we observed parallel actions undertaken in the arena of land policies.

Significant changes in policy date from the beginning of López Portillo's Government (1976–82). Health agencies attempted some reorganisation of the structure of medical care that placed more vigorous emphasis upon the need for local communities to have greater access to general services, and to 'soft-pedal' on costly investment programmes in the fields of intensive care and specialist treatment. In the Metropolitan Area the IMSS sought to respond to earlier criticism that it had neglected general medical care in favour of highly specialised treatment, and reorganised its health care system, establishing a new hierarchy of treatment. Both the IMSS and the Ministry of Health sought to develop the lower tiers of health care: family medical units comprising surgeries to provide out-patient treatment for IMSS affiliates. The Health Ministry developed programmes of education about health problems and preventive work within the *delegaciones*, and a new department was opened to attend 'marginal' areas. However, a lack of funds meant that by 1979 only 59 local health centres had been established out of the 700 required.

Access to health care within the Metropolitan Area of Mexico City

Access to adequate health care facilities is not simply a question of their availability or that they be of the right kind: it is also a matter of their being located at accessible points throughout the city. Large, intensive-care specialist hospitals form an integral part of any hierarchy of provision and can normally be expected to be located near the centre of the city or at a nodal point within the city's transport network. More important, however, is the need to achieve a balance and to ensure an adequate distribution of general treatment facilities (Eyles and Woods 1983).

In Mexico City a broad hierarchy exists comprising integrated medical centres – general hospitals – clinics and health centres. This is complemented by specialist hospitals and institutes. The latter, together with the multifaceted medical centres provide a service for the national and regional population. Given the enormous costs of establishing and maintaining these institutions it is reasonable to locate them in the largest urban centres. However, one may question the desirability of duplicating all levels of the hierarchy for each sector. IMSS, ISSSTE and SS each have large medical centres in Mexico City and, in some cases, more than one.

Here I am not concerned to explain why that situation has come about; rather my wish is to analyse the effectiveness of coverage that exists throughout the Metropolitan Area. If we examine more closely the location of public health services in the city the glaring inadequacy of coverage becomes apparent. In 1965 when rapid suburbanisation of low-income settlement had already been underway for two decades, there was minimal provision of health centres within easy reach of these poor districts. In the east, south east and north east there were virtually no public sector facilities (Figure 6.3). Most medical services were aligned in the shape of a horseshoe around Chapultepec Park with an especially large number situated around the city centre. In essence the older, established and richer parts of the city were well served.

Yet despite more than a doubling of population between 1965 and 1980, and the fact that most of the increase had been concentrated in the more suburban *delegaciones* and adjacent municipalities, the pattern established before 1965 has not altered appreciably (Figure 6.4). Although there has been some growth of new facilities in the periphery, they are widely scattered. Both ISSSTE and IMSS have done little more than consolidate their existing network, creating new medical centres and large hospitals but showing little real effort to decentralise coverage in the form of health centres and clinics to poor suburban districts. Granted, ISSSTE's unwillingness to shift is partly justifiable on the grounds that only a relatively small proportion of its affiliates live in the low-income settlements, but the same is not true for the IMSS. The Ministry of Health did make some attempt to increase access to their facilities and to shift the locus of services towards poorer areas. Between 1965 and 1971 the SS initiated a reorganisation of its facilities and closed several of their outlets downtown while opening others

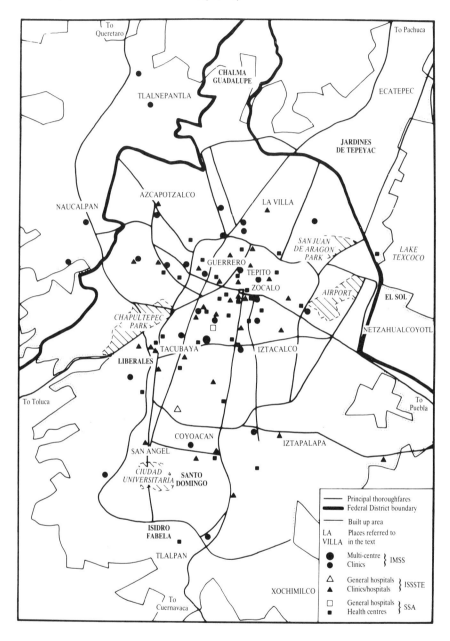

Figure 6.3 Location of institutions providing medical treatment in 1965

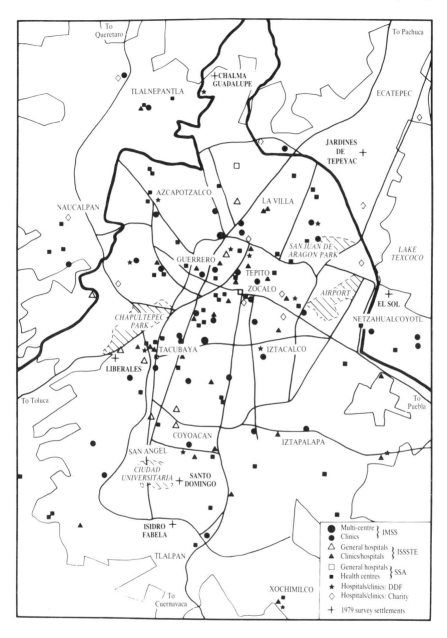

Figure 6.4 Location of institutions providing medical treatment in 1982

The reproduction of social inequality

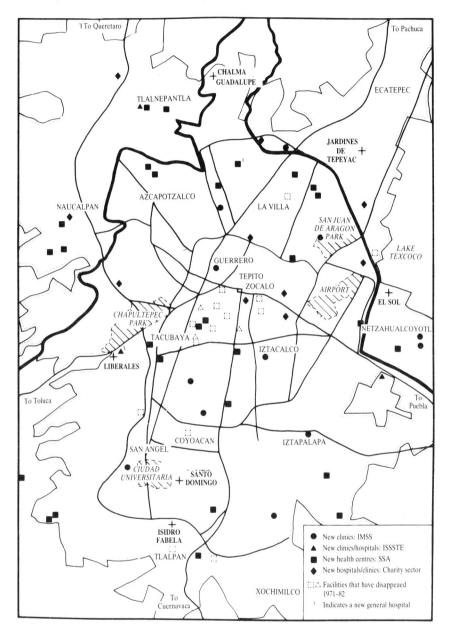

Figure 6.5   New locations for medical treatment established in Mexico City between 1971 and 1982

162

in the poorer districts of the Federal District: a process it extended during the 1970s (Figure 6.5). From 1977 there was a marked expansion of the charity sector. Between them, the SS and charity sector have taken the major initiatives in extending health care facilities to poor districts of the city.

Health care for residents of irregular settlements

In 1979 as part of the PIHLU study (see Chapter 2) some 630 households in six low-income irregular settlements in the periphery of the city were interviewed about matters relating to family health. Specifically the questionnaires contained a section about family illnesses suffered during the preceding twelve months, the treatment received, and opinions relating to the quality of medical attention. These data are partial in the sense that they only give an indication of health patterns for low-income residents in the *colonias populares* of Mexico City at a single point in time. However, they provide a basis for independent evaluation of the efficiency of the health care system, and several of the findings are interesting in the context of preceding discussion.

Of primary interest was the treatment sought both in spatial and sectoral terms. Inevitably, therefore, this led respondents to identify the more important illnesses suffered and to underreport minor or short-lived illnesses (such as colds or intestinal complaints). More than one-half of all household heads interviewed declared that at least one member of the immediate family had been ill during the previous twelve months. Mostly the person specified was either the wife (36 per cent) or a child (42 per cent). It often proved difficult to identify with any precision the true nature of the illness as many were 'minor' ailments that did not fit any easy categorisation. In those cases where the illness was specified a significant number related to some sort of natal care or to treatment for 'flu. Intestinal disorders also figured but were probably underreported or form a large part of an 'unspecified' illness category.

The source from which treatment was received appears to relate to two considerations. First, whether or not the individual was covered by any form of social security health care. Secondly, choice intervenes in so far as not everyone automatically used the cheapest system available to them. In Mexico City an estimated 66 per cent of the city population is covered by social security health care broadly similar to the proportion of heads of household in the sample: most of whom belonged to IMSS (Tables 6.1 and 6.2). Specifically, 60 per cent of those individuals for whom an illness was reported were covered by one of the social security organisations, though that coverage varied considerably between settlements. Yet despite the fact that the majority had social security, and that even those not covered had recourse to the government sector, many respondents opted for private treatment, usually by consulting a doctor at his surgery (Table 6.2). Indeed, almost two-fifths of all treatment was provided by the private

The reproduction of social inequality

Table 6.2 Type and institutional source of treatment for residents in irregular settlements

	Percentage	Number
Consultations:		
in a hospital	2.3	8
by a private doctor	26.9	94
in a health centre (SSA)	6.6	23
in a private clinic	2.3	8
in social security clinic	27.8	97
with a 'healer'	0.6	2
with a nurse	1.7	6
Consultations: sub-total	68.2	238
Hospitalisation:		
government or charity	7.7	27
private hospital	6.9	24
social security	16.9	59
Hospitalisation: sub-total	31.5	110

Source: PIHLU settlement survey, 1979.

sector. It appears that the poor often trade-off the use of public sector facilities in favour of the more conveniently located private service (see below). This is especially likely where the sickness is relatively minor and does not require intensive care or hospitalisation. For the latter, and for treatment that is likely to prove expensive, the official and social security sectors are used almost exclusively. By and large people can afford a one-off payment to a local doctor; but they cannot contemplate the high costs of hospitalisation or of sustained private treatment. This finding applies both to social security affiliates as well as those not covered, although not equally. Those with social security are more likely to use that service but 25 per cent of affiliates went 'private', compared with 82 per cent of those without cover whose only alternative was the official or charity systems (Table 6.3).

Two explanations may be advanced for the extensive use of private medicine by the poor. First, it may indicate dissatisfaction with the public sector brought about by earlier unsatisfactory treatment, long waits or because people feel culturally alienated from using modern medicine. Yet none of these reasons appear plausible given that practically everyone (over 80 per cent) expressed satisfaction with the treatment received regardless of the sector that provided it. This does not necessarily mean that the service offered is satisfactory: but simply that low-income residents expressed few complaints.

A second explanation relates to accessibility. I have shown that there is a marked discrepancy between the location of public health facilities and low-income housing areas. Invariably the latter are poorly served. Most people,

Table 6.3 Sector in which treatment was sought according to whether respondent had social security coverage

Sector in which treated	All (%)	Without social security (%)	Without social security (%)
Government and charity	17	32	7
Private	39	62	25
Social security	45	6	68
Total percentage	101	100	100
Total number	349	129	195

Source: PIHLU Settlement survey, 1979.

therefore, face a long journey on public transport or taxi to a government or social security clinic and, understandably, prefer to visit the local doctor, often in his consulting room in the same settlement. In most of the survey settlements the majority sought private treatment in the immediate vicinity of their homes. Alternatively, or in cases where specialist treatment was required, they went to the nearest appropriate institution (Figure 6.6). These are indicated by the thicker-line flows on the figure, and one can see that this often means a journey of considerable distance, especially in the most peripheral settlements such as Jardines and Isidro Fabela. The average (crow-flight) round-trip distance to the place of treatment in these two settlements was 12.5 and 10 kilometres respectively. Even residents in the better-served settlements such as Chalma and Santo Domingo had to travel an average of 6 km. Paradoxically, El Sol, which is one of the most poorly served of all, appears to be not so badly off (8 km) but this is because most residents have little alternative but to use the private **local** facilities, thereby reducing the settlement average travel distance recorded.[4] In this latter settlement, 19 households reported that they had used public facilities to treat the illness identified, and the average round trip (crow-flight) distance was 19 km. This compares adversely with the 5.4 km travelled by those 36 households who took advantage of private (and invariably local) facilities. Many of these people (21) were treated within their own neighbourhood.

The failure of the state to provide an adequate service of primary health care means that many of the poor are obliged to make their own arrangements and to provide for themselves. For the sake of convenience a substantial minority use private facilities and in the event of a relatively minor ailment most go to a nearby doctor. Although private consultations are relatively inexpensive in these districts, it is a paradox that the poor should make extensive use of this sector given that a comprehensive public system is purported to exist. It emphasises the need for a wider distribution of local health centres in peripheral areas of the city. In particular the IMSS and the SS should direct greater investment towards low-cost community

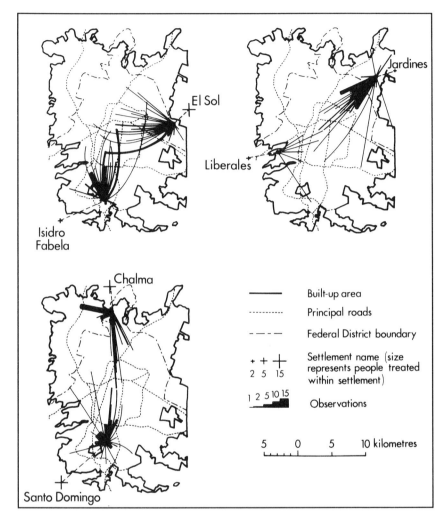

Figure 6.6 Place of medical treatment for residents of six irregular settlements in Mexico City

health care facilities given that it is the population dependent upon that sector which uses private doctors with greatest frequency.

The examination of access to health care in Mexico City demonstrates how various social groups are kept apart through separate 'tiers' of treatment available to them. Even the attempts to extend coverage of the IMSS to populations that were previously uncovered, although welcome, offered a minimal and inferior service to that received by existing members. This serves to create yet another tier within an already highly stratifed system and existing social inequalities are accentuated further.

Second, social inequalities are sustained through the sharply differentiated benefits that accrue to each 'tier' and the way in which each is financially regressive (Mesa Lago 1978). Contributions are a proportion of wages so that although better-off groups pay greater sums so do the other bipartite or tripartite contributor(s) be they government or employer (Midgley 1984). In the latter case contributions are usually generated from profits on goods so the consumer ends up paying. As a result those organisations which offer cover to better-paid workers and employees are most likely to build up their resources quickly. Clearly this multiplicity of structures is not an historical accident. It is a deliberate outcome of the political system and facilitates the manipulation of one sector or group of the population against another. It also makes the structure highly resistant to change. Few groups will wish to concede the advantage they hold.

This leads to my third general conclusion that a stratified structure has important ideological functions for the state. Covertly the health and social security systems serve to coopt the most powerful or organised groups in society. Thus federal workers are catered for through ISSSTE; those in strategic industries enjoy their own health care facilities as do the military. These conditions, together with wider benefits provided by each individual social security system, have evolved in response to pressure from these more powerful groups (Mesa Lago 1978). All along they have sought to maintain their relative advantage *vis-à-vis* other groups. IMSS offers the best medical service but its social security benefits are not as generous as others. The Ministry of Health which caters for the majority of the population is no more than a nominal health service. This situation would probably not persist if those people or communities without adequate coverage organised more effectively to make demands or displayed a propensity to protest. Currently the state can afford to offer the bare minimum without fear of generating strong protest. In addition it has created a range of one-off 'troubleshooting' institutions which appear to make concessions or provide relief where it is required.

Reproducing social inequality through state–community interaction

Another means through which social inequality can be sustained is through the arrangements that the state adopts towards engagement and interaction with local communities. As I argued in Chapter 3 in the context of the Federal District, these terms of engagement have changed over time from open-ended patron-client relations to a much more closely structured arrangement comprising the neighbourhood councils (*juntas de vecinos*). Indeed, a general review of channels of community action in three Latin American countries concluded that structures tended to be imposed top-down by the state rather than an expression of bottom-up mobilisation by the most disadvantaged (Gilbert and Ward 1984). The rationale for their the existence obeys state needs and criteria more than it reflects the needs of the poor. Of course, there are important exceptions to this highly constrained pattern but they tend not to be the rule. International agencies and many government agencies espouse the virtues of including community action and participation and expect it to figure as an element in the development projects that they sponsor (Skinner and Rodell 1983).

But if this somewhat cynical view reflects the practice, what about the theory? Surely organised struggle whether it be class-based in the classic sense or a 'Rainbow Coalition' of interest groups and political parties offers potential for overcoming social inequality? Over two decades ago there was a strong interest and belief in the possibilities that the *lumpenproletariat* (i.e. the masses in Third World countries who did not conform to a classic proletarian vanguard capable of promoting class struggle) would somehow rise up and destroy the repressive elites (Fanon 1967). Although an idealistic view, and one which failed to identify how a class in itself might become a class for itself, this work encouraged further investigation into the ways in which the poor mobilised themselves and extracted concessions from government (Goldrich, Pratt and Schuller 1967; Ray 1969; Cornelius 1975). However, these studies pointed not to radicalism of the poor, but to their conservatism. The privileged access of social and housing benefits offered by large urban centres, compared to what migrants had put up with in the provinces, encouraged support for the system. Moreover, the manner whereby these benefits were won through the exchange of political support also reduced the likelihood of the poor providing the vanguard for successful revolution or significant social change.

In this context Castells' work is very important. Indeed his own early thinking was strongly influenced both by orthodox theory about class struggle, combined with his experience in irregular settlements (*campamentos*) of Santiago Chile, during the Popular Unity Government 1970–3. But his contribution was that he was able to offer an attractive theory about the formation of social movements in relation to the growth of state intervention. A brief summary does not do justice to Castells' work, but the existence of other detailed evaluations (Lowe 1986) and the fact that Castells' own ideas about the nature and potential of urban social movements have turned almost full circle between 1971 and 1983, makes this brief treatment a little more justifiable. As I outlined earlier in this chapter Castells argued that the state's growing obligation to intervene to provide the 'means of collective consumption' in effect provides a point around which conflict can be forged against the dominant class or group who control those 'means' (in this case the state). Given appropriate leadership, and linkage to the advanced working classes (whose struggle around the capital relation – means of production – was paramount), an urban social movement could be forged that would lead to a 'qualitatively new effect' on the dominant structure of relations within that society (Castells 1977).

For several reasons Castells moved away from the strictures of this definition and began to give greater (equivalent) weight to the importance of 'secondary' or 'displaced' class struggle. Linkage to the capital relation through a proletarian vanguard was no longer paramount. Finally, faced with the extremely limited successes wrought by urban social movements during the 1970s, together with the growing internationalisation of the economic process, Castells backtracked and argued that social change is only possible when mobilisation around an issue of collective consumption is combined with political self-management and with the defence of cultural and territorial identity (Castells 1983: xviii, 328). But broadening the issue of mobilisation is not enough, he argues (p. 329), because urban movements can neither comprehend nor 'recognise the relationship between production, consumption and circulation' – a task that extends beyond the confines of the local community. At best, therefore, local groups are only likely to be effective in their resistance against 'exploitation – alienation – oppression that the city represents' (p. 330); therein lies their contemporary role and value.

Others have remained more steadfast in their belief in the possibility of achieving social change under conditions of 'flexible accumulation' and see the experience of the 'Greens' in West Germany and the 'Rainbow Coalition' in the US as promising in this respect (Harvey 1987). Harvey (1987: 283) also says that: 'true empowerment for the presently disempowered must be won by struggle from below and not given out of largesse from above'. In Mexico City the problem has been that *largesse* from above has consistently disempowered any serious movement towards social change. Nor do I see this situation changing significantly in the short to medium term.

How is this disempowerment achieved in the context of land policy, health care, housing and infrastructure servicing arrangements? There are three main mechanisms: through the structure of linkage and channels to the state; through tactics of divide-and-rule; and through the manipulation of popular ideology.

Control through linkages between state and the community/movement

The various types of control that may be exercised through different forms of state–community relationship are outlined in Table 6.4. Patron–clientelism involves an informal link between leader/community and a 'patron' in which goods and favours are distributed from the latter usually in exchange for political support (Grindle 1977). Co-option and incorporation occurs where the leader/community affiliates with a national organisation and thereby becomes subject to its orthodoxy, procedures, rules and so on. This is usually done because the co-opted party believes that s/he will win preferential treatment and benefit as a result of the link. In Mexico co-option is a classic strategy that the PRI uses in giving the impression that it has preferential access to resources. In fact co-option leads to a *reduced* likelihood of winning successful outcomes: what one

The reproduction of social inequality

Table 6.4 Methods of control exercised by different forms of community–state relationship

Nature of linkage	Way in which external control is exercised
Patron–client	Manipulation *ad hoc* concessions
Co-option/incorporation	Occasional 'lightweight' concessions Compliance with external orthodoxy
'Routinisation'	Queueing and concessions 'Gatekeepers' allocating resources 'Red tape' in order to delay and obstruct
Autonomy/independence	Concessions made in order to pacify Manipulation Repression; assassination of leaders, etc.

author appropriately calls the 'irony of organization' (Eckstein 1977). Routinisation is a form of integration sought by government agencies when communities are recognised and accommodated by the institution in order for it to fulfil its goals efficiently. Finally, communities may resist external mediation and, through their leaders, reject overtures that might lead to their loss of autonomy. This is done either for reasons of ideological purity, the group being wary of the undermining influence of the state; or it is born of a belief that independence and embarassment of local authorities will maximise the chances and speed of securing a desired outcome (Montaño 1976).

The ways in which land development issues and servicing have been managed through state–community relations in Mexico City offers insight into several of these processes. Here, for the sake of brevity I will deal only with land. Until the late 1970s the PRI used clientelism and co-option to good effect – often through the CNOP wing which was heavily involved as mediator between residents and the government (Cornelius 1975; Eckstein 1977; Alonso *et al.* 1980). In the Federal District land regularisation and service provision assumed importance as a means of ensuring and developing political control and support. Through the *Oficina de Colonias* residents were leant-on to attend political rallies and to vote for the PRI at elections; in exchange they could expect some form of government recognition for their settlement, and/or the installation of minor services and occasional handouts. This process of negotiation was mediated vertically through settlement leaders who acted as 'brokers' in informal patron–client networks involving the community and top-level politicians and government officials (Cornelius 1975).

Although the Party's direct control over settlement affairs suffered as a result of the creation of new agencies responsible for regularisation and housing and with whom it had little direct influence, the proliferation of factions and groups rife in each settlement before 1976 provided ample room in which the PRI could manouevre. Different leaders sought legitimacy through the creation of vertical clientelist links created with various 'patrons'. This 'splitting' or hiving-off of several factions within a single settlement was not seriously challenged until 1977 after which 'routinised' relationships between agencies and individuals became the order of the day. In the State of Mexico the Party's main task during the early 1970s was to penetrate the mass-based urban social movement (the MRC) and its sister organisation in the *Quinta Zona* of Ecatepec. By classic methods of co-option and infiltration, the CNOP successfully undermined the potency of these organisations by 1976 (Cisneros Sosa, no date).

However, radical social mobilisation has not always been headed-off by clientelism, co-option and routinisation (Montaño 1976; Ramírez Saíz 1983). In such cases government-sponsored repression either of the community or its leaders may be adopted in order to overcome opposition. The violence visited upon 2 de Octubre settlement in Ixtacalco and its leader Pancho de la Cruz during 1974–6 was also a warning to others of the ultimate deterrent.

Control through tactics of 'divide-and-rule'

The second principal mechanism whereby the state exercises control over potentially disruptive or threatening social movements is through dividing one group from another. Any attempt to weld a horizontal movement between different spatial or sectoral constituencies is likely to attract state concern. As I have just explained the state seeks vertically mediated links to individual leaders or communities. The MRC, the Urban Popular Movements Coordination (CONAMUP) and the Single Earthquake Refugees' Coordination (CUD) are examples of movements which broke the rules as far as the state is concerned. Government response is illuminating, and various mechanisms have been developed to drive a wedge between one group or faction and another.

One way is to systematically treat settlements differently. Thus deals are struck whereby water or land regularisation is provided to one area but not to another. Electricity here; but not there. This opens divisions between different settlement leaders over their settlement priorities for improvements and was an important way in which settlements in Ecatepec were set against each other during the 1970s (Guerrero *et al.* 1974). Also, as I outlined earlier, links between agencies and local constituencies accentuate these divisions particularly where the inter-agency rivalries exist – as was the case under Echeverría. Sometimes, too, local officials will deal differentially to deny one settlement any benefits, while apparently meeting the needs of a similar adjacent area. The aim here is to undermine the settlement leadership considered by the state to be non-compliant, and to encourage incipient factions in that settlement, in order to strip away the recalcitrant leader's support base. In the 'treatment' of such areas Machiavelli is alive and well.

Elsewhere it is unneccessary to create divisions between constituencies as these exist already. Renters and owners within irregular settlements will have very different priorities about government intervention. Similarly, the different types of land acquisition processes described earlier will require resolution through different agencies: CoRett for *ejidal* land, other federal and state agencies elsewhere depending upon the jurisdiction. Also, on *ejidal* land the 'regularisation' interests often lead in various directions depending upon how land was acquired: by invasion, concession, purchase by an *avecindado* and so on.

Whether or not the good is consumed collectively or individually will also shape the opportunities for collaboration. For example unlike water, electricity, drainage and perhaps, regularisation, which are 'collectively consumed' (i.e. consistently required by the large majority of the community), health and education are 'consumed' individually and ephemerally. Those who have children of school age send them to school; and demands vary according to the presence or absence of children and according to their ages. Not everyone has an interest in school provision. The same argument applies to health: not everyone has a need for medical treatment. Most tend to trust their luck and to hope that a member of their family will not fall seriously ill. If they do, then that **individual** seeks appropriate medical attention. Hence settlement leaders identify only those services which they know are likely to evince widespread support as the principal focus of mobilisation. Here, too, scale is important. In Mexico the smallest institutional level of health care service commonly found is that of a clinic or health centre. Usually these are designed to serve several settlements. Therefore, if pressure is to be applied to persuade government to provide a facility, it must be coordinated between several communities at the same time. Several factors militate against this happening. Few settlements are at the same level of 'integration' in terms of service provision. Even in adjacent communities the local leadership will generate a different rank order of priorities for future actions. Moreover, the vertical nature of relations between individual settlements and individual politicians and agencies in Mexico acts, quite deliberately, against communities working together in unison. From a leader's point of view, mobilisation around a health care issue which requires collaboration with neighbouring communities is usually a non-starter.

Control through the ideology of social welfare provision

Another basis for division among people whose class status is similar is to shape popular ideology in a way that is non-threatening to the state. The demand for services or goods may be socially constructed by government. For example the current content of the ecological debate within the Federal District has largely been appropriated from radical and green groups, thereby upstaging their arguments and hijacking their momentum.

Likewise, in this chapter I have demonstrated how full legalisation of 'clouded' land title in Mexico has been raised by government as a popular 'need'. The ways in which popular ideology is created and sustained has received inadequate attention in contemporary research in Mexico and elsewhere.

Moreover, in the context of health care in Mexico City one should not underemphasise the ideological role that a stratified social security system exercises in preventing the emergence of social action around health care issues. The population in irregular settlements in Mexico City is deliberately split several ways: some have full IMSS coverage; others have partial IMSS coverage; and a few belong to ISSSTE. Everyone else knows that should they fall ill then the Ministry of Health or a local private doctor will provide appropriate attention. There is not likely to be a single view about the necessity for improved facilities nor about the type of provision that should be sought. In addition, as we have observed, people do not perceive health care provision as a problem. Most are satisfied with the treatment that they receive. Although objective criteria suggest that health care in Mexico City is inadequate and unequal, the very existence of several different sources of treatment encourages satisfaction with the status quo. Those who want health care benefits offered through social security schemes know that the most feasible way to achieve it is by securing a job where it is provided automatically, and not by pressing the state to provide it to the whole population.

Neither are existing pressure groups which have won social security benefits for their members likely to press for changes that would make the system more equitable. They will continue to press only for improvements for their membership and fight to maintain their relative advantage over competing pressure groups. As in the past, any future significant change in the nature of health care provision for the majority will derive from governmental initiative and *largesse*, rather than as a result of organised trades union or settlement mobilisation.

The paradox: improving or worsening social inequality in Mexico City?

The improvement of urban living conditions

The academic literature on Mexico and elsewhere is replete with assertions that urban living conditions are deteriorating. The provision of housing and services falls behind demand, densities rise, land prices show a dramatic increase, journey to work lengthens, and people slowly choke to death from pollution and contamination. Throughout this book I have challenged such assertions at least *a priori*. If conditions *are* getting worse in Mexico City and elsewhere then let us, as academics, show the extent and rate of that

Table 6.5 Changing levels of dwelling ownership and service provision in Mexico City 1970 and 1980

	Total number of homes (thousands)		Percentage of owners[1]		Percentage of homes:					
					without electricity		without interior water supply[2]		without drainage[3]	
	1970	1980	1970	1980	1970	1980	1970	1980	1970	1980
Total country	8286.4	12074.6	66	68	41	25	61	50	59	43
Metropolitan Area	1477.3	2528.2	42	54	9	3	40	31	25	14
DF	1219.4	1747.1	38	48	5	3	36	30	22	14
Ecatepec	34.5	130.2	67	69	27	4	61	36	55	11
Naucalpan	65.3	134.4	57	59	15	3	47	36	33	13
Netza.*	90.3	214.1	66	63	40	4	68	40	41	2
Tlanepantla	60.4	138.8	56	63	17	3	49	32	35	15
Atizapán*	—	36.2	—	77	—	4	—	34	—	20
Coacalco	—	17.7	—	79	—	2	—	12	—	8
Tultitlán	—	24.0	—	76	—	6	—	31	—	32
Cuatitlán Iz.	—	31.7	—	82	—	4	—	26	—	25
Nicholas Romero	—	19.4	—	79	—	15	—	65	—	54
La Paz	—	16.9	—	67	—	7	—	49	—	24
Texcoco	—	17.6	—	66	—	8	—	36	—	42

* Netza.: Netzahualcóyotl; Atizapán: Atizápan de Zarágoza.

Those *municipios* for which data are not provided for 1970 were not included in the 'Metropolitan Area' at that time. The minimum threshold for inclusion was a population of 100 000 people.

(1) The classification of tenure altered between 1970 and 1980. In 1970 a two-fold classification was adopted: owners and non-owners (which included accommodation that was rented, loaned or acquired through work). In 1980 the census identifies owners, renters, and 'others'. Because of the ambiguity on the census forms it is likely that some 'sharers' were included under the owner category. The figure of 68 per cent is, therefore, probably a slight overestimation. Nevertheless it appears that the proportion of owners has continued to rise since 1960.
(2) In both 1970 and 1980 more than 50 per cent of households had access to a piped water supply outside the dwelling – either elsewhere in the building or in the same plot.
(3) In 1970 drainage was defined as a 'hygienic system' for removing *aqua negras* (waste waters). In 1980 it was defined as a hygienic system with drainage pipes. (The latter would include connections to mains drainage, a septic tank, or occasionally, a hole in the ground.)

deterioration. One area where I believe significant improvements may be observed since the 1960s is that of servicing levels.

Once land has been acquired, the poor turn their attention towards the introduction of urban services such as water, electricity, public transport, paved roads, street lighting, and to other public utilities including schools, covered markets, and health centres. Unlike middle-income subdivisions where most of these services are provided from the outset, in irregular settlements they are usually provided only when the area is fully settled, and there may be long delays before an adequate service is obtained – if at all. Whether or not a settlement receives a service, and the time it takes before it is provided, relates to a number of complex factors. Resident priorities, total costs and ease of installation, local leadership attributes, community adherence to the politiking rules may all be important considerations (Ward 1981a, 1986).

The delivery of public services: electricity and water

Industralisation during the 1940s and 1950s required, among other things, provision of an adequate and reliable power supply. For many years federal investment in the Electricity Generating Commission (CFE) was a priority area and, once industrial and commercial needs had been met, there was ample supply to meet domestic needs as well. As a result most households in Mexico City enjoy a private metered service (Table 6.5). Although Mexico City's population is privileged in this respect, and a much higher proportion of dwellings nationally lacked a formal supply even in 1980, most urban areas throughout the country appeared to be reasonably well provided (Ward 1986). Most places, and the country as a whole, experienced a significant absolute and relative improvement in the distribution of domestic supplies between 1970 and 1980.

By and large, supply has managed to keep pace with rapid city growth, both in the Federal District and the surrounding municipalities. Moreover, many of those households recorded to be without an electricity supply will in fact receive current through informal illegal hook-ups. This practice is especially common in recently formed settlements where groups of residents collaborate to buy cable and splice into a nearby overhead supply.

The provision of water and drainage both nationally and in Mexico City is much less widely available than electricity. Overall in 1980 almost one-third of dwellings in the Metropolitan Area lacked an interior water supply, although approximately one-half of these households did have access to a piped supply outside the dwelling – usually in the same plot. At a national level, and in most other cities, provision is not as widespread as in the capital. The record for dwellings without a drainage system appears to be better but this lower figure relates primarily to the broad definition of what constitutes a drainage system under the Mexican Census (a 'hygenic system for the removal of waste waters', see Table 6.5).

Significantly, too, there is marked spatial variation in the level of service provision. At a national level rural areas are less well served than urban centres, State capitals appear to be better off than other large urban centres, and cities in the traditionally poorer regions such as Oaxaca, Chiapas and

Guerrero are poorly served (Ward 1986: 88). Those areas in Mexico City with extensive irregular settlement experience the highest levels of relative deprivation (cf. Figures 2.5 and 2.6).

However, although adequate drainage and interior water supply is still lacking in many settlements, it would be churlish not to note the significant improvements registered since 1970 (Table 6.5). Nationally and in the Metropolitan Area the number of dwellings with an interior supply of water and a drainage system doubled between 1970 and 1980: a considerable achievement. This contributed to the relative improvement in servicing levels that is apparent in Table 6.5. Yet it is also important to recognise that, despite this investment, in **absolute** terms the position in 1980 was actually **worse** than a decade before. In 1980 there were more dwellings without an interior supply of running water than in 1970. The same feature appears in relation to dwellings with a drainage system with the exception of the Metropolitan Area of Mexico City which had approximately the same number of dwellings inserviced as a decade previously.

These figures also tell us nothing about the quality of the service. Without a purifier, water is not, strictly speaking, drinkable. Most Mexico City residents who can afford it buy purified water in bottles or flaggons. Also, the water supply itself is often irregular. During the dry season a common feature of water provision to some of the survey settlements was the irregularity with which it flowed. In Santo Domingo, for example, residents complained that the authorities may as well not have bothered to install a domestic supply as water flowed only in the early hours of the morning and was rarely sufficient to fill their tanks. Similarly, in many settlements in Netzahualcóyotl and Ecatepec where water and drainage networks were installed during the mid-1970s, the drainage system has broken down. Subsequent urbanisation works and heavy traffic have ruptured pipes; inadequate maintenance means that many drains are choked; and the lack of water means that the system is not flushed clear.

Given these failings we must treat the substantial improvements achieved between 1970 and 1980 with a degree of caution. Nevertheless, living conditions recorded for Mexico City do point towards a marked improvement during the 1960s and 1970s. Whether this improvement has continued during the austerity programmes of the 1980s remains unclear, but initial indications are not positive (Perló 1988).

In this Chapter I have shown that any serious attempt to improve social conditions in Mexico City and to reduce existing patterns of inequality are likely to be constrained by the nature of political mediation and the way in which the bureaucracy is structured; by the stratification of delivery systems in many arenas of social welfare provision; and by the disempowering mechanisms that the state adopts towards social groups that might develop a head-of-steam directed towards mobilisation and social change. Each mechanism has, I argue, an overall regressive effect even though the actual content of policies has usually improved, as have the way in which agencies are charged to carry out their functions more expeditiously and efficiently.

Overall, the Mexican system has emerged to deliver a better service *peso* for *peso* in real terms than it did, say, at the end of the Echeverría term. But this has only negligible effect when viewed against the wider structures and underlying state rationale which act to sustain social inequality in the city.

7
The reproduction of urban form: Modern, vernacular and post-modern environments in Mexico City

---

The relationship between urban form and social process

Architecture as the spirit of its time

At the beginning of this book I discussed recent theory about the way in which urban environments are created and reproduced. I speculated, also, about the impact of the so-called New International Division of Labour upon urban environments such as Mexico City. I hope by now the reader will appreciate that economically determinist explanations of the city tell only part of the story. Although a marxist framework acknowledges the importance of social and political and ideological processes, the economic (capital) relation remains paramount. But in recent years greater explanatory weight has been given to processes of social production of the built environment and to the role of human agency (Castells 1983; Gregory 1987).

In Mexico City I have argued that while economic processes have fuelled the engine of urban growth, the levels of poverty, bases of social differentiation, together with the actual nature of city expansion owe as much to political and social factors as to the purely economic. There is nothing new about this argument – as I will demonstrate in a moment. Mexico City, like all cities and urban-based populations, is a product of historical processes. History is reflected in the ground plan, collective memory, physical structure, design, and monuments of a city. Thus, it reflects the spirit of the time (*zeitgeist*): the nub of Mumford's (1938) argument more than fifty years ago. Other writers such as Glass (1968: 48) have described the 'urban' as 'a mirror . . . of history, class structure and culture', while more recently Simmie (1986) in an introduction to a *Sociology, Politics and Cities* series which he edits, stated that cities 'are the places where the results of past and present economic and political conflicts leave their most obvious marks'. However, it is not just the physical environment that is an outcome of historical processes; the population imbibe that local history and create a new history of the city through their own actions or *praxis*. There is, therefore, a collective consciousness of the people in the city or, as Castells (1983: 302) argued, when seeking to redefine the 'urban', is 'the social meaning assigned to a particular spatial form by a . . . historically defined society'. Urban meaning is the synthesis of the historical social form and the specific goal of a society – fashioned through conflict between different groups with different stakes.

Whether there is anything intrinsically urban about these processes compared with processes operating in non-urban environments is a moot, and hotly debated point. Harvey (1985) reduces the analysis to questions of the built environment and the reproduction of labour power, and underplays the importance of any rural–urban dialectic, except in the realm of ideology, where, he says, it remains significant. Saunders (1986) goes further and rejects the notion of the urban as a spatial object. He proposes that the distinctiveness of urban sociology is not a particular concern with space, and still less with the city as a spatial entity. Rather it is concerned with a focus upon one aspect of social organisation (the state) inscribed in space. He writes (1986: 287) that 'the work of writers such as Pahl and Castells has been enormously suggestive in terms of substantive focus but has ultimately collapsed in the face of the attempt to tie social processes to spatial form'. I do not agree. In the words of one author 'Space matters' (Massey and Allen 1984) and, as I will show in this chapter, the physical form of the city is another means whereby social inequality is reproduced and sustained. But this is not new: Harvey's earlier work in Baltimore demonstrated the same proposition. Fortunately, resolution of these debates is not essential to the argument that I wish to develop here.

Although the importance of seeking to understand the conditioning relationship between economic, social and other processes and resultant urban form is widely recognised, relatively little research has explicitly addressed the ways in which, once produced, the urban structure in turn reproduces social relations in the city. In particular if we look at a city's architecture we may discover both past philosophies and rationale for urban development, and also the way in which the physical structure of the city cumulatively helps to shape contemporary social patterns and behaviour. The city is both a product of the past and, mediated through its architecture and design, assists in creating the now and the tomorrow. This is not to fall into the trap of architectural or design determinism, even though I believe that both may exercise an important but not crucial conditioning of human behaviour (Lynch 1981; Newman 1972; Dicken 1986b). Rather, it is to argue that the physical structure of the city (i.e. its ground plan representing past design philosophy [or absence] as well as its architecture) helps to articulate and to reproduce a wide range of processes.

In an excellent review of the 'post-modern' city Knox (1987) identifies how architecture can be construed as shaping urban reproduction. First, architecture both expresses and shapes culture in so far as it 'fixes' ideas about ideology and aesthetics in the urban environment, so that it becomes part of us, and we it. Second, architecture expresses the social construction of how things get built in terms of a society's laws, regulations and so on; but it also articulates strong *political* themes: of *laissez faire* (irregular settlement for example); of **modernisation** (such as Lucio Costa's 'aeroplane' design for Brasilia's ground plan and Oscar Niemeyer's modernist buildings); of **repression** (apartheid cities in South Africa, and in the UK and the US a growing tendency for exclusive and policed zones within residential areas); of **environmentalism**; of **populism** and so on. In many respects 'post-modern' architecture, discussed later in this chapter, reflects and reinforces contemporary liberal and individualist political philosophies (O'Connor 1984; Harvey 1987; 1989). Third, architecture shapes the process of capital accumulation through its representation of new fashions and the fresh opportunities they offer for investment in the built environment. Harvey (1987: 265) argues that 'spatial practices' are not innocent of capital accumulation processes and that 'Those who have the power to command and reproduce space possess a vital instrumentality for the reproduction and enhancement of their own power.'

A fourth relationship identified in Knox's paper is the one between architecture, legitimation and social reproduction. Building and urban design shape the ideology of urban citizenry or, as Porphyrios (in Knox 1987: 366–7) has it: 'architecture gives back to reality an imaginary coherence that makes reality appear natural and eternal'. Personally I'm not sure about the eternal aspect since contemporary modern and post-modern architecture may also reinforce the idea of temporal change, transitoriness and redundancy, but the point about architecture's role in shaping reality as it is perceived, is both powerful and important. Buildings carry messages. We need to know much more about the rationality, and about the authors of those messages. That is the main purpose of this penultimate chapter. I want to explore the extent to which the architecture of Mexico City carries a message, and what that message means.

In earlier chapters I have argued that social and spatial inequality in Mexico City are an outcome of economic and political processes mediated through a range of sectoral activities: planning, the provision of land, housing and health care delivery systems, through its transportation structure and so on. Now the aim is to identify the currents in Mexico's recent architectural history and to evaluate the influence of architects in shaping the nature of the city. Here, of course, one must examine both 'informal' architecture embodied in self-help, as well as the more formal elements embodied in urban design. I want to know how far the physical design of the city reinforces existing structures of social inequality. Do they, in Harvey's terms, represent and reproduce the 'violence' enacted against the working classes?

Mexico City: the bases of social stratification and their representation in past city form

The focus of this text has been unambiguously and unapologetically contemporary. However, Mexico City's 'biography' spans a greater range and intensity of history than any other city in the world: from pre-Columbian Aztec glory, to colonial capital for New Spain, through independence and occupation in the nineteenth century, through Social Revolution and upheaval in the first two decades of the twentieth century (Kandell 1988). All this and much more, before the material considered in this book even begins. Mexico City is a palimpsest of these past struggles and, to a greater or lesser extent, these influences remain embedded in the city today.

Tenochtitlán – the city discovered, conquered and razed by Cortes – formed the centre of Aztec culture and its empire. Emerging as an all powerful force in the fourteenth century, the Aztecs founded their city upon a site on which, as was foretold, they saw an eagle devouring a snake (today symbolised and depicted in the national flag). That it was located in the middle of a network of lakes some of which were saline, has meant that from the very first Mexico City's history has been concerned with the procurement of fresh water and this has remained a key issue in the present day (Perló 1988). Part of the original aqueduct still remains. Food was produced intensively on the 'floating' gardens (in fact man-made islands of silt) of Xochimilco on the southern freshwater perimeters of the lake. But the city was built upon violence and conquest of neighbouring (and distant) territories in order to provide tribute, slaves and male warriors for human sacrifice. The social organisation was geared to this project. A king priest was selected from a Council of all the Clans formed of those who had progressed through the ranks of individual clans or *calpulli* as they were known. Each *calpulli* was spatially separate, occupied a particular neighbourhood, educated its children, dedicated itself to a particular trade or set of functions, and, most important of all, operated as a fighting unit: a sort of batallion-cum-guild (Valiant 1972; Offner 1984). Social mobility was achieved through leadership promotion within each *calpulli*.

The cosmology of the Aztecs was clearly reflected in city form. It was a remarkable city: one of great splendour and violence. Pyramids and palaces were covered in stucco and painted predominantly white with fiercely coloured adornments (Plate 7.1). The Aztecs were sun worshippers and the daily procession of human sacrifices quickened during the instability associated with the latter years of the 52 year cycle at the end of which all fire would be extinguished only to be relit if the world did not end (Soustelle 1971). Fortuitously, Cortes' arrival coincided with the instability associated with the end of one of these cycles. In pride of place before the main temple were the skull racks of thousands of human sacrifices.

The project of the *conquistadores* and subsequent colonial administration was the subjugation of the indigenous population, their conversion to

Plate 7.1 Mural of Tenochtitlán by Diego Rivera in the National Palace

Plate 7.2 Colonial 'Baroque' architecture: the front of the Cathedral, Zocalo, Mexico City

Christianity, and the exploitation of agricultural and mineral wealth that Mexico offered. The town was the instrument of this process. Churches were raised on the sites of Aztec temples. The symbolism of defeat and subjugation were reinforced by the massiveness and splendour of these churches, particularly during the later Baroque (Plate 7.2). The city plan conformed with the guidelines of the day and subsequently laid down in the 1573 Ordinances or 'Laws of the Indies'. Streets were laid out on a grid-iron pattern, with principal administrative and ecclesiastical buildings around a central *plaza*: or *Zocalo* in Mexico. The rich built mansions and palaces adjacent to the central plaza; while the poor lived in hovels and encampments at the periphery.

The social structure was built around an elite administrative *cadre* of appointees from Spain, the peninsular people (*peninsulares*), who dominated both politically and socially, and lived primarily in urban areas. The agricultural economy came increasingly to be dominated by a pure blood Spanish descendent group in Mexico. Conflict developed between this *criolla* population and the *peninsulares* whose domination and control was increasingly resented and, ultimately, was overthrown by independence in 1821. Below the *criollas* in the social pyramid came *mestizos* (mixed Spanish/Indian); and blacks and miscengenated black groups (*mulattos*); and, at the bottom of the pyramid, the Indians – or at least those who had survived the frequent epidemics of illnesses previously unknown to them. But this was not a rigid caste system; there was some opportunity for social mobility and 'passing' based upon economic wealth (Chance 1975).

The nineteenth century, too, saw an inflow of other Europeans: from France during Napoleon III's imposition of Maximilian as 'Emperor'; and others from Britain and elsewhere associated with large-scale infrastructural developments undertaken in Mexico City and throughout the territory during the Díaz dictatorship of the last two decades. As I will demonstrate below, the beginning of the twentieth century was marked by an inflow of European ideas and inspiration in art and architecture. Moreover, the original cultural and phenotype mixing has been further overlain by other population streams of Jews from Eastern Europe, Lebanese, and Spaniards fleeing Franco. During the 1960s and 1970s there was a small inflow of refugees from the southern cone of Latin America. Although in terms of total numbers these twentieth-century immigration streams have been relatively insignificant, most groups have settled into a particular (and often important) niche within Mexican economy and society.

Today the majority of the population is *mestizo*. Pure Spanish descendency carries slight anti-nationalist overtones and is not highly desired. But Mexicans, while being intensely nationalist, appear subconsciously to deprecate 'Indianness' and 'blackness' and to reify 'whiteness' and European or North American influences. This is manifest in a variety of ways. The rich are most likely to be fair and phenotypically European, than dark and Indian. The converse also applies. In advertising, too, sexist and racist images predominate in a much more pervasive way than, say, in the UK or the USA.

In particular the relationship with the USA is highly ambivalent. Mexicans feel an admiration for North American consumerism and wealth; yet resentment at their own nation's poverty, nineteenth-century losses of territory, and at the contemporary cultural and economic dominance posed by the USA. This, together with the intense mixing of earlier cultural traditions, has led to what some have described as a rather 'masked' and contradictory national personality (Franco 1967; Paz 1961). It is also an intensely patriarchal society in which *machismo* (male dominance) remains entrenched, and *marianismo* (motherhood, passivity, and long-suffering 'earth mother' syndrome within the family unit) are esteemed.

The important point to recognise is that Mexicans have a long, racially and culturally very diverse history. It is also one that has been particularly violent. While there is intense national pride at being Mexican, there are also many contradictions. A love/hate relationship towards consumerism and the north; vitality and exhuberance combined with fatalism and a morbid preoccupation with death; male dominance fronting male inferiority and feelings of impotence; national pride yet ambivalence towards the US; passivity and violence. As we shall observe below, an appreciation of these attributes and elements of personality is important in any interpretation of Mexico City's built environment.

Vernacular architecture rules OK?

Mexico City's contemporary built form may be examined both by looking at formal architecture and its inspiration, as well as by informal and traditional building processes. Naturally, given its sequent occupance, and a highly diverse culture, it is a city with an especially rich architectural history. But it is rich in another respect: that of popular initiative and vernacular housing traditions. Although irregular settlements are not strictly 'vernacular' environments in the sense of their being indigenous to a particular place or culture, they are sometimes conceived as such. 'Spontaneous settlements . . . are next only to preliterate and traditional vernacular settlements in their supportiveness of culture' (Rapoport 1988: 59). In terms of the processes underpinning their creation, and the positive outcome ('product characteristics') that arise for user/inhabitants, the two are, he argues, very similar. He concludes that these self-shaped environments are frequently of higher quality than those of designers working within developed or wealthy societies, and that one can learn a great deal by analysing them (ibid: 72–3). My purpose here is to analyse irregular settlement not through such rose-tinted cultural spectacles, but to identify the relationship between social process and spatial form and to ask how the process of **physical design** and development of self-help settlement in Mexico City reproduces social inequality.

The reproduction of urban form

Mobility without moving

In terms of population and the built-up area I have emphasised from the beginning of this book that Mexico City is primarily one of poverty and social inequality. Around 50 per cent of the population (i.e. 9 millions) and 60 per cent of the built-up area of Mexico City occupy settlements that have emerged illegally through one form or another (Chapter 5). Estimates about the proportion of the city population earning around the minimum wage vary between 45 per cent and 66 per cent (Stolarski 1982: 61). Many households have more than one earner and earn somewhat more, but the previous chapter demonstrated how most low-income city residents are obliged to turn to illegal methods of land acquisition in order to get access to housing. Once a plot of land is secured and households feel a modicum of security that no-one is going to take steps to evict the fledgling community, the settlement is upgraded through mutual aid on the part of residents' cooperative efforts, and through government intervention to install basic services, public utilities and to guarantee security of tenure.

At the individual plot level, households take responsibility for overseeing the construction of their dwelling, each making individual decisions about matters of design, layout, sequence of room construction, materials used and the level of labour power that will be hired, or put up by themselves through self-help. One observes a process of 'consolidation' over time, so that, provided no barriers are put in the way, individual settlements pass through various levels or 'stages' of physical development. Agglomerations of unserviced shacks are replaced by brick-built rooms with laminated roofs, until after fifteen or twenty years they comprise 'consolidated' often two-storey dwellings with all services on line (see Plates 2.9 and 2.10). Given that the people who develop and live in their homes are purported to be one-and-the-same, the process is sometimes viewed as offering social mobility through the medium of upgrading without having to trade up and move from one neighbourhood to another (Turner 1963, 1968b).

As I will argue below, this portrayal is both simplistic and disingeneous. It is a portrait which emerged during the late 1960s and early 1970s as a result of research that sought to identify the underlying processes of irregular settlement development and their populations (Turner 1968a, 1968b, 1969; Leeds 1969; Abrams 1966). The research findings were partly a response to the repressive policies of many governments of the day, and probably deliberately overstated the positive aspects of self-help in order to turn governments away from policies of squatter settlement eviction and the construction of relatively expensive project housing that accommodated only a small porportion of the total demand. In quantitative and qualitative terms these policies were inadequate (Gilbert and Ward 1978).

Working specifically in Mexico City, Turner (1976) and his colleagues differentiated between the 'supportive shack' and the 'oppressive house'. The former provide shelter at a cost that the poor could just about afford, in locations that dovetailed with their employment, social interaction and other needs. Instead of evicting squatters and razing such areas, governments should seek to support irregular settlers in doing what they know how to do best: design and manage the construction of their own homes themselves, and volunteer labour and time for local community development initiatives. Governments, for their part, should intervene not through full-blown housing developments but to provide housing 'elements' that self-builders could not readily provide for themselves: 'lumpy' services which required large investment and some degree of monopoly control and coordination such as water, drainage, electricity. Given that security of tenure was argued to be paramount before residents would invest in permanent building materials, the 'regularisation' of 'clouded' land tenure was required to give legal title to *de facto* owners. In Mexico the actual manner through which title transfer is achieved has enjoyed different social constructions over time. Today, the usual practice is to expropriate illegally occupied lands, compensate the original owners, and to sell back to individual self-builder occupiers (Varley 1989).

Gradually the arguments of Turner, Abrams and others gained powerful backers, most notably through international agencies seeking to intervene in urban development processes in developing countries (World Bank 1972; UNCHS 1982; Linn 1983). By the mid- to late-1970s two types of self-help supported programmes emerged in Mexico and elsewhere. First, sites-and-services comprised the advanced acquisition of land and installation of basic services before self-builders were allowed to purchase and occupy individual plots. Because of high land values in Mexico City, the existing huge demand and the fear that it might encourage further cityward migration, local authorities have been reluctant to develop sites-and-services in the city to any significant extent. Upgrading is the second type of policy prescription which, in Mexico City, was politically much more acceptable and desperately needed given the large number of unserviced settlements and the high levels of insecurity and conflict that prevailed in those neighbourhoods. As I identified in the previous chapter, Mexico City, like most Mexican cities, experienced significant relative improvements in its level of servicing during the 1970s.

But this positive appraisal of irregular settlement has not gone unquestioned. In the past decade many analysts have questioned the wisdom and analytical utility of this approach from a variety of perspectives. Here, in reviewing the critique, I want to identify also how the physical characteristics of irregular settlement **reproduce** social inequality.

The limits to self-help: how inequality begets inequality

(1) Through romanticising reality

As I suggested above, the argument that squatter settlements offered an 'architecture that works' (Turner 1968b), could be excused, at least in part, by the desirability of turning around many of the stereotypical views of self-build processes and low-income populations. But to sustain the argument that it reflects a medium through which self-expression, mobility, and dwelling adjustments to family size and employment situation could be achieved, is to confuse **choice** with **constraint**. It also belies the enormous social costs that arise from living in irregular settlements. People opt for the insecurity associated with illegal land occupations only because they have to, not because they want to (Harms 1976). Setting-up house on land invariably unsuited to urbanisation, without services, and with young (often infant) children in tow is a decision not taken lightly and one which involves ongoing sacrifice and hardship. One settler described to me how it was to squat on the Pedregal, a lightly vegetated recent lava flow in the south of the city: 'There were snakes and scorpions. We lived in dwellings open to the skies; there were no roads and no buses. There was nothing at all for us in those early days.' For some of us 'camping out' may be fun for a day or two, but we cannot easily imagine the day-to-day and day-long difficulties associated with raising a family in such an environment.

Living in irregular settlements invokes enormous social costs, and is one way in which inequality and hardship are sustained and reproduced through the physical environment. Conditions may improve gradually, but the lack of services and failure to provide adequate living environments for workers mean that the home is the principal medium through which poverty is experienced and reproduced. These social costs weigh especially upon women who carry out domestic tasks and whose workplace is the dwelling (Chant 1985; Chant and Ward 1987).

As well as a gender differentiation there is also a household division of labour, so that these social costs do not fall only upon women. Children, too, are expected to assist usually in fetching water from standpipes. Men give up their 'spare time' in order to extend and improve the house; while both men and women may be engaged in the Sunday morning *faenas* or task groups organised by the settlement improvement association. Men and women are involved in the often protracted negotiations with local authorities for legal recognition, services and public utilities (Gilbert and Ward 1985). Although men often 'front' these organisations, women tend to predominate and do most of the work (Moser 1989). In the *Asamblea de Barrios* organisation, for example, created in 1986, 80 per cent of the members are women, yet its leader 'Superbarrio' (who appears dressed in a Superman-type outfit and mask) is a man.

However, despite this hardship there is an apparent paradox that overall residents seem satisfied with their efforts, and are reluctant to condemn the state or local authorities for failing to provide adequate housing. Viewed in retrospect, all the blood, sweat and tears seem worth while, and in my various settlement surveys few respondents have expressed regret at their decision to participate in capturing land whether through illegal purchase or invasion. Most people state that their principal gains have been a *patrimonio* (inheritance) for their children; and the feeling that they could live more easily (*más tranquilo*) in their plots without the inter-family arguments associated with life in a shared plot and especially in a *vecindad* (tenement). Also, while irregular settlements in Mexico City display especially high intestinal disease and illness levels compared with, say, downtown areas where respiratory illnesses have a higher occurrence due to the higher densities and contamination (Fox 1972), it is probably true that children enjoy a better living environment than those who live in downtown tenements. They have more space, the streets are safer, and there is a higher level of surveillance over the street by neighbours. Also many Mexico City citizens living in irregular settlements today arrived as migrants from provincial areas during the 1950s and 1960s. Their move to the city often from impoverished rural areas, together with the relative concentration of resources in the capital, the opportunities for work, and ultimately the chance of securing a foothold in the land and housing markets, persuade them that they have fared pretty well. Whether, ultimately, their children will be as satisfied is another question.

(2) Through the predations of other interest groups

A second major area of criticism of self-help as a mechanism for reproducing inequality relates to the failure to recognise the 'functionality' of illegal settlement for a wide variety of other interest groups in addition to some of the urban poor (Connolly 1982). Specifically, it is argued that the relatively cheap 'solution' that self-help settlements provide is an important element in the mechanism in which the state reproduces labour power effectively. New generations of workers are born and bred in these neighbourhoods, providing the labour for the future. These settlements also provide a means whereby labour power may reproduce itself on a daily basis: as an environment in which to live. The low costs of acquiring land illegally and the practice of investing one's time and money in gradual improvement of dwelling and environment, make it a process that is just about affordable to many. But it is also exploitative in several respects. By cheapening the costs of housing (an important component of labour reproduction costs and therefore wage demands), the internal pressures to raise real wages is eased and alleviated. Also, labour is exploited twice over: in the workplace, and then at home as 'spare time' is turned over to dwelling production and improvement. Hardship – 'violence' to use Harvey's (1985) term – is exercised both at the place of work and through the home. In Mexico City the rapid expansion of irregular settlement from the mid-1940s was the mechanism through which the urban labour force was accommodated in the absence of employer or public sector housing provision (Azuela and Cruz Rodríguez 1989). That it was affordable to workers earning a minimum wage meant that demands for higher wages were not allowed to intensify, especially given union leadership's highly

highly conciliatory relations with the state. Similarly, middle-income groups benefit in so far as low wages allow them to enjoy cheap services from domestic labour, gardeners, chauffeurs, home decorators, etc.

In addition to industrial capital other interest groups have also benefited. The market for construction materials has increased as have multiplier linkages with local retailers and distributors (Ball and Connolly 1987). Although large-scale construction interests would have been equally served by major public projects, the same does not apply to local suppliers and producers. Irregular settlements also offered a reserve of cheap construction labour that could be hired and fired depending upon major contracts at any one point in time. When the large firms did not need their services, there were opportunities for casual hirings in the 'self-build' sector (Ball and Connolly 1987).

Government officials and politicians may benefit to the extent that irregular settlement offers opportunities for political patronage (through clientelism), empire building, or simply a mechanism whereby pressure from local groups may be mediated and dissipated (Ward 1986). Only when demands threaten to overload the capability of the system to respond and lead to upwellings of unrest do the costs begin to outweigh the benefits (Gilbert and Gugler 1982). Yet this is rarely allowed to happen. On such occasions as the 'Movimiento Restaurador de Colonos' movement in Netzahualcóyotl and Ecatepec in 1969–70 and the upsurge of protest groups in the downtown area after the 1985 earthquake, the government acted decisively to head off unrest: usually by striking a deal with the protestors, and subsequently seeking to deform their movement (Gilbert and Ward 1985).

(3) Exploiting the poor through helping them

Irregular settlement development also offers a mechanism whereby capital may penetrate peripheral areas of the urban environment which were previously 'informal' and partially protected from direct capital accumulation processes. This process is referred to as commodification. A key criticism that was levelled at Turner was his focus upon **use** values of property and for ignoring the fact that even recently established irregular settlements have an **exchange** value in the market. The process of illegal settlement and self-help, albeit informal, is firmly situated within the sphere of capital accumulation and is subjugated to the logic of the dominant mode. For the squatter, Burgess (1982: 66) argues:

> . . . it is not the absence of a technocratic and bureaucratic system, or the (absence of) legal housing norms, or the sequence of building operations that have cheapened his house, it is merely *the fact that he is operating in a different sphere of circulation of capital – that covered by the petty commodity production of*

housing. He has not escaped capitalism – he is merely in another part of it. [Emphasis in the original]

Dualist models of development theory and employment structures have been superceded since the late 1970s in favour of approaches which emphasise the integration and domination of peripheral structures within a wider system (Corbridge 1986; Bromley 1978). Equally, it is erroneous to conceive housing or land markets in Mexico City as somehow separate from overall land and housing production processes. With certain notable exceptions (such as the preferential access to some *ejidal* land) the poor are at the end of the queue for land and bid for those areas in which other groups have little interest (Gilbert and Ward 1985). The point here is to appreciate that access to land for irregular settlement has become increasingly difficult in recent years, and the costs associated with consolidation have risen sharply in real terms.

In earlier work I sought to analyse the determinants of 'successful' upgrading in Mexico City and compared three squatter areas at different 'stages' of their physical development trajectory (Ward 1978). I wanted to know whether consolidation was largely a product of years of 'sweat equity' invested in improving one's home, family size and structure, employment type; or what? Through an analysis of indices of dwelling 'consolidation' and the characteristics of individual (owner) households it became apparent that ability to create an 'investment surplus' was most closely related to higher levels of dwelling improvement. This directed me to examine more closely the relationship between economic factors and consolidation: number of workers, nature of cost sharing, wage levels, etc. In short I found that income levels, access to employment (wage type and job stability), and inflation rates relative to wages and the costs of building material, were the factors which were most likely to affect consolidation. Thus I concluded that economic structural determinants of poverty at the national and regional level inhibit the potential success of self-help.

From the early 1970s onwards residents of irregular settlements in Mexico City will have found it more difficult to achieve the same rates and levels of successful consolidation than did previous generations between 1950 and 1970. This, despite (and in part because of) the more enlightened and efficient government policies adopted since 1971 (discussed in the previous chapter). Recent generations are caught in two jaws of a vice. On the one hand access to wage employment has tightened and real wages have declined, particularly since 1982. Thus the ability to create an investment surplus has been eroded. On the other, the costs of irregular settlement housing production have risen significantly in real terms. Land costs have increased, albeit not as sharply as might have been expected given the growing scarcity of land (Gilbert and Ward 1985). The costs of building materials rose well ahead of inflation during the 1970s (Ward 1978). Moreover, the introduction of government policies to regularise land title, provide services and public utilities, and to **recover the costs** from beneficiaries has meant that a battery of new costs have appeared as a direct result of 'enlightened' support for self-help. (However, it must be noted that these new costs are often subsidised and may not greatly exceed the 'informal' supply costs to which residents are subject before receiving a formal supply [Ward 1986: 102]. This point is one that is frequently conveniently forgotten by critics of government intervention and by those wishing to emphasise the commodification argument [Burgess 1985].) In addition, there are concerted attempts to integrate irregular settlements into the tax base of the city by including them on the cadastral register (Linn 1983). In Mexico City under Hank González there was an active campaign to integrate the legalisation programme with property tax assessment and levies. The current (1989) Federal District administration has also resolved not to raise the **rates** of property taxation and service consumption charged, but to ensure registration and regular **revision** of the basis of valuation upon which payments are assessed in order to ensure that the real value of levies is not eroded by inflation.

My inclination, therefore, is broadly to support the commodification thesis of Burgess and others (Burgess 1985; Angel *et al.* 1983; Fiori and Ramírez 1987). Residents of irregular settlements are increasingly exposed to capital penetration processes at the periphery. Thus, as well as cheapening the reproduction costs of labour power, low-income groups are more actively exposed to capital accumulation processes from real estate agents, the construction materials industry, public and private utility industries and from the state itself. Self-help is both a response to poverty but also reproduces it.

(4) Reproducing inequality through the ideology of self-help

It is not a new argument that a shift towards widespread ownership in society leads to the adoption of more conservative, status-quo seeking and petit-bourgeois values (Bassett and Short 1980). The equity component cultivates a belief in the defence of private property; it secure votes; and it individualises property relations. The struggle for housing as a collective good which is socially produced is thereby undermined (Burgess 1985).

In Mexico City, housing provision is closely tied to a state project of social control. This is achieved in a variety of ways. First, as we saw in the previous chapter the stratification of housing provision and land entitlement programmes divides low-income (and other) groups into different interest groups which often have to compete with each other for scarce resources. The issue becomes one not of the size of the overall cake, but of negotiating and competing for a slice of it.

Second, ideological and social control is exercised through PRI manipulation and electoral control mediated through the process of self-help (Eckstein 1977; Azuela and Cruz Rodríguez 1989). Popular struggles for land acquisition, regularisation, services, and other urban resources have systematically been penetrated and shaped by clientelist community–state relations initially through the CNOP and the 'Oficina de Colonias'; then more broadly through a variety of political and executive 'patrons' and agency heads (not all of whom were priísta affiliates or militants) under President Echeverría; and latterly through more technical and less overtly partisan agencies. Where social peace or popular mobilisation have threatened to get out-of-hand or to demonstrate a cross-settlement collective response, then the government has acted sharply to head-off unrest through negotiation and subsequent co-optation, using violence and repression as a last resort (Montaño 1976).

Third, the hetereogeneity of irregular settlement also undermines collective response by dividing settlements on the basis of mode of land acquisition, the 'stage' of consolidation, the servicing priorities of residents, community leadership structures, social classes, and above all tenure relations (owners-v.-sharers-v.-renters: see Gilbert and Varley 1990; Coulomb 1989). These tenure splits multiply still further the constituencies into which people fall or may be divided. One's ideological perspective is likely to be shaped by one's housing status. Renters, harrassed squatters, displaced downtown tenants are likely to be more radical and disposed to anti-government demonstration than are those who have, in effect, been bought-off by the government through successive housing policies.

Finally, social relations are reproduced through the physical structure of the dwelling environment. Social interaction patterns vary according to the physical design characteristics as well as settlement type and location. For example because of their locational advantages, downtown vecindades display considerable population stability. Social interaction patterns are strongly localised **within** the tenement (Lewis 1961; Valencia 1964). None the less apart from contact with kinsfolk in other tenements or neighbourhoods much of the day-to-day interaction takes place within the same tenement (especially among women). Solidarity in defence of one's own vecindad is high. More recently established tenements in peripheral or past-peripheral irregular settlements are smaller, relatively more expensive, and have a higher population turnover (Gilbert and Varley 1990). With the exception of single female-headed households, relations between families in these vecindades appear to be more restrained (Chant 1985).

In irregular settlements people come from a wide variety of regional backgrounds and the relatively large size of most Mexico City settlements makes it unlikely that any one cultural or family group from a single region will dominate. Yet even here, too, social interaction patterns are constrained to the immediate locality. In three squatter settlements analysed in 1973 social interaction patterns showed a high level of localisation, which was particularly marked among the poorest households and between women (Ward 1976a; see also Lomnitz 1977). Men tended to be more outwardly oriented, as did better-off households. Thus the physical environment, be it the squatter settlement or a vecindad, has an important effect upon the way in which social relations are articulated and reproduced. But in this case the social interaction patterns probably serve to reduce intra-group inequalities through mechanisms of sponsorship and exchange (Lomnitz 1977; Kemper 1974).

Thus, I have identified four principal mechanisms whereby 'vernacular' architecture acts as an important mechanism of reproducing social and economic relations in Mexico City. It achieves this at an ideological level through romanticising poverty and by focusing attention upon use rather than exchange values; through the privatisation and individualisation of housing provision; through generating different and competing constituencies; and through day-to-day social interaction patterns which emerge in low-income settlements. At an economic level I have shown how 'vernacular' housing intensifies commodification and opens up the low-income settlement process to the predations of capital accumulation. Although the adverse outcomes of this process have probably been overstated and remain to be analysed properly, it seems inevitable that the earlier successes of upgrading and self-build are being constrained by conditions of austerity, rising construction costs, and sometimes by cost recovery and taxation arising from government policy. Low-income settlement production at costs that are broadly affordable to the poor facilitates the reproduction of labour power which, in turn, benefits a wide range of other social and economic interest groups. While in Mexico City vernacular architecture 'rules', it is definitely not OK.

The creation of inequality through earthquake reconstruction

Perhaps the most clear-cut example of how Mexico City's government has acted through physical design to reproduce social inequality and to (inadvertently) create social divisions that did not exist before is provided by the post-earthquake reconstruction programme. This programme was focused largely upon rehousing low-income residents most affected by the earthquake in the downtown area of the City. Many of the old tenements were destroyed or damaged irreparably in the September 1985 earthquakes and despite its strong public commitment to a decentralisation policy, the government opted for the politically more acceptable solution of rehousing *in situ*. The basis for inclusion in the programme carried out by a specialist agency created for the purpose (RHP) was the expropriation decree issued very soon after the disaster (Mexico RHP 1988).

The housing reconstruction programme undertaken by RHP in the Federal District enjoyed huge resources and was financed through a World Bank loan and from national fiscal resources (in approximately equal amounts). Although not openly admitted, the government did not expect to recover its own real capital investment, while the World Bank only expected a 50 per cent return. In effect this meant that the housing was very heavily subsidised, and the opportunity for developing a capital basis for an ongoing rolling housing programme was eroded.

When it finally came on-line in 1986–7 the housing 'solution' was most impressive. Some 28000 previous *vecindad* tenant households were re-housed almost always on their previous sites, now in **owner**-occupied two-bedroom accommodation following one of four design prototypes. A further 11650 dwellings were rehabilitated and 4500 homes were subject to minor repairs (Mexico RHP 1986). 'Traditional' components of Mexican architecture (strong vivid colours, central patios, large common entrance archways (*portón*), and window surrounds were incorporated very success-fully into these designs. The result, therefore, was a high standard dwelling, with an exchange value of around (then) 6 million pesos, yet each dwelling cost little more than 3 million pesos to be paid over an eight year period. The fact that most residents identified strongly with a sense of *barrio* that prevails in the area (broadly equivalent to 'Cockney' pride in London); together with their being rehoused *in situ*, and continuing to work in the central area, means that very few have sold out. Most were eager to stay and to enjoy the 'windfall' that, perversely, the earthquake had provided. So how did this replicate and intensify social inequality?

It has done so through the arbitrary way in which the benefits of reconstruction fell among people with an identical class and cultural background. Before the earthquakes everyone rented accommodation, which was often very dilapidated and unsalubrious. This was a stable working-class area in which people lived and worked in services, or in the host of small workshops and enterprises which abound. Fate determined where the earthquake did most damage, but it was an inadequate govern-ment instrument (the expropriation decree) that determined exactly which families would benefit. Thus, families living cheek by jowl in adjacent *vecindades* found themselves in one of two camps: either included in the group to become owner occupiers and windfall beneficiaries of underpriced, high-quality housing; or excluded from the RHP programme and at best likely to be included in the less well financed 'Phase 2' programme designed in part to 'mop up' those who were excluded. What was previously a broadly homogeneous social class was split irrevocably.

From the outset a high level of insecurity emerged among the *damnificado* (refugee) population about who, exactly, would benefit. After several false starts, Camacho (then an underminister at SPP), moved to head the Urban Development and Ecology Ministry and brought in a new team to run the RHP. The social unrest and the numerous defence groups that had been spawned in the central area were successfully appeased through a Camacho-inspired 'Democratic Accord' (*Concertación Democrática*) whereby benefi-ciaries were given guarantees about their inclusion in the programme, the nature of the housing they would receive, its costs and completion schedule (Mexico RHP 1988). Thus, many groups were in effect bought off, while the minority that were excluded continued to fight on, but now in a severely weakened and badly divided form.

This particular experience also sheds light on how a major government programme can come to **shape** people's aesthetic tastes in housing. The brightly coloured and reasonably sensitively designed apartment blocks are what people throughout Mexico now claim they want: completed housing (rather than self-help), and bold bright colours (*vivienda de colores*). In the next section I will examine the roots and formal architectural trditions of these designs.

Reproducing the city: modern and post-modern architecture

Although many buildings in the city today are 'international' in style and would not look out of place in London, Frankfurt or Los Angeles, they have usually been developed by Mexican-based architects and practices rather than by transnational or US firms and consortia (Plates 7.3 and 7.4). Indeed, some of the most successful and imaginative Mexican architects have won commissions in the US and a few have successful practices in both countries. To the extent that MacDonalds, Colonel Sanders, FuddRuckers and others have extended their franchise, logos and exterior and interior designs to the city, this has been done through local firms. As I will explain below, it would be quite misleading to understate this Mexican dominance. The following analysis is based in part upon discussions and interviews that I was priviledged to enjoy with many contemporary Mexican architects. Specifically, I was interested to discover the architectural and intellectual sources of urban design (past and present) in Mexico City as manifest through its buildings and monuments. I wanted to know how far building design was largely shaped by intellectual currents, or was subject to strong 'suggestive influence' by a state seeking congruence and mutual reinforcement between its development 'project' and the physical structure of the city. That is to say who creates the ideology of urban form and why? And once created, is it self-sustaining?

Eclectism and denying the past

Before the beginning of the Revolution in 1910 architectural influences were dominated by European styles – especially from London, Paris and Berlin (Ricalde and Sánchez 1984). Centralisation, expansion, and European cultural ideas dominated during the *Porfiriato* at the beginning of the century, and this was reflected in large scale, sumptuous public and private buildings that reproduced among other styles elegant French eighteenth-century designs. Sometimes, too, one observes Art Noveau influences, particularly in window embellishments and in the glass of the windows themselves (Hernández 1981). Congestion in the old 'First Quarter' (*Primer Cuadro*) of the city, electrification of tramways, the emergence of private transport for the rich and the desire to reflect one's social position through palatial houses and gardens had, by the late nineteenth century, set in train a centrifugal movement to high-income residential subdivisions. Excellent examples of these mansions may still be observed in Colonias Juárez, Cuauhtemoc and Roma Norte, and which were developed during the first two decades.

Many public buildings also drew upon neo-romantic and neo-gothic inspiration. The Palace of Fine Art (begun 1904) and the Central Post Office (completed 1907) were both designed by Adamo Boari and provide excellent examples (Plates 7.5 and 7.6). Classical styles were adopted for public buildings such as the Geology Institute and the Ministry of Communications and Public Works (1902–11) and this is also a feature of monuments erected at the time. For example one of the most famous and loved monuments – The Angel – dates from this time and is a replica of the original which is in Berlin. Others such as 'El Caballito' (actually Carlos IV of Spain and erected in 1802), the monument to Benito Juárez (1910) and to Cristopher Columbus also drew heavily upon the classical style (Plates 7.7–7.9). Such representations were politically respectable in that their source of inspiration did not portray indigenous origins. Rather, they reflected the grandeur that Porfirio Díaz wished to project, together with the strong sense of affinity with Europe and a rejection of national roots. Mexico began with Columbus' discovery and the failure to erect monuments dedicated to Pre-Columbian traditions constituted an attempt to erase from the collective memory the violence of the conquest.

Revolution and modernism

The social tensions entrained during the Revolution are clearly represented in the urban fabric. So, too, is the upsurge of a new middle class during the 1920s, and the large throughflow of provincial population associated with the conflict and with the camp-followers of various leaders who came to the city in order to vie for power and to forge the new Constitution. There was a reaction against the reproduction of European 'Academy' styles even though these continued to be adopted for some private houses, albeit with less ostentation. Of growing importance, especially for public buildings and monuments, were designs which sought a return to national bases of inspiration incorporating colonial and vernacular styles.

Not only was this a period of social change, but the Revolution and the broadening of Mexico's development base heralded the emergence of a middle class who needed also to display their new-found status through residential segregation and private house design. Colonia Roma, particularly its southern section, was developed at this time, as were the new residential districts of Condesa-Hipódromo begun during the 1920s. Architectural designs which predominated at this time comprised houses which gave straight onto the street, and which sometimes had interior patios. Facade adornment was less grandiose and included narrow 'false'

Plate 7.3 International logos and international styles: FuddRuckers hamburgers in Mexico City

Plate 7.4 Modernist architecture and sculpture along Paseo de la Reforma

Plate 7.5 Palace of Fine Art (Adamo Boari 1904. Completed by Mariscal in the early 1930s; the interior is

Plate 7.6 Italianesque influence: the Central Post Office (Adamo Boari 1907)

Plate 7.7   'The Angel', Paseo de la Reforma

Plate 7.8 Statue to Columbus, Paseo de la Reforma

Plate 7.9 Monument to Benito Juárez, Alameda Park

balconies, 'colonial' stucco work, and even occasional pre-hispanic elements. Now that pre-hispanic roots were respectable, monuments depicting Aztec heroes were raised, and in emphasising indigenous images there was a conscious attempt to recast national culture recognising those origins. The violence of the conquest remained a problem, however, given that most of the population was *mestizo* rather than pure Indian. Cortes went uncelebrated, and it was left to muralists such as Diego Rivera to blend depictions of the violence of conquest with the violence of industrial exploitation. In his work, in particular, the struggle for national identity became enmeshed with a depiction of revolutionary and class struggle.

Modernism of the 1920s, proselytising as it did the principles of functionalism and of anti-bourgeois sentiment, required an architecture that would serve the needs of the modern age without adornment. Knox (1987) describes the emergence of modernism as a rejection of the pitched roofs, ornate cornices and so on which represented the 'crowns' of the old nobility which the bourgoisie had imitated. Flat roofs, clean right angles to sheer facades offered a pure interpretation of the spirit of the age – exemplified in the Ministry of Health and Social Security Building completed in 1926 (Plate 7.10) and the Tuberculosis Sanatorium in Tlalpan (then a small town several miles to the south of the built-up area). In Mexico City the inspiration for these developments came from the revolutionary and socialist spirit of the Revolution and from a nationalism that was struggling to define itself. Artists such as Dr Atl, Diego Rivera, Siquieros, Clemente Orozco and the generation which surrounded them used their skills and historical (often indigenous) images to fire that definition. Murals on public buildings, popular sculpture and monuments all sought to cement this ideology in national and city culture. In some respects these monuments and art closely resemble Soviet socialist realism such as the monument to the Revolution itself (designed initially to be the cupola of a new Congress building but restructured into a monument in 1935–6 when funds ran short Plate 7.11) and that of the monument to Alvaro Obregón (1934) in San Angel. The Open Air Theatre in Hipódromo-Condesa was laid out in 1927 in the Parque España (Plate 7.12). Many cinemas, hotels such as The Prado, and the national stadium then in Orizaba Street, were influenced by modernism but imbued with a heavy nationalist spirit. Sometimes this even recast modernism altogether, as in Diego Rivera's wonderful but all too little visited Anahuacalli Museum hidden in the south of the city, and aptly described by one informant as 'pre-post-modern' (Plate 7.13).

For the elite, new residential areas began to be developed during the 1930s in a 'leapfrogging' pattern of residential estate development that continued until the 1970s. For example, Polanco and Lomas de Chapultepec were developed at this time with further infilling of more modest middle- and upper-middle-income housing in Condesa and Cuauhtemoc. Although Mexican modernism continued to dominate throughout the 1930s and 1940s it was also accompanied by some degree of eclecticism which adds to the rich variety of architectural styles observed

Plate 7.10 Ministry of Health (Santacilia 1926)

Plate 7.11   Monument to the Revolution (Santacilia 1935–6)

Plate 7.12 Open Air Theatre, Parque España (1927)

Plate 7.13 Pre-post-modernism: Diego Rivera and Juan O'Gorman's Anahuacalli Museum, Coyoacan

Plate 7.14   Art Deco residence in Colonia Condesa/Parque España

Plate 7.15   Modernist homes in Parque Melchor Ocampo
(Luis Barragan 1940s)

Plate 7.16 Eclecticism: 'Colonial Californian' style home, Polanco

Plate 7.17 Eclecticism: English mock Tudor, in Virreyes

Plate 7.18 'The Diana'. Classicism with a modern touch by Juan Olaquibel, Paseo de la Reforma (1946)

Plate 7.19   Monument to the Mexican Race 'La Raza' (1940). Insurgentes
Norte

in these areas today. 'Art Deco' buildings abound (Plate 7.14) and this style was adopted also by Mariscal in his completion of the interior of Boami's Palace of Fine Arts upon which work had been suspended since the *Porfiriato*. 'Functionalist' house designs also incorporated intensely Mexican ideas of texture, movement and above all deep colour epitomised in Luis Barragan's buildings and gardens and which have become the inspiration to many contemporary Mexican architects (see Plate 7.15 and Plate 7.25).

It is from the 1940s that architectural 'fashion' developed a quickening dynamic of its own as both the elite and the upper-middle-classes tried to outdo their peers through status displays in house design, and through residence in the most 'chic' areas of the day. Thus, there is a sequence of residential developments: Virreyes, extensions to Lomas, Jardines de San Angel during the 1950s and 1960s, Tecamachalco in the 1970s, and more recently the infilling and luxurious house developments in and around the old 'pueblo' cores to the south of the city (San Angel Inn), Tlalpan, and Coyoacan. House design in each of these areas reflects particular fashions that emerged or were created. During the 1940s for example this was a process 'prostituted by the bourgeois aberration of "Colonial Californian" ' (Ricalde and Sánchez 1984:54) style of open ranch home which was becoming popular especially among private residences in Polanco and in Lomas de Chapultepec (Plate 7.16). Oddly enough the popularity of this style was encouraged by a radical in the person of ex-President Cárdenas himself, and this led to his taste in architecture feeling the brunt of Juan O'Gorman's caustic irony. Visiting these areas today the heavy eclecticism of different styles (Californian 'ranch', English 'Tudor', 'Colonial', French eighteenth century with Mansard Roofs, 'modern', etc.) may be clearly seen – sometimes mixed together in a single house (Plate 7.17).

A parallel sequence emerges for the middle classes. On the one hand social groups wishing to live as close to their would-be peers moved a generation or so later by 'filtering' into formerly elite housing. This accounts for the densification in Polanco, and other areas, as well as a turnover and subdivision of dwellings into apartments in Condesa, Roma Sur and other similar areas from the 1960s onwards. On the other hand the middle classes could emulate in a less grandiose manner the elite's move to the suburbs. Residential areas that developed in this way were Del Valle, and Napoles during the 1950s, Satélite in the 1960s and a series of subdivisions beyond Satélite in Naucalpan (State of Mexico).

This eclecticism is also to be seen in the monuments of the 1940s notably in the assertion of national pride through the monument to the Mexican Race ('La Raza' 1940) and the 'Diana' huntress statue which is a modern (and rather beautiful) representation of a classical image (Plates 7.18 and 7.19). But although some private houses went overboard to embrace the architectural 'fetishism' during the 1940s and 1950s most houses, public buildings and monuments of the day represent an intensely nationalist interpretation of modernism. It blended indigenous and vernacular architecture with the wider principles of modernist functional thinking.

The legacy of modernisation

Within the public sphere, however, modernism and functionalist orthodoxy prevailed during the period of rapid economic growth and increased state intervention in the 'modernisation' process (1945–70). Architecture and city design reflect and reinforce this image and statism is redolent in the early monuments of the period dedicated to the Petroleum Workers, the Child Heroes and to the Roadbuilders (Plates 7.20–7.22). Buildings constructed by the state sector were almost exclusively in the orthodox modernist mould, such as the Social Security Institute on Reforma (1947: Plate 7.23), the Social Sciences building at the National University (1946–52), Miguel Aleman housing project (1949) and that of Nonoalco Tlatelolco in 1960. These were often very large-scale projects comprising high-rise housing developments, multiple-department medical centres (Centro Médico), government buildings (Centro SCOP) and the massive campus of University City. Although orthodox modernist in style, Mexican nationalism once again was not averse to experimentation: for example, through large-scale mosaic murals on building facades (of which Juan O'Gorman's adornment of the old library building at the University City is probably the most famous). To some extent this modernisation was accompanied by an era of populism especially under President López Mateos (1958–64).

Since the 1960s Mexico City has become part of the international scene. Although as I argued in Chapter 1 it is unhelpful to consider it a 'World City', it nevertheless moved firmly onto the world centre stage not least through events such as the Olympic Games (1968), and the World Cup (1970 and 1986: Plate 7.24). Indeed, for the Olympic Games each participating country was requested to provide a large piece of commemorative sculpture distributed alongside the southern ringroad. Generally the purpose of monuments constructed since the 1960s appears to be one of reinforcement: of the modern, of the abstract, and of the international. Later in the 1960s and 1970s these came to reflect an even greater 'international' content of geometric sculptures, and modern high-tech fountains (Plates 7.4 and 7.24).

Modernism and internationalism

As the 'international' style (glass and cement tinted buildings: Plates 7.3 and 7.4) began to dominate, this diluted somewhat the strong national essence in design that had existed previously. Architects began to move away from a preoccupation and interest in local materials such as stone and marble and indigenous representation towards industrialised materials such as concrete and glass. Of course, this was in part related to the growing influence of the Association (Camara) of the Construction Materials Industry and the role of large national firms within it (COPEVI 1978). The state reinforced the

Plate 7.20   Monument to the Petroleum Workers (Juan Olaquibel 1952)

Plate 7.21 Monument to the Child Heroes

Plate 7.22 Monument to the Roadbuilders

process through standardisation of designs for hospitals, IMSS and ISSSTE social security buildings, schools (through CAPFCE) and so on. Although most bread-and-butter design contracts for private sector development adopted the international style (albeit through Mexican architectural practices) this was not exclusively the case. The principal Mexican architects of the day adopted the international style but often in ways which made the outcome distinctively a Mexican adaptation. In particular one architect Ricardo Legoretta, following Barragan's work of the 1940s, looked to traditional Mexican architecture for inspiration. Following Mexican traditions of strong bright colours (purples, mauves, blues and ochre browns) used on exterior walls in provincial towns, together with the love of large archways, he has developed an architectural style epitomised by large rough concrete textures, elaborate colour, free-standing walls, interplay of bright light and dark shadow and heavy flowing waterscapes (Plate 7.25). Deservedly, his work is internationally renowned and he also runs a successful practice in the United States.

In essence two broad types of architecture feature today. There are the buildings for large-scale national and international firms, banks and so on which often have a particular 'signature' which they wish to sustain. Internationalist in style, these buildings would not look out of place alongside their counterparts in any other large city of the world. They reinforce the ideas of modernity, functionality, domination (of finance and commerce) and a lack of humanism. There are also those buildings that, as one architect respondent stated, 'try to make a statement'. I have already mentioned the work of Legoretta in this context but there are several others whose work represents a genuine reworking of modernism incorporating traditional or indigenous elements from the past in a way that avoids being 'kitch'. Another foremost contemporary architect (González de Leon) explained to me that the pyramids of Teotihuacán, and the palpable sense of mass epitomised in churches and monasteries of the sixteenth century had entered his subconscious from an early age. The use of different levels, ramps, pyramidal form, large free-standing walls, heavy shadow and so on are features of recent buildings such as the Military College, the Colégio de México, the INFONAVIT building, the Rufino Tamayo Museum and many others (Plates 7.26–7.28). Furthermore as I mentioned earlier in this chapter, rich colours, a range of entrance porches and arches, emboldened surrounds for exterior windows were all traditional features that were embodied in the housing reconstruction programme for low-income groups in the inner city. This not only reinforced local residents' links with the past, it has shaped the future demand for state housing. Today people not only want affordable low-cost housing, but they want it to embrace heavy colours.

Plate 7.23   Modernism par excellence: the Mexican Social Security Institute Building (Santacilia 1947), Paseo de la Reforma

Plate 7.24 Modernism and Internationalism: the Aztec (football) Stadium (Ramírez Vázquez 1968)

Plate 7.25 Hotel Camino Real, Mexico City (Ricardo Legoretta 1968. The walls are bright yellow and pink. Note shadows created by free standing walls.)

Plate 7.26 The Colégio de México building (González de Leon and Zabludovsky 1975)

Plate 7.27 INFONAVIT building (González de Leon 1978)

Plate 7.28 Rufino Tamayo Museum (González de Leon and Zabludovsky 1980)

227

Plate 7.29 Post-modernism: pediments, pillars, artisanal bricks. The Episcopal Church, Chapultepec

Plate 7.30   The Banco de México building (González de Leon 1989). Mexican architecture with a hint of post-modernism (Pergola style roof garden and steel tube railings.)

The reproduction of urban form

Eschewing post-modernism

This strong element of tradition that is characteristic of contemporary Mexican architecture goes some way to explaining why 'post-modern' architecture and patterns of social organisation do not figure in Mexico City. The term 'post-modernism' is rather elusive to define – despite its wide usage (Harvey 1987, 1989; Gregory 1987). Broadly it comprises an intellectual and aesthetic current associated with the condition of late capitalism. It is a reaction against the past philosophy that planning and development should be on a large scale, technologically rational, austere and functionally efficient. In architectural terms it is a response to the 'crisis' of modernism and its impersonality. Instead, post-modernism emphasises the small-scale, the community level, neo-vernacular styles and the playful and eclectic use of historical imagery. Pediments, columns, arches, scrolls, lanterns, Venetian colours are in vogue – often in a single collage (Plate 7.29). As Knox (1987: 359) states: 'Post-Modernist architecture is characterized by the self-conscious and ironic use of historical styles and imagery, an emphasis on the scenographic and the decorative (as opposed to the compositional) properties of the built environment, and a rejection of the social objectives and determinist claims of Modernism.'

But it is more than an architectural or design fetish. It must also be seen as a condition associated with the regime of 'flexible accumulation' that has emerged since 1973, and it is an important mechanism whereby capital investment in the built environment may be recycled, thereby conditioning social relations around the renewed processes of accumulation (Harvey 1989; Dear 1986). In the United Kingdom inner-city gentrification is but one expression of post-modernist aesthetics and revitalisation of capital accumulation. Harvey describes other more contrived schemes (through 'spatial fixes') of consumption and spectacle (US shopping malls; Baltimore's Harbour; Liverpool's garden festival and so on).

Mexico City does not appear to have 'enjoyed' a surplus of capital investment that was unable to find a ready outlet in urban development. Prime redevelopment sites have usually become available often through buying out large (but now unfashionable) homes along main throughfares such as Insurgentes. Recently, too, the 1985 earthquake has provoked considerable opportunities for redevelopment. Plenty of outlets have existed for commercial capital without the need aggressively to seek to evict people from inner-city sites (Ward and Melligan 1985). Nor has the state-initiated remodelling in the historic core (*Primer Cuadro*), accompanied by the construction of a new wholesale market on the periphery to replace the downtown Merced led to a Covent Garden-style gentrification and land-use changes. If this was the intention behind Mayor Hank González' development plans, and if the investment capital was available in the late 1970s, then it quickly evaporated during the crisis and has not resurfaced until very recently (1988–9). There is no significant gentrification in the downtown area. Thus, although it is more hypothesis than proof, one crucial reason why no post-modernist current exists in Mexico City is because the logic and imperatives of capital accumulation do not demand it.

However, on its own this would not explain why contemporary public and private buildings, shopping malls and so on have not adopted post-modern 'self-conscious imagery'. I explored this question in my interviews with leading architects. It would appear that one important reason for its non-appearance is that there is **no aesthetic need**. As I have demonstrated earlier in this chapter, a concern with the vernacular would not be new in Mexico City. Much of the built-up area is developed through self-build. Moreover, middle-income private homes have widely adopted eclectic styles throughout the modernist period. More significantly in the case of industrialised building projects is the fact that Mexican architects have always successfully interpreted modernism using traditional and local imagery. Thus 'post-modern' architectural design would offer little that was either new, or significant, to Mexico City residents. Some people might argue that several features of contemporary architecture are post-modern: González de Leon's steel tubes trim, and roof gardens on the recently completed Banco de México building (Plate 7.30). But these features are always integrated into a conception that is Mexican. It is not pastiche; nor 'kitch'.

Economically, too, post-modern ornateness, ostentation and higher construction costs would not sit comfortably in the climate of austerity that has dominated Mexico City through the 1980s. Even large-scale private investment projects appear unwilling to flaunt themselves and follow the latest imported 'fad' from the United States. If Mexican architects have never entirely eschewed overseas architectural influences neither have they wholeheartedly embraced US orthodoxy. While the 'international style' may still dominate today it is the fact that it is not unequivocally North American that has made it acceptable for most Mexicans.

It would seem, therefore, that Mexico City's architecture is a very important medium whereby the reigning philosophy and ideology of development are read and made legible to the general public. But this reading of buildings is not mindless nor is it directed by the state authorities. Top architects such as Legoretta and González de Leon profess to listening to their clients about details but not to being instructed about how their designs should look. If a client has a clear idea of the sort of building to be built then they seek out the architect whose past work is most likely to reproduce that preconception. Architects, and not the state, determine the design form of the city although the state may have a great influence when it regularly repeats a particular style or 'signature': for example the schools built by CAPFCE according to Artigas' original design prototype.

Where the state may be more directly influential is in its commissioning of monuments which represent a more clear-cut opportunity to create an ideological imprint in people's minds. We have seen how monuments in

Mexico City deliberately turned away from indigenous origins before the Revolution, but were warmly embraced thereafter – at least until the influence of modernism and internationalism took over. Monuments are probably a better guide to what the state thinks, and what it wants the people to think.

8
Mexico City: a conclusion or an epitaph?

In this final brief chapter I want to offer an interpretation of the likely direction of Mexico's City's future development during the 1990s. The massive changes that I have observed during the many years that I have been acquainted with the city advise caution about the accuracy of any crystal ball gazing. Nevertheless, I hope that in preceding chapters I have mapped out the directions in which existing problems are likely to lead, as well as demonstrated the ways in which citizens, politicians and urban managers have tended to respond as the city evolves. This ought to provide us with a surface upon which we can obtain sufficient purchase to make some interpretation about the future. I do not propose to repeat or to summarise findings relating to individual chapters. Rather, the intention is to draw those separate conclusions together into a wider interpretation of what the future may hold. It is a personal view, not one taken from other texts. Nor is it one that I have discussed with key contemporary decision makers in Mexico. As I stated in the Preface, my intention was always to 'call things as I saw them', and, having come this far, I figure that I'm in as good a position as anyone to do that.

In 1978 I wrote a journalistic article entitled 'Mexico City: the city the world will watch'. Rather a pretentious title you might think, and you are probably right. In some ways, though, I was anticipating Mexico becoming the largest city in the world. More importantly, given that rapid urban expansion in the future will occur largely in developing nations, it was to be a test case of whether large cities could survive in contexts where resources were scarce and poverty widespread. In short, if the consequences of megacity growth are dire, they will first come unstuck in Mexico City. Much of the subsequent reporting has, exaggeratedly, focused upon crisis flashpoints and visions of an 'ecological Hiroshima' (*Time* 2 January 1989, see the Preface to this volume).

Although these crises are real they are not new. One of the advantages of researching back through government reports, newspaper articles and commentaries, and academic journal articles since the 1950s is that one observes that the crisis is ongoing. During the 1950s, when the city was already large by world standards (then 3.1 million), writers found difficulty in comprehending a metropolitan area with a predicted population of 5 million and 8.5 million by 1960 and 1970 respectively. In the same manner, people gasp at the inevitability of there being around 26 million living in the Metropolitan Area by the turn of the century (Delgado 1988). I am sure, too, that historians could provide evidence of similar preoccupations in earlier decades, and even earlier centuries. Although distant-past crises have not always been associated with issues of growth, the content of debates has invariably focused upon servicing, upon getting water into the city, and sewage and wastes out. Echeverría's monument to the deep drainage system situated in Gustavo Madero *delegación* is not only a tribute to the huge investment undertaken during the 1970s. It is a tribute to several centuries of labour and preoccupation about water and drainage issues.

Also, academics are not even clear about whether or not cities should be allowed to grow. Some argue that the larger the city, the greater the economies of scale; the higher the productivity of labour; and that infrastructural costs do not increase with city size per capita. Therefore cities should be left to grow (Richardson 1973, 1976). Others urge caution and suggest that there are 'intervening variables' that determine greater productivity (such as better labour supply and infrastructure) which do not relate to large city size and agglomeration economies. Smaller cities are easier to 'manage' and less likely to be dependent upon sophisticated planning devices (Gilbert 1976b). Better, therefore, where possible, to keep them small. Others argue that city growth, left to its own devices, may undergo 'polarisation reversal' whereby previous tendencies towards regional divergence are turned around as the growth rates of secondary cities located outside come to exceed those of the metropolitan centre (Townroe and Keen 1984; but cf. Gwynne 1985).

It may be important to resolve these questions in the context of decentralisation efforts and contemporary patterns and policies of city growth in developing countries. But in the context of Mexico City they do not matter a jot. The city is already enormous, and will continue to grow further. The crisis is ongoing and irreversible. But so, too, are citizens' responses and initiatives. Therefore, we need to recast the question. To what extent will future populations of Mexico City be capable of confronting and coping with city growth? And what measures, if any, will improve the chances of success?

In response to the first question I am cautiously optimistic, despite my criticisms throughout this book about the underlying lack of political commitment demonstrated by successive governments towards the resolution of city problems and inequality. Nor do I believe in the inevitability of deteriorating living conditions that many contemporary marxists espouse. I am optimistic for two basic reasons. First, because Mexican citizens are enormously resourceful and have survived rapid and dysfunctional urban growth in the past – albeit at enormous social costs. Secondly, because the political commitment will have to emerge if the broad current political structure in Mexico is to survive. It must, and will I am sure, adjust, and not, one hopes, in the direction of repression (although that is always a possibility). Whether it will adjust far enough, and quickly enough, is the critical question.

In terms of the city's growth and physical expansion the crisis turns, really, on what is achieved outside the DF. If there is no major amalgamation of the DF and Estado de México political entities, then really success or failure will depend upon what the State of Mexico government is capable of achieving. In 1984 64 per cent of the population lived in the DF; the remainder outside. By the year 2000 it will be roughly 50:50. Between 1980 and 2000 most *delegaciones* will grow slowly if at all. The large proportion of growth, therefore, will take place in the State of Mexico – especially in those outer ring municipalities of the Metropolitan Zone (see Figure 1.1). Thus far, however, I have observed little evidence of any capacity and vision from the State of Mexico authorities to plan that growth. Most of my focus in this book and that of government and academic analysts has been towards the past and current weighting of population in the city. We have failed to look, adequately, at the precise area where the battle over future city growth will be won or lost.

In terms of city structure my optimism is based upon the evidence that I have identified (largely in Chapter 2) for a reordering of land uses that has occurred in the past. Sub-centres in the city often built around old *pueblo* cores have become the important foci in people's daily lives. This process has been harnessed and stimulated by planning policy throughout the Metropolitan Area during the past ten years. The city has become multi-centred, and people have adjusted to its growth by relating increasingly to a relatively small part. This has been accompanied by important shifts in the appropriate location of industry and other land uses. Another reason for my optimism relates to the emergence of a planning process in the Federal District although this has been ephemeral. Exhortation from technicians and academics about the virtues and need for planning will not count for terribly much. But I am confident that politicians will realise that the political advantages outweigh any loss of personalistic and idiosyncratic control. I am not especially encouraged by the early actions of the present DF planning team and its Mayor who, given their previous experience of physical planning, ought to know better, and also ought to have greater vision about the city's development. It appeared that their approach was to respond reflexively through political management to problems as they arose or were constructed from the wider debate (public security, ecology, etc.). Initiatives in urban development amounted to superficial 'bread and festival'-type actions (*mini-urbanismo*) which, patently, are not good enough.

The second principal consideration central to Mexico City's future relates to changes achieved in its political structure. In Chapter 3 I identified how popular social mobilisation in Mexico has been mediated by the state first through clientelism, and more recently through civic neighbourhood councils. But neither mechanism has proved adequate in circumventing either the emergence of independent urban social movements such as the CONAMUP, the CUD and the *Asamblea de Barrios*; nor has it offset the electoral swing to the opposition parties. Attempts by government to extend political representation through initiatives such as the Representative Assembly of the DF seek, in my view, to head-off demands for a fully elected local congress and direct elections for City Hall officials along the lines that exist in all other Mexican states. I expect some movement towards a local congress: but remain less sanguine about direct elections for the Mayor and sub-mayors. However, if the current momentum can be maintained, the national government and the PRI may be obliged to give up what is, fundamentally, an anti-democratic political structure.

In my view there are two imperatives if Mexico City is to move forward developmentally and politically. The first relates to the allocation of responsibility for the built-up area/metropolitan Zone. This must take the form of a **single political entity** capable of creating acomprehensive and integrated strategy of metropolitan development. As I mentioned above, events are occurring outside the DF which affect both it and the Metropolitan Area at large; yet the DF is currently powerless to respond. Moreover some hard decisions about financing overall city development have to be taken and these can only be confronted by a single executive charged with responsibility for the whole area. Perhaps some sort of Greater London Council (GLC)-type arrangement would serve. This 'tier' of metropolitan government might even leave the municipal structure broadly intact and not require major revision to the political administrative organisation of the State of Mexico. But it would require a new level of executive authority responsible for overall strategy and direction to which municipalities or their borough equivalents would be bound. The fact that the GLC was wound up by the Conservative Government was not because it was ineffective or moribund; but rather, that it worked too well! Central government resented its power and the fact that it was able to present strategies and policies that were anathema to the Conservatives. For Mexico City it is **precisely** this sort of metropolitan executive authority and leadership that is required.

The second imperative comprises the relationship between that hypothetical metropolitan executive and the public. Only a strategy that forms part of an agenda or manifesto of a political party elected to power has the ultimate authority and legitimacy to be implemented. If it falls short in its implementation then people will want to know why. Thus it is imperative for the government/PRI to accept in principle an electorally contested basis of executive authority; first in the DF, but subsequently also at the level of a metropolitan government. We are talking here of empowerment: of the people; of their elected representatives; and of the **government**.

The adoption of these two imperatives requires considerable political will on the part of the government and PRI. The current political climate of genuine pluralism and democratisation offers an opportunity for these possibilities to be broached and acted upon. As is readily apparent throughout this book, governing Mexico City is likely to prove far from easy, and there is no assurance of success. An opposition party if given a chance to accept the challenge, might easily (and inevitably?), fall flat on its face. Perhaps the city is ungovernable.

My third proposition regarding the city's future relates to the content of policies and their implementation. I have argued in this volume and elsewhere that government in Mexico is becoming more technocratic in its approach. Nowhere is this more obvious than in the Federal District where politicians, agency heads and functionaries depend far less upon PRI patronage for their jobs. More important is the fact that, in most realms of city and sectoral management, policies are much more in tune with people's needs and with a state-of-the-art technical understanding of policy alternatives. There is greater efficiency; tighter budgetary controls: and above all more appropriate policies to affect people's needs. In real terms, peso for peso, citizens do far better today than during the 1970s.

The improvement in servicing levels; the more sensitive and realistic housing policies; the emergence of a planning structure and process; and the vastly extended and improved transportation system, have all had real and positive impact upon the lives and life chances of Mexico City citizens. In none of these cases is there any cause for complacency but the achievements are real. That they have occurred at all may be explained by the intensifying crisis during the 1960s and 1970s and the need for the state to respond. In so doing, the state was obliged to confront interest groups, which, earlier, it might have protected. Also, as we have seen throughout this book, the state has undertaken action in ways that have sought to improve objective conditions while at the same time pacify, divide and stratify low-income populations.

Whether future Mexico City governments will be able to continue to offset social unrest through efficient management and improved delivery of urban goods, I very much doubt. The 1988 election results suggest that people are no longer impressed that they can, nor convinced that they will. The city will survive, but unless change along the lines that I have identified is undertaken soon, it will never thrive. My optimism, my admiration for the resourcefulness of Mexican people, and my analysis of Mexico City's recent past suggest that I should not write its epitaph: at least, not yet.

Notes

Chapter 5

1. In part the views expressed in this chapter are informed by my own participation within that process. In 1978–9 I was engaged full time as advisor to the department concerned with the elaboration of urban development plans in the then recently established Urban Planning Ministry (SAHOP). I am grateful to Arq Roberto Eibenshutz (then General Director of Population Centres) and to Arq Javier Caraveo a colleague at that time and subsequently director of the DF Urban Development Plan and its first chief executive as Head of Planning 1980–4. Multiple discussions with both have informed much of the analysis (although responsibility for the opinions expressed are entirely my own).

2. Although still important, the final version was a substantially diluted version of an earlier draft which contained a wide range of radical proposals aimed at confronting land speculation and the imposition of some form of urban land reform (Saldivar 1981). Passage of the law generated intense conflict between the state and the more powerful oligarchic groups but this probably emanated more from the latter's hatred of Echeverría and his economic policies than from an intrinsic reaction to the proposals contained in the draft legislation. Whichever, the Executive backpedalled, and the law that was passed contained a large number of general objectives to regulate and order human settlements into urban systems, to plan for improved access to employment and public utilities, to conserve the environment, to exercise control over the real estate market, and to encourage public participation in the resolution of urban problems (Mexico SAHOP 1979).

3. These data are derived from a content analysis of all legislation about planning published in the *Diario Oficial* since 1928. (See also Gil Elizondo, 1987.)

4. The overall director of this programme was Manuel Camacho while he was undersecretary at SPP. His immediate boss was Carlos Salinas, now President.

5. A further reason for low levels of collaboration is that it is unlikely that two planning departments at any point in time will have roughly equal status. The influence of one group is likely to be waxing or waning with respect to the other. It would be a magnanimous gesture for that department which was on the 'up' to assist its less fortunate counterpart. Therefore, at best one is likely to find little more than active communication between departments; at worst each will attempt to undercut the initiatives of the other. The recent (post-1982) evidence of more active informal collaboration between the Planning Department

of the Federal District and the Directorate of Urban Development and Housing in the State of Mexico is the exception that proves the rule. Both 'teams' emerged from the same group of one directorate in SAHOP and were, therefore, ex-colleagues and often personal friends.

6. At this time I was full-time adviser to the responsible officer at SAHOP and I am, therefore, in a position to speculate about the reasons for this rather unprecedented request to another ministry to prepare the Federal District Plan. It appears to have been prompted by the continuance in office of the planning chief whom the Mayor Hank González did not trust, but in the event she was eventually replaced yet responsibility for the Plan remained primarily with SAHOP. Undoubtedly an important consideration was the close political alliance between personnel in DDF and in SAHOP. For a fuller discussion see Ward (1981b: 56–7). However, by the time that SAHOP officials had submitted estimates and outlines of the new plan it appears that the Mayor had won his battle within the cabinet and secured the necessary financial appropriations. As for protest on the streets and in the press, the DF made minor concessions: the trees were removed for 'replanting' in Chapultepec Park; residents and tenants were compensated or bribed to leave. The proposal to place the contract with SAHOP was, therefore, withdrawn although it was later revived.

Chapter 6

1. The reader is referred to a previous version of this matrix, together with the counterparts for Bogotá and Valencia (Gilbert and Ward 1985).
2. The history of land transfers before they came to be in the hands of the developers is interesting. Briefly, it was originally federal land which was privatised during the 1920s at low cost on the understanding that it would be improved for agricultural purposes (*bonificación*). These improvements were not undertaken and the government sought the restitution of the lands under its ownership. This led to litigation and the Supreme Court found against the Government (Guerrero *et al.* 1974). Thereafter, during the 1940s, the land began to change hands and prices rose.
3. A similar stratification pattern exists for housing provision and if space permitted a parallel argument could be developed similar to that of health care. See Ward (1990) for details and a figure showing the stratification and levels of housing production by institution over time.
4. At first sight these distances may appear not unreasonable. However, they are conservative estimates based upon crow-flight distances and make no allowances for inefficient transport networks and transport systems. They are also averages and include the low distances associated with intra-settlement treatment. Also, one should bear in mind that few people in London would expect to travel more than 2 kilometres to see their doctor and not a great deal further to a hospital casualty department.

References

Aguilar Martínez, G. 1984. Política y planeación urbana en el Distrito Federal. Evolución y actualidad. Paper presented to the Anglo-Mexican Symposium of Geographers in Mexico City, September. Mimeo.

——. 1987. Urban planning in the 1980s in Mexico City: operative process or political facade? *Habitat International*, **11** (3), pp. 23–38. Spanish translation in *Estudios demográficos y urbanos*, 1987, **5**, pp. 273–99.

——. 1988. Community participation in Mexico City: a case study. *Bulletin of Latin American Research*, **7** (1), pp. 22–46.

Alonso, J., *et al.* 1980. *Lucha urbana y acumulación de capital*. Mexico DF: Ediciones de La Casa Chata.

Amin, S. 1974. *Accumulation on a world scale: a critique of the theory of underdevelopment*. New York: Monthly Review Press.

Angel, S. 1983a. Upgrading slum infrastructure: divergent objectives in search of a consensus. *Third World Planning Review* **5**, pp. 5–22.

——. 1983b. Land tenure for the urban poor. In *Land for housing the poor*, S. Angel *et al.* (eds.), pp. 110–42. Singapore: Select Books.

Angel, S. Archer, R. Tanphiphat, S. and Wegelin, E. (eds.) 1983. *Land for housing the poor*. Singapore: Select Books.

Arias, P. and Roberts, B. 1985. The city in permanent transition. In *Capital and labour in the urbanized world*, J. Walton (ed.), pp. 149–75. London: Sage.

Arizpe, L. 1978. *Migraciones, etnicísmo y cambio económico: un estudio sobre migrantes campesinas a la Cd. de México*. Mexico DF: El Colégio de México.

Azuela, A. 1983. La legislación del suelo urbano: auge o crisis? In Ediciones SIAP, *Relación campo-ciudad: la tierra, recurso estratégico para el desarrollo y la transformación social*, pp. 514–31, Mexico DF: Ediciones SIAP.

Azuela, A. and Cruz Rodríguez, M.S. 1989. La institicionalación de las colonias populares y la política urbana en la ciudad de México (1940–1946). *Sociológica*, **4** (9), pp. 111–33.

Badcock, B. 1984. *Unfairly structured cities*. Oxford: Blackwells.

Balán, J., Browning, H., and Jelin, E. 1973. *Men in a developing society: geographic and social mobility to Monterrey, Mexico*. Austin: University of Texas Press.

Balán, J. 1982. Regional urbanization and agricultural production in Argentina: a comparative analysis. In *Urbanization in contemporary Latin America*, A. Gilbert *et al.* (eds.), pp. 35–58. Chichester: Wiley.

Ball, M. and Connolly, P. 1987. Capital accumulation in the Mexican construction industry 1930–82. In *International Journal of Urban and Regional Research*, **11**, pp. 153–71.

References

Barberán, J., Cárdenas, C., López Monjardin, A. and Zavala, J. 1988. *Radiografía del fraude: análisis de los datos oficiales del 6 de julio.* Mexico: Nuestro Tiempo.
Barkin, D. and Esteva, G. 1978. *Inflación y democracía: el caso de México.* Mexico DF: Siglo XXI.
Baross, P. 1983. The articulation of land supply for popular settlements in Third World cities. In *Land for Housing the Poor*, S. Angel *et al.* (eds.), pp. 180–210. Singapore: Select Books.
Bassett, K. and Short, J. 1980. *Housing and residential structure.* London: Routledge & Kegan Paul.
Bataillon, C. and D'Arc, H. 1973. *La Ciudad de México.* Mexico DF: Sepsententas.
Batley, R. 1982. Urban renewal and expulsion in São Paulo. In *Urbanization in contemporary Latin America*, A. Gilbert *et al.* (eds.), pp. 231–62. Chichester: Wiley.
Bazant, J. 1979. *Rentabilidad de la vivienda de bajos ingresos.* Mexico DF: Editorial Diana.
Bazdresch, C. 1986. Los subsidios y la concentración en la ciudad de México. In *Decentralización y democracía en México*, B. Torres (ed.), pp. 205–18. Mexico: El Colégio de México.
Beltran, U. and Pórtilla, S. 1986. El proyecto de decentralización del Gobierno Mexicano (1983–84). In *Decentralización y democracía en México*, B. Torres (ed.), pp. 91–118. Mexico: El Colégio de México.
Benton, L. 1986. Reshaping the urban core: the politics of housing in authoritarian Uruguay. *Latin American Research Review*, 21 (2), pp. 33–52.
Birkbeck, C. 1978. Self-employed proletarians in an informal factory: the case of Cali's garbage dump. *World Development*, 6, pp. 1173–85.
Boonyabancha, S. 1983. The causes and effects of slum eviction in Bangkok. In *Land for Housing the Poor*, S. Angel *et al.* (eds.), pp. 254–83. Singapore: Select Books.
Bortz, J. 1983. La cuestión salarial actual. *Análisis Económico*, vol. 2, pp. 103–20. Mexico DF: UAM Azcapotzalco.
Brambila, C. 1987. Ciudad de México; la urbe más grande del mundo? In *El atlas de la Ciudad de México*, G. Garza (ed.), pp. 146–51. Mexico DF: Departamento del Distrito Federal and Colégio de México.
Bromley, R. 1978. Organization, regulation and exploitation in the so-called 'urban informal sector': the street traders of Cali, Colombia. *World Development*, 6, pp. 1161–71.
Brown, J. 1972. *Patterns of intra-urban settlement in Mexico City: an examination of the Turner theory.* Dissertation Series 40. Ithaca: Cornell University Latin American Studies Programme.
Burgess, J. 1978. Conflict and conservation in Covent Garden. *L'Espace Géographique*, 2, pp. 93–107.
Burgess, R. 1982. Self-help housing advocacy: a curious form of radicalism. A critique of the work of John F.C. Turner. In *Self-help housing: a critique*, P. Ward (ed.), pp. 55–97. London: Mansell.
——. 1985. The limits to state-aided self-help housing programmes. *Development and Change*, 16, pp. 271–312.
——. 1986. The political integration of urban demands in Colombia. *Boletin de estudios latinoamericanos y del caribe*, 41, pp. 39–52.
Burgess, R. 1990. *Labour, shelter and global capitalism.* London: Methuen.
Butterworth, D. 1972. Two small groups: a comparison of migrants and non-migrants in Mexico City. *Urban Anthropology*, 1 (1), pp. 29–50.
Calnek, E. 1975. The organization of food supply systems: the case of Tenochtitlán. In *Las ciudades de América latina y sus áreas de influencia a través de la historia*, J. Hardoy, and R. Schaedel, (eds.). Buenos Aires: Ediciones SIAP.
——. 1976. The internal structure of Tenochtitlán. In *The valley of Mexico*, E. Wolf (ed.). Albuquerque: University of New Mexico Press.

241

References

Camacho, C. 1987. La ciudad de México en la economía nacional. *El atlas de la Ciudad de México*, G. Garza, (ed.), pp. 95–99. Mexico DF: Departamento del Distrito Federal and Colégio de México.

Campbell, T. and Wilk, D. 1986. Plans and plan making in the Valley of Mexico. *Third World Planning Review*, 8 (4), pp. 287–313.

Carr, B. 1986. The Mexican left, the popular movements, and the politics of austerity. In *The Mexican left, the popular movements, and the politics of austerity*, B. Carr (ed.). San Diego: Centre for US-Mexican Studies, University of California, Monograph Series No. 18.

Castells, M. 1977. *The urban question: a marxist approach*. London: Edward Arnold.

———. 1979. *City, class and power*. London: Macmillan.

———. 1983. *The city and the grassroots*. London: Edward Arnold.

Castillejos, M. 1988. Efectos de la contaminación ambiental en la salud de niños escolares en tres zonas del area metropolitana de la ciudad de México. In *Medio ambiente y calidad de vida*, S. Puente, and J. Legoretta, (eds.), pp. 301–30. Mexico City: Plaza y Vanes and Departamento del Distrito Federal.

Castillo, H., Camarena, M. and Ziccadi, A. 1987. Basura: procesos de trabajo e impactos en el medio ambiente urbano. *Estudios Demográficos y urbanos*, 2 (3), pp. 513–43.

Chance, J. 1975. The colonial Latin American city: pre-industrial or capitalist? *Urban Anthropology*, 4 (3), pp. 211–23.

Chant, S. 1984. Las olvidadas: a study of women, housing and family structure in Querétaro, Mexico. Unpublished PhD Thesis. University of London.

———. 1985. Family formation and female roles in Querétaro, Mexico. *Bulletin of Latin American Research*, 4 (1), pp. 17–32.

Chant, S. and Ward, P. 1987. Family structure and low-income housing policy. *Third World Planning Review*, 9 (1), pp. 5–19.

Chant, S. ·(forthcoming). 'Sisters of the shaking earth': women, low-income households and urban labour markets in Mexico.

Cibotti, R. *et al.* 1974. Evolución y perspectivas de los procesos de planificación en América Latina. In ILEPES, OEA, BID, *Experiencias y problemas de planificaión en América Latina*. Mexico: Siglo Vientiuno Editores.

Cisneros Sosa A. No date. La colonia el Sol. Mexico DF: mimeo.

———. 1983. Los ciudadanos del Distrito Federal. *Revista de Ciencias Sociales y Humanidades*, p. 9. UAM, Iztapalapa.

Cockcroft, J.D. 1983. *Mexico. Class formation, capital accumulation and the state*. New York: Monthly Review Press.

Collier, D. (ed.) 1979. *The new authoritarianism in Latin America*. Princeton University Press.

Connolly, P. 1981. Towards an analysis of Mexico City's local state. Mimeo.

———. 1982. Uncontrolled settlements and self-build: what kind of solution? The Mexico City case. In *Self-help housing: a critique*, P. M. Ward (ed.), pp. 141–74. London: Mansell.

———. 1984. Finanzas públicas y el estado local: el caso del DDF. *Revista de ciencias sociales y humanidades – UAM*, 5 (11), pp. 57–91.

———. 1988a. Crecimiento urbano, densidad de población y mercado inmobiliario. *Revi..ta A*, 9 (25), pp. 61–85.

———. 1988b. Productividad y relaciones laborales en la industria de la construcción. *Vivienda*, 13 (1), pp. 82–99.

COPEVI, 1977a. *La producción de vivienda en la zona metropolitana de la ciudad de México*. Mexico DF: COPEVI AC.

———. 1977b. *Investigación sobre vivienda: las políticas habitacionales del estado mexicano*. Mexico DF: COPEVI AC.

———. 1978. Estudio de densidades habitacionales y revisión de la zonificación secundaria. Mimeo various volumes. Mexico DF: COPEVI AC.

Corbridge, S. 1986. *Capitalist world development: a critique of radical development geography*. Basingstoke: Macmillan.

Cordera, R. and Tello, C. 1983. *México: la disputa por la nación*, 4th edition. Mexico: Siglo XXI.

Cornelius, W. 1973. Contemporary Mexico: a structural analysis of urban caciquismo. In *The caciques: oligarchical politics and the system of caciquismo*, R. Kern (ed.), pp. 135–91. Albuquerque: University of New Mexico Press.

——. 1975. *Politics and the migrant poor in Mexico*. California: Stanford University Press.

——. 1989. Political change in Mexico: what is happening, and why? Mimeo.

Cornelius W. and Craig, A. 1988. *Politics in Mexico: an introduction and overview*. San Diego: Centre for US–Mexican Studies, University of California, Reprint Series No. 1.

Cornelius, W., Gentleman, J. and Smith, P. (eds.). 1989. The dynamics of political change in Mexico. In *Mexico's alternative political futures*, pp. 1–55. San Diego: Centre for US–Mexican Studies, University of California, Monograph Series No. 30.

Coulomb, R. 1989. Rental housing and the dynamics of urban growth in Mexico City. In *Housing and land in urban Mexico*, A. Gilbert (ed.), pp. 39–50. San Diego: Centre for US–Mexican Studies, University of California, Monograph Series No. 31.

Cruz Rodriguez, M. no date. El ejido en la urbanización de la ciudad de México. Mexico DF: Licenciatura thesis, UAM, Azcapotzalco.

De la Madrid, M. 1982. *Los grandes retos de la Ciudad de México*, Mexico DF: Grijalbo.

Dear, M. 1986. Post-modernism and planning. *Society and Space*, 4, pp. 367–84.

——. 1988. The post-modern challenge: reconstructing human geography. *Transactions of the Institute of British Geographers*, 13, pp. 262–74.

Delgado, J. 1988. El patron de ocupacional territorial de la Ciudad de Mexico al año 2000. In *Estructura territorial de la Ciudad de México*, O. Terrazas, and E. Preciat (eds.), pp. 101–41. Mexico City: Plaza y Janes and Departamento del Distrito Federal.

Dicken, P. 1986a. *Global shift: industrial change in a turbulent world*. London: Harper & Row.

Dicken, P. 1986b. Review of *Utopia on Trial*. *International Journal of Urban and Regional Research*, 10, pp. 297–300.

Domínguez, L. 1987. Sistema de transporte colectivo el metro. In *El atlas de la Ciudad de México*, G. Garza, (ed.), pp. 198–201. Mexico DF: Departamento del Distrito Federal and Colégio de México.

Dos Santos, M. 1970. The structure of dependence. *American Economic Review*, 60, pp. 231–6.

Drakakis-Smith, D. 1981. *Urbanisation, housing and the development process*. London: Croom Helm.

Duran, D. 1967 *Historia de las Indias de Nueva España*. 2 vols. Mexico: Editorial Porrúa.

Durand, J. 1983. *La ciudad invade el ejido*. Mexico DF: Ediciones de la Casa Chata.

Eckstein, S. 1977. *The poverty of revolution: the state and the urban poor in Mexico*. Princeton University Press.

Eyles, J. and Woods, K. 1983. *The social geography of medicine and health*. London: Croom Helm.

Fagen, R. and Tuohy, W. 1972. *Politics and privilege in a Mexican city*. California: Stanford University Press.

Fanon, F. 1967. *The wretched of the earth*. Harmondsworth: Penguin.

Ferras, R. 1978. *Ciudad Netzahualcóyotl: un barrio en via de absorción por la ciudad de México*. Mexico DF: Centro de Estudios Sociológicos, El Colégio de México.

References

Fiori, J. and Ramírez, R. 1987. Notes for comparative research on self-help housing policies in Latin America. Mimeo.

Flores Moreno, J. 1988. El transporte en la zona metropolitana de la Ciudad de México. In *Grandes problemas de la Ciudad de México*, R. Benítez and J. Benigno (eds.), pp. 265–80.

Fox, d. 1972. Patterns of morbidity and mortality in Mexico City. *Geographical Review*, **62**, pp. 151–86.

Franco, J. 1967. *The modern culture of Latin America: society and the artist*. London: Pall Mall Press.

Fried, R. 1972. Mexico City. In *Great cities of the world*, W. Robson and D. Regan (eds.), 3rd edition, pp. 645–88. Beverly Hills: Sage.

Frieden, W. 1965. The search for a housing policy in Mexico City. *Town Planning Review* **36**, pp. 75–94.

Friedmann, J. and Wolff, G. 1982. World city formation: an agenda for research and action. *International Journal for Urban and Regional Research*, **6** (3), pp. 309–43.

Furtado, C. 1971. *Economic development of Latin America: a survey from colonial times to the Cuban Revolution*. Cambridge University Press.

Garavita Elias, R. 1983. La protección al salario. *Análisis Económico* vol. 2, pp. 121–50. Mexico: UAM, Azcapotzalco.

García, B. and Muñoz, H. and de Oliveira, O. 1982. *Hogares y trabajadores en la Ciudad de México*. Mexico DF: El Colégio de México and the Instituto de Investigaciones Sociales, UNAM.

Garza, G. 1978. *Ciudad de México: dinámica económica y factores locacionales*. Mexico DF: Temas de la Ciudad, DDF.

——. 1986. Ciudad de México dinámica industrial y perspectivas de decentralización después del terremoto. In *Decentralización y democracía en México*, B. Torres (ed.), pp. 219–36. Mexico: El Colégio de México.

——, 1987. Distribución de la industria en la ciudad de México. In *El atlas de la Ciudad de México*, G. Garza (ed.), pp. 102–07. Mexico DF: Departamento del Distrito Federal and Colégio de México.

Garza, G. and Schteingart, M. 1978. *La acción habitacional del estado mexicano*. Mexico DF: El Colégio de México.

Gil Elizondo, J. 1987. El futuro de la ciudad de México. Metrópoli controlada. In *El atlas de la Ciudad de México*, G. Garza (ed.), pp. 415–18. Mexico DF: Departamento del Distrito Federal and Colégio de México.

Gilbert, A. 1976a. *Development planning and spatial structure*. Chichester: Wiley.

Gilbert, A. 1976b. The arguments for very large cities reconsidered, *Urban Studies* **13**, pp. 27–34.

Gilbert, A. 1978. Bogotá: politics, planning and the crisis of lost opportunities. In *Latin American urban research*, W. Cornelius and R. Kemper (eds.), vol. 6, pp. 87–126. London: Sage.

——. 1981. Bogotá: an analysis of power in an urban setting. In *Urban problems and planning in the modern world*, M. Pacione, (ed.), pp. 65–93. London: Croom Helm.

——. 1983. The tenants of self-help housing: choice and constrait in the housing market. *Development and Change* **14**, pp. 449–77.

——. 1984a. Self-help housing and state intervention: illustrated reflections on the petty-commodity production debate. Paper presented to Colloquium of British-Mexican Geographers, Mexico City, September.

——. 1984b. Planning, invasions and land speculation: the role of the state in Venezuela. *Third World Planning Review*, **6**, pp. 11–22.

Gilbert, A. and Goodman, D. (eds) 1976. *Development planning and spatial structure*. Chichester: Wiley.

Gilbert, A. and Gugler, J. 1982. *Cities, poverty and development: urbanization in the Third World*. Oxford University Press.

Gilbert, A. and Varley, A. 1990. *Landlord tenant: housing the poor in Urban Mexico*. London: Routledge.

Gilbert, A. and Ward, P. 1982a. The state and low-income housing. In *Urbanization in contemporary Latin America*, A. Gilbert *et al.* (eds.), pp. 79–128. Chichester: Wiley.

———. 1982b. Residential movement among the poor: the constraints on housing choice in Latin American cities, *Transactions of the Institute of British Geographers*, New Series, 7, pp. 129–49.

———. 1984. Community action by the urban poor: democratic involvement, community self-help or a means of social control? *World Development*, **12** (8), pp. 769–82.

———. 1985. *Housing, the state and the poor: policy and practice in three Latin American cities*. Cambridge University Press.

Gilbert, A and Ward, P. 1986. Latin American migrants: a tale of three cities. In *People and environments*, F. Slater (ed.), pp. 24–42. London: Collins Educational.

Glass, R. 1968. Urban sociology in Great Britain. In *Readings in urban sociology*, R. Pahl (ed.), pp. 21–46. Oxford: Pergamon.

Goldrich, D., Pratt, R. and Schuller, C. 1967. The political integration of lower-class urban settlements in Chile and Peru, *Studies in Comparative International Developments*, 3, 1.

González Casanova, P. 1970. *Democracy in Mexico*. New York: Oxford University Press.

González de la Rocha, M. 1988. Economic crisis, domestic reorganisation and women's work in Guadalajara, Mexico. *Bulletin of Latin American Research*, 7 (2), pp. 207–23.

González Rubí, R. 1984. La vivienda, un desafío atroz. *Comércio Exterior*, **34** (May, July and August issues), pp. 390–96, 592–98, 728–34.

Gottlieb, 1976. *Long swings in urban development*. New York: NBER.

Goulet, D. 1983. *Mexico: development strategies for the future*. Indiana: University of Notre Dame Press.

Graizbord, B. and Arias, R. 1988. Prospectiva del crecimiento de la Zona Metropolitana de la ciudad de México. *Vivienda*, **13** (1), pp.100–7.

Gregory, D. 1987. Post-modernism and the politics of social theory. *Society and Space*, 5, pp. 245–48.

Grindle, M. 1977. *Bureaucrats, politicians and peasants in Mexico: a case study in public policy*. Berkeley: University of California Press.

Guevara, S. and Moreno, P. 1987. Areas verdes de la zona metropolitana de la ciudad de México. In *El atlas de la Ciudad de México*, G. Garza (ed.), pp. 231–6. Mexico DF: Departamento del Distrito Federal and Colégio de México.

Guerrero, Ma. T. *et al.* 1974. La tierra, especulación y fraude en el fraccionamiento de San Agustin. Mexico DF: mimeo.

Gunder Frank, A. 1967. *Capitalism and underdevelopment in Latin America*. New York: Monthly Review Press.

Gwynne, R. 1985. *Industrialisation and urbanisation in Latin America*, London: Croom Helm.

Hansen, R. 1974. *The politics of Mexican development*, 2nd edition. Baltimore: Johns Hopkins University Press.

Hardiman, M, and Midgley, J. 1982. *The social dimensions of development: social policy and planning in the Third World*. Chichester: Wiley.

Hardoy, J. 1967. *Urbanization in Pre-Columbian America*. London: Studio Vista.

Harloe, M. 1977. *Captive cities*. Chichester: John Wiley.

Harms, H. 1976. The limitations of self-help. *Architectural Design*, **46**, pp. 230–1.

Harvey, D. 1973. *Social justice and the city*. London: Edward Arnold.

References

Harvey, D. 1985. *The urbanization of capital.* Oxford: Basil Blackwell.
———. 1987. Flexible accumulation through urbanization: reflections on 'post-modernism' in the American City. *Antipode*, **19** (3), pp. 260–86.
———. 1989. *The condition of post modernity.* Oxford: Blackwells.
Heath, J. 1985. Contradictions in Mexican food policy. In *Politics in Mexico*, G. Philip (ed.), London: Croom Helm.
Henderson, J. 1986. The new international division of labour and urban development in the world system. In *Urbanisation in the developing world*, D. Drakakis-Smith (ed.), pp. 63–84. London: Croom Helm.
Hernandez, V. 1981. *Arquitectura doméstica de la ciudad de México (1890–1925).* Mexico City: UNAM.
Herzog, L. 1990. *Where North meets South: cities, space and politics on the United States–Mexico border.* Austin: University of Texas Press.
Huntingdon, S. 1968. *Political order in changing societies.* New Haven: Yale University Press.
Jackson, H. 1973. Intra-urban migration of Mexico City's poor. Unpublished PhD dissertation, University of Colorado.
Jáuregui, E. 1969. Aspectos meteorológicos de la contaminación del aire en la ciudad de México. *Igeniería Hidráulica en México*, **23**, 1.
———. 1971. *Mesoclima de la Ciudad de México.* Mexico DF: UNAM, Instituto de Geografía.
———. 1973. The urban climate of Mexico City. *Erdkunde*, **27** (4), pp. 298–307.
———. 1987. Climas. In *El atlas de la Ciudad de Mexico*, G. Garza (ed.), pp. 37–40. Mexico DF: Departamento del Distrito Federal and Colégio de México.
Jeannetti Davila, E. 1986. Decentralización de los servicios de salud. In *Decentralización y democracía en México*, Torres, B. (ed.), pp. 91–118. Mexico: El Colégio de México.
Jiménez, E. 1988. New forms of community participation in Mexico City: success or failure?. *Bulletin of Latin American Research*, **7** (1), pp. 17–31.
———. 1989. A new form of government control over *colonos* in Mexico City. In *Housing and land in urban Mexico*, A. Gilbert (ed.), pp. 157–72. San Diego: Centre for US-Mexican Studies, University of California, Monograph Series No. 31.
Johnston, R. 1973. Towards a general model of intra-urban residential patterns. Some cross-cultural observations. *Progress in Geography*, **4**, pp. 84–124.
———. 1980. *City and society: an outline for urban geography.* Harmondsworth: Penguin.
Judisman, C. 1988. Empleo y mercados de trabajo en el area metropolitana de la ciudad de México 1975–88. In *Medio ambiente y calidad de vida*, S. Puente and J. Legoretta (eds.), pp. 225–50. Mexico City: Plaza y Vanes and Departamento del Distrito Federal.
Kandell, J. 1988. *La capital: the biography of Mexico City*, New York: Random House.
Kaplan, M. 1972. *Aspectos políticos de la planificación en América Latina.* Montevideo: Biblioteca Científica.
Kemper, R. 1971. Migration and adaptation of Tzintzuntzán peasants in Mexico City. Unpublished PhD thesis, Berkeley.
———. 1974. Family and household organization among Tzintzuntzán migrants in Mexico City: a proposal and a case study. In *Latin American Urban Research*, W. Cornelius and F. Trueblood (eds.), vol. 4, pp. 23–46. California: Sage.
———. 1976. *Campesinos en la Cd. de México: gente de Tzintzuntzán.* Mexico DF: Sepsententas.
Knox, P. 1987. The social production of the built environment: architects, architecture and the post-modern city. *Progress in Human Geography*, **11**, pp 354–77.
Kouyoumdjian, A. 1988. The Miguel De la Madrid *sexenio*: major reforms or

foundation for disaster? In *The Mexican economy*, G. Philip (ed.), pp. 78–94. London: Routledge.

Kowarick, L. 1975. *Capitalismo e marginalidade na América Latina*. Rio de Janiero: Paz e Terra.

Lamarche, F. 1976. Property development and the economic foundations of the urban question. In *Urban sociology: critical essays*, C. Pickvance (ed.). London: Tavistock.

Lavell, A. 1973. Capital investment and regional development in Mexico. *Area*, 5, 1.

Legoretta, J. 1983. *El proceso de urbanización en ciudades petroleras*. Mexico City: Centro de Ecodesarrollo.

———. 1988. El transporte público automotor en la ciudad de México y sus efectos en la contaminación atmosférica. In *Medio ambiente y calidad de vida*, S. Puente and J. Legoretta (eds.), pp. 262–300. Mexico City: Plaza y Vanes and Departamento del Distrito Federal.

Lewis, O. 1964. *The children of Sánchez: autobiography of a Mexican family*. Harmondsworth: Penguin.

Linn, J.F. 1983. *Cities in the developing world: policies for their equitable and efficient growth*. Oxford University Press.

Lizt Mendoza, S. 1988. Respuestas del transporte urbano en las zonas marginadas. In *Grandes problemas de la Ciudad de México*, R. Benítez Zenteno and J. Benigno Morelos (eds.), pp. 215–42. Mexico DF: Plaza y Janes and Department of Federal District.

Lojkine, J. 1976. Contribution to a Marxist theory of capitalist urbanization. In *Urban sociology: critical essays*, C. Pickvance (ed.), pp. 119–46. London: Tavistock.

Lombardo, S. 1987. Esplendor y ocaso colonial de la ciudad de México. In *El atlas de la Ciudad de México*, G. Garza (ed.), pp. 60–3. Mexico DF: Departamento del Distrito Federal and Colégio de México.

Lomnitz, L. 1977. *Networks and marginality*. New York: Academic Press.

López Acuña, D. 1980. *La salud desigual en México*. Mexico DF: Siglo XXI Press.

López Diaz, C. 1978. La intervención del estado en la formación de un asentamiento proletario: el caso de la colonia Ajusco. Mexico DF: Licenciatura thesis, Department of Anthropology, Unversidad Iberoamericana.

Lowe, S. 1986. *Urban social movements: the city after Castells*. Basingstoke: Macmillan.

Lynch, K. 1981. *A theory of good city form*. Massachusetts: MIT Press.

MacPherson S. and Midgley, J. 1987. *Comparative social policy and the Third World*. Brighton: Harvester Press.

Makin, J. 1984. Self-help housing in Mexico City, and the role of the state. Unpublished PhD Thesis, Heriot Watt University.

Martin, R. 1987. The new economics and politics of regional restructuring: the British experience. Paper presented at the International conference on 'regional Policy at the Cross Roads', University of Leuven, 22–24 April.

Martín de la Rosa, 1975. *Netzahualcóyotl: un fenómeno*. Mexico DF: Testimonios del Fondo.

Massey, D. and Allen, J. (eds.) 1984. *Geography matters*. Oxford University Press.

de Mattos, C. 1979. Plans versus planning in Latin American Experience. *CEPAL Review*, 8.

Mele, P. 1987. Urban growth, illegality and local power in the city of Puebla. Paper presented to the Annual Conference of the Institute of British Geographers, 9 January, Portsmouth.

Mesa Lago, C. 1978. *Social security in Latin America: pressure groups, stratification and inequality*. University of Pittsburgh Press.

Mexico, BNH. 1952. *El problema de la habitación en la Ciudad de México*. Mexico DF: BNH report.

References

——. COPLAMAR, 1982. *Necesidades esenciales en Mexico: Salud.* Mexico DF: Siglo XXI.

——. DDF. 1980. *Plan de desarrollo urbano: plan general del Plan Director, Versión abreviada.* Mexico DF: DDF publication.

——. DDF. 1982. *Sistema de planificación urbana del Distrito Federal.* Mexico DF: DDF publication.

——. INVI. 1958. *Las colonias populares de la Ciudad de México: problemas y soluciones.* Mexico DF: INVI publication.

——. RHP (Renovación Habitacional Popular). 1986. *Programa operativo.* Mexico DF: RHP Agency Publication.

——. RHP. 1988. *Housing reconstruction program: a memoir.* Mexico DF: RHP Agency Report.

——. SAHOP, 1978. *Plan nacional de desarrollo urbano, Versión abreviada.* Mexico DF: Agency publication.

——. SAHOP, 1979. La incorporación de los procesos que generan los asentamientos irregulares a la planeación de los centros de población. Mexico DF: SAHOP, DGCP.

——. SPP. 1983. *Plan nacional de desarrollo, 1983–88.* Mexico DF: SPP publication.

Meyer, L. 1987. Sistema de gobierno y evolución política hasta 1940. In *El atlas de la Ciudad de México*, G. Garza (ed.), 372–5. Mexico DF: Departamento del Distrito Federal and Colégio de México.

Midgley, J. 1984. *Social security, inequality and the Third World.* Chichester: Wiley.

Montaño, J. 1976. *Los pobres de le ciudad de México en los asentamientos espontáneos.* Mexico DF: Siglo XXI.

Moore, R. 1978. Urban problems and policy responses for Metropolitan Guayaquil. In *Latin American urban research*, W. Cornelius and R. Kemper (eds.), vol. 6, pp 181–204. Beverly Hills: Sage.

Morales, M.D. 1987. La expansión de la Ciudad de México (1858–1910). In *El atlas de la Ciudad de México*, G. Garza (ed.), pp. 64–8. Mexico DF: Departamento del Distrito Federal and Colégio de México.

Moreno Toscano, A. 1979. La 'crisis' en la ciudad. In *México Hoy*, P. González Casanova and E. Florescano, (eds.), pp. 152–76. Mexico DF: Siglo XXI.

Morse, R. 1971. Trends and issues in Latin American urban research, 1965–70. *Latin American Research Review*, **6**, (3), pp. 3–52.

Mumford, L. 1938. *The culture of cities.* London: Secker and Warburg.

Muñoz, H. and de Oliveira, O. 1976. Migración, oportunidades de empleo y diferencias de ingreso en la Ciudad de Mexico, *Revista Mexicana de Sociología*, 1, pp. 51–83.

Muñoz, H., Oliviera, O. and Stern, C. (eds.) 1977. *Migración y marginalidad ocupacional.* Mexico DF: Universidad Nacional Autónoma de México.

Navarette, I. Martinez de. 1970. La distribución del ingreso en México: tendencias y perspectivas. In *El perfil de México en 1980*, D. Ibarra *et al.* (eds.), vol. 1, pp. 15–71. Mexico DF: Siglo XXI.

Navarro Benítez, B. 1988a. Sistemas de transporte y metropolización en la ciudad de México. In *Estructura territorial de la Ciudad de México*, O. Terrazas, and E. Preciat (eds.), pp. 143–60. Mexico City: Plaza y Janes and Departamento del Distrito Federal.

——. 1988b. El transporte público en la Zona metropolitana de la Ciudad de México. *Vivienda*, **13** (1), pp. 34–47.

——. 1989. *El traslado masivo de la fuerza de trabajo en la Ciudad de México.* Mexico DF: Plaza y Janes and DDF.

Needler, M. 1982. *Mexican politics: the containment of Conflict.* New York: Praeger.

Negrete, M.E. and Salazar, H. 1987. Dinámica de crecimiento de la población del la ciudad de México (1900–1980). In *El atlas de la Ciudad de México*, G. Garza (ed.), pp. 125–8. Mexico DF: Departamento del Distrito Federal and Colégio de México.

Newman, O. 1972. *Defensible space*. New York: Macmillan.

Nuñez, O. 1983. Causas sociales y políticas en las movilazaciones de los colonos en el DF, 1970–73. *Tabique*, 2, pp. 3–33.

O'Connor, J. 1973. *The fiscal crisis of the State*. New York: St Martin's Press.

——. 1984. *The accumulation crisis*. Oxford: Basil Blackwell.

O'Donnell, G. 1974. Corporatism and the question of the state. In *Authoritarianism and corporatism in Latin America*, J. Malloy (ed.), pp. 47–87. University of Pittsburgh Press.

Offner, J. 1984. *Law and politics in Aztec Texcoco*. Cambridge University Press.

de Oliveira, O. and García, B. 1987. El mercado de trabajo en la ciudad de México. In *El atlas de la Ciudad de México*, G. Garza (ed.), pp. 140–5. Mexico DF: Departamento del Distrito Federal and Colégio de México.

Orellana, C. 1973. Mixtec migrants in Mexico City: a case study of urbanization. *Human Organization*, 32, pp 273–83.

Padgett, L.V. 1966. *The Mexican political system*. Boston: Houghton Mifflin.

Padilla Aragón, E. 1981. *Mexico: hacia el crecimiento con distribución del ingreso*. Mexico DF: Siglo XXI.

Pahl, R. 1975. *Whose city?*. Harmondsworth: Penguin.

Palma, G. 1978. Dependency: a formal theory of underdevelopment or a methodology for the analysis of concrete situations of underdevelopment? *World Development*, 6, pp. 881–924.

Partida, V. 1987a. El proceso de migración a la ciudad de México. In *El atlas de la Ciudad de México*, G. Garza (ed.), pp. 134–40. Mexico DF: Departamento del Distrito Federal and Colégio de México.

——. 1987b. Projecciones de la población de la zona metropolitana de la Ciudad de México. *El atlas de la Ciudad de México*, G. Garza (ed.), pp. 410–14. Mexico DF: Departamento del Distrito Federal and Colégio de México.

Paz, P. 1961. *The labyrinth of solitude*. New York: Grove Press.

Perlman, J. 1976. *The myth of marginality*. Berkeley: University of California Press.

Perló, M. 1979. Política y vivienda en México, 1910–1952. *Revista Mexicana de Sociología*, 3, pp. 769–835.

——. 1980. Los problemas finacieros de la Cd. de México. *El Día*, 7 June 1984.

——. 1981. *Estado, vivienda y estructura urbana en el Cardenismo*. Mexico DF: UNAM, Cuadernos de investigación social 3, Instituto de Investigaciones Sociales.

——. no date. De como perdío la Cd. de México su municipalidad sin obtener un cambio ni una democracía de manzana. Mexico DF: mimeo.

——. 1988. Historia de las obras, planes y problemas hidráulicos en el Distrito Federal. Mimeo.

Pezzoli, K. 1989. Irregular settlement and the politics of land allocation in Mexico City: the case of Ajusco. Mimeo.

Pickvance, C. (ed.) 1976. *Urban sociology: critical essay*. London: Tavistock.

Pommier, P. 1982. The place of Mexico City in the nation's growth: employment trends and policies. *International Labour Review* 121, pp. 345–60.

Pradilla, E. 1976. Notas acerca del 'problem de vivienda'. *Ideología y Sociedad*, 16, pp. 70–107.

——. 1988. Crisis y arqitectura de subsistencia en México. In *Estructura territorial de la Ciudad de Mexico*, O. Terrazas, and E. Preciat (eds.), pp. 45–77. Mexico City: Plaza y Janes and Departamento del Distrito Federal.

Puente, S. 1987. Estructura industrial y participación de la zone metropolitana de la ciudad de Mexico en el producto interno bruto. In *El atlas de la Ciudad de México*, G. Garza (ed.), pp. 92–5. Mexico DF: Departamento del Distrito Federal and Colégio de México.

References

Purcell, S. and Purcell, J. 1980. State and society in Mexico. *World Politics*, **32**, pp. 194–227.

Ramírez Saíz, J. 1983. *Carácter y contradiciones de la ley general de asentamientos humanos*. Mexico DF: Instituto de Investgaciones Sociales, UNAM.

Rapoport, A. 1988. Spontaneous settlements as vernacular design. In *Spontaneous shelter: international perspectives and prospects*, C. Patton (ed.), pp. 51–77. Philadelphia: Temple University Press.

Ray, T. 1969. *The politics of the barrio*. Berkeley: University of California Press.

Ricalde, H. and Sánchez, F. 1984. *Arquitectura Mexicana: Siglo XX*. Mexico DF: Asociación de Ingenieros y Arquitectos de México AC, pp. 48–80.

Richardson, H. 1973. *The economics of urban size*. Saxon House and Lexington Books.

——. 1976. The arguments for very large cities reconsidered: a comment, *Urban Studies*, **13**, pp. 307–10.

Roberts, B. 1978. *Cities of peasants: the political economy of urbanization*. London: Edward Arnold.

Rodríguez, V. 1987. The politics of decentralization in Mexico. Unpublished PhD dissertation, University of California, Berkeley.

Rodríguez Araujo, O. 1979. *La reforma política y los partidos en México*. Mexico DF: Siglo XXI.

Rodwin, L. (ed.). 1988. *Shelter, settlement and development*. Boston: Allen & Unwin.

Rodwin, L. *et al.* 1969. *Planning urban growth and regional development*. Cambridge Mass.: MIT Press.

Roth, G. 1987. *The private provision of public services*. Washington: Oxford University Press and the World Bank.

Roxborough, I. 1979. *Theories of underdevelopment*. Basingstoke: Macmillan.

Ruvacalva, R.M. and Schteingart, M. 1985. Diferenciación socioespacial intra-urbana en el área metropolitana de la ciudad de México. *Estudios Sociológicos*, 9.

——. 1987. Estructura urbana y diferenciación socioespacial en la zona metro-politana de la ciudad de México (1970–80). In *El atlas de la Ciudad de México*, G. Garza (ed.), pp. 108–15. Mexico DF: Departamento del Distrito Federal and Colégio de México.

Saldivar, A. 1981. *Ideología y política del estado mexicano 1970–76*, 2nd edition. Mexico DF: Siglo XXI.

Sanders, W. and Price, B. 1968. *Mesoamerica: the evolution of a civilization*. New York: Random House.

Sanders, W., Parsons, J. and Santley, R. 1979. *The basin of Mexico: ecological processes in the evolution of a civilization*. New York: Academic Press.

Saunders, P. 1979. *Urban politics: a sociological interpretation*. London: Hutchin-son.

——. 1986. *Social theory and the urban question*, 2nd edition. London: Hutchin-son.

Schafer, R. 1966. *Mexico, mutual adjustment planning*. New York: Syracuse University Press.

Schers, D. 1972. The popular sector of the PRI in Mexico. Unpublished PhD dissertation, University of New Mexico.

Schnore, L. 1966. On the spatial structure of cities in the two Americas. In *The study of urbanization*, P. Hauser and L. Schnore (eds.). New York: Wiley and Sons.

Schteingart, M. 1987. Expansión urbana, conflictos sociales y deterioro ambiental en la Ciudad de México. El caso del Ajusco. *Estudios demográficos y urbanos*, **2** (3), pp. 449–78.

——. 1988. Mexico City. In *Mega-cities*, M. Dogan and J. Kasada (eds.), vol. 2, pp. 268–93. Beverly Hills: Sage.

Scobie, J. 1974. *Buenos Aires: plaza to suburb 1870–1910*. New York: Oxford

University Press.

Scott, I. 1982. *Urban and spatial development in Mexico*. Baltimore: Johns Hopkins University Press.

Scott, R. 1964. *Mexican government in transition*. Illinois: University of Illinois Press.

Simmie, J. 1986. General Editor's Preface to S. Lowe, *Urban social movements: the city after Castells*. Basingstoke: Macmillans.

Skidmore, T. and Smith, P. 1989. *Modern Latin America*, 2nd edition. New York: Oxford University Press.

Skinner, R. and Rodell, M. (eds.) 1983. *People, poverty and shelter: problems of self-help housing in the Third World*. London: Methuen.

Sklair, L. 1988. Mexico's *maquiladora* programme: a critical evaluation. In *The Mexican economy*, G. Philip (ed.). London: Routledge.

——. 1989. *Assembling for development: the maquila industry in Mexico and the United States*. Boston: Unwin Hyman.

Smith, P. 1979. *Labyrinths of power: political recruitment in twentieth century Mexico*. New Jersey: Princeton University Press.

——. 1989. The 1988 Presidential succession in historical perspective. In *Mexico's alternative political futures*, Cornelius W., et al. (eds.) pp. 391–416. San Diego: Centre for US-Mexican Studies, University of California, Monograph Series No. 30.

Soustelle, J. 1971. *The four suns*. London: Andre Deutsch.

Stanislawski, D. 1947. Early Spanish town planning in the New World. *Geographical Review*, 37, pp. 94–105.

Stern, C. 1977. Cambios en los volumenes de migrantes provenientes de distintas zonas geoeconómicas. In *Migración, y desigualdad social en la Ciudad de Mexico*, C. Stern et al. (eds.), pp. 115–28. Mexico: UNAM/El Colégio de México.

Stolarski, N. 1982. *La vivienda en el Distrito Federal: situación y perspectivas*. México DDF: General Directorate of Planning.

Suárez Pareyón, A. 1978. La colonia Guerrero: un caso de deterióro en la Ciudad de México. *Arquitectura Autogobierno*, 9, pp. 36–44.

Sudra, T. 1976. Low-income housing system in Mexico City. Unpublished PhD dissertation, MIT.

Sutherland, L. 1985. Informal paratransit in Mexico City. Unpublished PhD dissertation, University of Zurich.

Teichman, J. 1988. *Policy making in Mexico: from boom to crisis*. Boston: Allen & Unwin.

Tello, C. 1978. *La política económica en México, 1970–1976*. Mexico DF: Siglo XXI.

Townroe, P. and Keen, D. 1984. Polarization reversal in the State of São Paulo, Brazil. *Regional Studies*, 18 (1), pp. 45–54.

Turner, J. 1963. Dwelling resources in South America. *Architectural Design*, 37, pp. 360–93.

——. 1968a. Housing priorities, settlement patterns and urban development in modernizing countries', *Journal of the American Institute of Planners*, 34, pp. 354–63.

——. 1968b. The squatter settlement: architecture that works. *Architectural Design*, 38, pp. 355–60.

——. 1969. Uncontrolled urban settlements: problems and policies. In *The city in newly developing countries*, G. Breese (ed.), pp. 507–31. Englewood Cliffs NJ: Prentice Hall.

——. 1976. *Housing by people*. London: Marion Boyars.

Turner, J. et al. 1972. Government policy and lower-income housing systems in Mexico City. Agency Report to AURIS. Mexico City and Cambridge, Mass.: Mimeo.

References

Unikel, L. 1972. *La dinámica del crecimiento de la Ciudad de México*. Mexico DF: Fundación para Estudios de Población.

Unikel, L. and Lavell, A. 1979. El problema urbano regional en México. *Gaceta UNAM*, cuarta época, vol. 3, suplemento número 20, 9 de agosto.

United Nations. 1980. *Yearbook of national accounts statistics*. New York: United Nations.

United Nations Centre for Human Settlements (UNCHS). 1982. *Survey of slum and squatter settlements*. Dublin: Tycooly International Publishing Ltd.

Valencia, E. 1965. *La Merced: estudio ecológico y social de una zona de la Ciudad de México*. Mexico DF: Instituto Nacional de Anthropología e História.

Valiant, G. 1972. *Aztecs of Mexico: origin, rise and fall of the Aztec Nation*. Harmondsworth: Penguin.

Varley, A. 1985a. 'Ya somos dueños'. Ejido land regularization and development in Mexico City. Unpublished PhD Thesis, University of London.

———. 1985b. Urbanization and agrarian law: the case of Mexico City. *Bulletin of Latin American Research*, **4** (1), pp. 1–16.

———. 1987. The relationship between tenure legalization and housing improvements: evidence from Mexico City. *Development and Change*, **18**, pp. 463–81.

———. 1989. Settlement, illegality, and legalization: the need for reassessment. In *Corruption, development and inequality*, P. Ward (ed.), pp. 143–74. London: Routledge.

Vaughn, D. and Feindt, W. 1973. Initial settlement and intra-urban movement of migrants in Monterrey, Mexico. *Journal of the American Institute of Planners*, **39**, pp. 388–401.

Vernez, G. The residential movements of low-income families; the case of Bogotá, Colombia. Mimeo: the New York City Rand Institute.

Vidrio, M. 1987. El transporte de la Ciudad de México en el siglo XIX. *El atlas de la Ciudad de México*, G. Garza (ed.), pp. 68–71. Mexico DF: Departamento del Distrito Federal and Colégio de México.

Villegas, J. 1988. Zona metropolitana de la Ciudad de México: localización y estructura de la actividad industrial. In *Estructura territorial de la Ciudad de México*, O. Terrazas, and E. Preciat (eds.), pp. 161–88. Mexico City: Plaza y Janes and Departamento del Distrito Federal.

Wallerstein, I. 1974. *The modern world system: capitalist agriculture and the origins of the European world economy in the sixteenth century*. New York: Academic Press.

Ward, P. 1976a. In search of a home: social and economic characteristics of squatter settlements and the role of self-help housing in Mexico City. Unpublished PhD Thesis, University of Liverpool.

———. 1976b. The squatter settlement as slum or housing solution: the evidence from Mexico City. *Land Economics*, **52**, pp. 330–46.

———. 1976c. Intra-city migration to squatter settlements in Mexico City. *Geoforum*, **7**, pp. 369–82.

———. 1978. Self-help housing in Mexico: social and economic determinants of success. *Town Planning Review*, **49** (1), pp. 38–50.

———. 1981a. Political pressure for urban services: the response of two Mexico City administrations. *Development and Change*, **12**, pp. 379–407.

———. 1981b. Mexico City. In *Urban problems and planning in Third World cities*, M. Pacione (ed.), pp. 28–64. London: Croom Helm.

———. 1982. Informal housing: conventional wisdoms reappraised. *Built Environment*, **8**, pp. 85–94.

———. 1986. *Welfare politics in Mexico: papering over the cracks*. London: Allen & Unwin.

———. 1989a. Land values and valorisation processes in Latin American cities: a research agenda. *Bulletin of Latin American Research*, **8** (1), pp. 47–66.

——. 1989b. Political mediation and illegal settlement in Mexico City. In *Housing and Land in Urban Mexico*, A. Gilbert (ed.), monograph Series No. 31, pp. 135–55. University of California at San Diego: Centre for US–Mexican Studies.

——. 1990. Mexico. In *International handbook of housing policies and practices*, W. van Vliet (ed.) Connecticut: Greenwood Press.

Ward, P. and Melligan, S. 1985. Urban renovation and the impact upon low-income families in Mexico City. *Urban Studies*, **22**, pp. 199–207.

Weisskoff, R. and Figueroa, A. 1976. Traversing the social pyramid: a comparative review of income distribution in Latin America. *Latin American Research Review*, **2**, pp. 71–112.

Whitehead, L. 1980. Mexico from bust to boom: a political evaluation of the 1976–9 stabilization program. *World Development*, **8**, pp. 843–63.

——. 1981. On 'governability' in Mexico. *Bulletin of Latin American Research*, **1**, pp. 27–47.

——. 1984. Politics of economic management. Seminar given in 'Mexico 1984' conference held at the Institute of Latin American Studies, London, 4–5 June.

Whitehead, L. 1989. Political change and economic stabilization: the 'Economic Solidarity Pact'. In *Mexico's alternative political futures* Cornelius W., *et al.* pp. 181–214. San Diego: Centre for US-Mexican Studies, University of California, Monograph Series No. 30.

Wollch, J. and Dear, M. (eds.) 1989. *The power of geography: how territory shapes social life*. Boston: Unwin Hyman.

World Bank. 1972. *Urbanization*. Sector Policy Paper. Washington: World Bank.

World Health Organisation (WHO). 1978. *Primary health care*. Geneva: WHO.

——. 1981. *Global strategy for health for all by the year 2000*. Geneva: WHO.

Wynia, G. 1972. *Politics and planners: economic development policy in Central America*. Madison, Wisconsin: University of Wisconsin Press.

Index

254

Index

model, Turner's, 53, 93
monuments:
  'La Raza', *215*
  to the Revolution, 207, *232*
Montevideo, 101
MRC (Moviemento Restaurdor de Colonos),
  149, 171, 190
mulattos, 184
multiple employment strategies, 25
'mutual adjustment', 117

Nacional Financiera, 6, 117
Napoles, 59, 216
National:
  Action Party (PAN), 27, 64, 65–6
  Democratic Planning System, 134
  Economic Development Plan, 126
  Industrial Development Plan, 119
  Population Commission (CONAPO),
    33–4
  Revolutionary Party (PNR), 64
  University, 130
  Urban Development Plan, 118, 119, 120
  Urban and Housing Programme, 120
nationalisation, 139
Naucalpan, 34, 40, 56, 58, 94, *174*
nepotism and sinecures (in government), 69
networks, 25, 108
Netzahualcóyotl, xvii, 23, 34, 40, 82, 96,
  146, 155, *174*, 176, 190
New International Divison of Labour, 3
New York, xviii, 3, 29
Newly Industrialised Countries (NICs), 3
Nicaragua, 116
nicknames, 26
NICS, 3
NIDL, 3
north west, 56

Oaxaca, 118, 175
Obregon, Alvaro, 73, 205
Oficina de colonias, 151, 170, 193
O'Gorman, Juan, 217
oil, 10–11, 13–14
Ordaz, Díaz, 8, 112
Olympic Games, 217
Organic Law (1970), 86
Orozco, Clemente, 205
out-lying towns, 93
over accumulation, 5
owners, 172, 174

Pachuca, 97
Palace of Fine Arts, 197, 216
PAN (National Action Party), 27, 64, 65–6,
  82, 84–5
Panista, 66
Pantitlán, 94
PARM, 82
Parque Melchor Ocampo, *211*
partial plans, 127

participation, active, 117, 132–4, 137
particularistic design making, 114
party politics in Mexico, 65–9
patron-client, 86, 130, 154, 155, 169, *170*
patronage, 25, 237
PCM (Mexican Communist Party), 66
PCP *see* Procuraduria de Colonias Populares
PDM (Mexican Democratic Party), 66
PEMEX, 13–14, 119
'pendulum politics', 72
peninsulares, 184
periférico, 97, 105
periphery, 1, 2, 27, 53
permuta, 56, 148
peso, 7, 177
Petroleum Workers, 217, *218*
PFCRN, 82, 84
Phase 2 rehousing programme, 195
Philip II, King of Spain, 30
PIHLU (study), 98, 163, 165
Pino Súarez Station, 109
piped water supply, 57
planes parciales, 125
planning:
  agencies, 115
  emergence of, 117–20
  function of, 135–7
  impediments to structural, 116–20
  initiatives, 120–8
  legislation, 121
  process, 235
  public participation in, 132–4
  structure in Mexico City, 100, 114–37
plaza, 184
PMS, 82
PNR *see* National Revolutionary Party
Polanco, 59, 61, 100
'polarisation reversal', 234
policy making, 71–3, 90
political:
  control, 137
  manipulation, 155
  mediation, 138
  space, 114
  themes, 180
politicians, background of, 70
politicians, 'old style', 63
políticos and *técnicos*, 78, 117
politics of plan and implementation, 129–32
pollution, xvii–xviii, 58
Popocáteptl, xvii
Population Centres Directorate, xxi
population densities, 40–2, 118
population target, 124
Porfiriato, 6
Porfirio Díaz, 30, 197
Portillo, José López *see* López Portillo,
  José
'post-modernism', 180, *229*, 230–2
poverty, 186–7
PPS, 82, 84

Index

Index

wage(s):
    amount spent on transportation, 96–7
    employment and, 14–15
    inequality, 23
    inflation and, 16–17
    levels, 7, 8, 11, 15, 21, 23, 190
    real, 191
Washington, D.C. 87
water and drainage:
    agencies in Mexico, 128, *142*, 175
    delivery, 175–7
    provision to low-income settlements,
        57–8, 175–7
welfare *see* social welfare
welfare protection, 25
workers, male and female, 22–3
working-class districts, 95, 101

working-class organised, 139
World bank, 28, 100, 194
World Cities, 3
World Cup, 217
World Health Organisation (WHO), 99, 155
Wynia, G, 117

Xalostoc, 58
Xochimilco, 40

Yokohama, 29
Yucatán, 65, 118

Zeitgeist, 178
Zocalo, 35, 184
zona urbana ejidal see ejido
zoning, 124, 134, 141